Jung, Gods,
& Modern Man

Jung, Gods, & Modern Man

Antonio Moreno, O.P.

UNIVERSITY OF NOTRE DAME PRESS
NOTRE DAME   LONDON

Nihil obstat: Paul Scanlon, O.P., Provincial
Bede Wilks, O.P., S.T.Lr.
David K. O'Rourke, O.P., S.T.Lr.

Imprimatur: ✝ Leo A. Pursley, D.D.
Bishop of Fort Wayne-South Bend
July 31, 1970

Library of Congress Catalog Card Number: 73-122047
Manufactured in the United States of America by
NAPCO Graphic Arts, Inc.

Acknowledgments

The author wishes to thank the following publishers for permission to quote from various works to which they have rights:

ABP International

From *Contact with Jung,* edited by Michael Fordham, published by Tavistock Publications, London, 1963.

George Allen & Unwin Ltd.

From *The Complete Works of Friedrich Nietzsche,* edited by Oscar Levy, New York, 1924.

Barrie & Jenkins Ltd.

From *Jung and the Problem of Evil* by H. L. Philp. Copyright © 1958 by H. L. Philp.

Beacon Press

From *Man's Search for Meaning* by Viktor E. Frankl, translated by Ilse Lasch, Boston, 1968. Copyright © 1959, 1962 by Viktor Frankl. Reprinted by permission of the Beacon Press.

Doubleday & Company, Inc.

From *Dreams, The Dark Speech of the Spirit* by Morton T. Kelsey. Copyright © 1968 by Morton T. Kelsey.

Harcourt, Brace & World, Inc.

From *The Sacred and the Profane* by Mircea Eliade, New York, 1961.

From *The City in History* by L. Mumford, New York, 1961.

Harper & Row

From *Myth and Reality* by Mircea Eliade, New York, 1963. Copyright © 1963 by Harper & Row, Publishers, Inc.

The Harvill Press Ltd.

From *Soul and Psyche* by Victor White, O.P., London, 1960.

Herder and Herder

From *Existential Psychology* by I. A. Caruso, New York, 1961.

sonality (© 1954 and 1964 by Bollingen Foundation). Reprinted by permission of Princeton University Press. (U. K. and British Commonwealth rights by Routledge & Kegan Paul Ltd.)

From *Complex/Archetype/Symbol in the Psychology of C. G. Jung* by Jolande Jacobi, translated by Ralph Manheim, Pantheon Books, New York, 1959. Copyright © 1959 by Bollingen Foundation. Reprinted by permission of Princeton University Press.

From *The Myth of the Eternal Return (Cosmos and History)* by Mircea Eliade, translated by Willard R. Trask, Bollingen Series XLVI, New York, 1954. Copyright © 1954 by Bollingen Foundation. Reprinted by permission of Princeton University Press. (U. K. and British Commonwealth rights by Routledge & Kegan Paul Ltd.)

Random House, Inc.; Alfred A. Knopf, Inc.

From *Memories, Dreams, Reflections* by C. G. Jung, edited by Aniela Jaffé, published by Pantheon Books, a Division of Random House, Inc., New York, 1963.

From *The Antichrist* by Friedrich Nietzsche, translated by H. L. Mencken, Alfred A. Knopf, Inc., New York, 1941. Copyright © 1918 by Alfred A. Knopf, Inc.

Henry Regnery Company

From *Disputed Questions on Truth* by St. Thomas Aquinas, Chicago, 1952–1954.

Routledge & Kegan Paul Ltd.

From *The Integration of the Personality* by C. G. Jung, translated by Stanley Dell, London, 1940.

From *Psychological Types* by C. G. Jung, translated by H. G. Baynes, London, 1923.

Sheed & Ward Inc.

From *Mephistopheles and the Androgyne: Studies in Religious Myth and Symbol* by Mircea Eliade, © in the English translation Harvill Press, London, and Sheed & Ward, Inc., New York, 1965. English title *The Two and the One.*

From *Images and Symbols* by Mircea Eliade, © Librairie Gallimard 1952, © in the English translation Harvill Press 1961, published by Sheed & Ward, Inc., New York.

The Society of Authors

From *Christianity and the New Age* by Christopher Dawson, London, 1934.

To My Parents

Contents

Preface

The obscurity and tremendous complexity of Jung's voluminous works make the task of anyone trying to write a book on his ideas a difficult one. Jung deals with depth psychology; but, since depth psychology touches the deeper recesses of our mysterious self, evidently it cannot be an isolated and simple phenomenon, easy to discover and simple to understand. On the contrary, depth psychology necessarily has to be connected with all the important factors making up our personality and bearing upon man as man. Hence Jung embraces in his views a diversity of sources and elements which he believes are connected with the activity of the unconscious. This complexity, on the one hand, and the extent of his writings, on the other, makes the problem of selection and synthesis a crucial one. Even more, the cautious reader may perhaps detect a few basic ideas underlying the tremendous variety of elements around which much of Jung's thought actually revolves, especially archetypes, individuation, religion, mental health, and his views of the problem of evil.

In dealing with Jung we are not trying to delve into every aspect of his pioneer work in detail, but rather to investigate his main ideas about religious factors and the elements related to them. After many years of painstaking empirical investigation, Jung reached the conclusion that religion is a human instinct as real as the instinct of self-preservation or sex and the most important factor influencing the behavior of man. So disregarding side details and accidentals, we have first endeavored to give a synthetic explanation and exposition of Jung's ideas on religion and their psychological presuppositions, beginning with the collective unconscious and individuation. Without a clear knowledge of Jung's collective unconscious and individuation, his ideas on religion can hardly be understood, for the former is the source of religious factors and revelation; the latter, as the human process of growth, is intimately associated with the development and assimilation of certain archetypes, especially the archetype of the self which Jung identifies with Christ. Then we have made a critical analysis of Jung's controversial ideas about religion, namely, the Trinity, Christ, the Holy Ghost, myth, and God as a quaternity including evil in his nature as a factor as important as is good. We have to study also the implication of morality and religion in neurosis and therapy. Finally, we have closed our work with an essay on Nietzsche. Using the principles established by Jung, we find in the psychology of Nietzsche's personality the ultimate explanation for his "death of God" attitude, and in the similarity between Nietzsche's unconscious and the unconscious of contemporary man the explanation of the present death of God attitude as a social phenomenon.

As mentioned above, this volume has been written intentionally in a condensed and synthetic fashion. The reader will not find here an exhaustive analysis of anything written by Jung on any topic. We have simply tried to summarize what we believe to be the essence and core of his thought in conjunction with the psychological phenomenon of religion. Neither have we attempted to prove all of our philosophical and theological presuppositions, for this would have led us far beyond the initial scope of our endeavor. For those who want to investigate topics left unexplained or principles taken for granted, I have supplemented the text by indicating in the footnotes the principal sources and references bearing upon the subjects.

For the philosopher not familiar with depth psychology, Jung's methodology will at first be difficult to comprehend. Here lies, perhaps, the main difficulty of any philosophical or theological analysis of Jung's ideas on religion; hence the reader should be warned beforehand, for Jung's approach to religion and man is mainly psychological and empirical. Consequently, for those trained in abstract speculation in theology and philosophy or any similar discipline, Jung's approach to religion will be foreign, hard to understand, and likely to lead to semantic and methodological difficulties. We have tried, if this is possible, to be objective in our exposition and critical evaluation and have sought what we believe to be the truth and Jung's genuine interpretation.

In addition to Jung, the reader will find many references to St. Thomas Aquinas and St. Augustine as the main sources of philosophical and theological evaluation. Concerning the problem of myth and its anthropological implications, the reading of Mircea Eliade's volumes has been the source of much historical data and of many valuable philosophical insights concerning myth and religion.

Four of the chapters of the present volume already have been published in English and Spanish. All of them, however, have been slightly revised for this volume with the exception of the chapter on Jung's ideas on religion—ideas which have been profoundly modified and enlarged. These chapters are included in the present volume with permission of the editors to whom many thanks are due.

I

The Collective Unconscious

In the realm of psychology, the present century has been characterized by important research on the layers of the human psyche we call the unconscious, on the methods of dealing with it, and on the relation between mental health and the contents of the unconscious psyche. Nobody denies the existence of consciousness, because everybody possesses certitude of his own. But in the literature concerning this subject, consciousness remains a vague concept, and so does unconsciousness. Aristotle seems to relate consciousness to knowledge, for consciousness is the awareness immanent in cognitive acts, not exclusively those cognitive acts ordained to the knowledge of external objects, but any human acts of which we are aware. There is not only consciousness of thinking, but there is also consciousness of feeling, of anxiety, of suffering, as well as other vital phenomena. Consciousness is a special kind of reflective knowledge which is obtained by the mere perception of the activity of human functions. The acts may be of different kinds, but the awareness is a common cognitive perception underlying all of them. Not every vital act is conscious, as, for instance, sleep; but the vital conscious acts are such on account of the special cognitive awareness which grasps their existence by means of their activity. For example, we are conscious of suffering because we perceive the existence of human vital acts connected with it.

Jung identifies consciousness with the relation between the ego—which he defines as a complex of representations which constitutes the centrum of the field of consciousness—and the psychic contents—an inward perception of the objective life

process.[1] Thus, he points out the intimate connection of consciousness with the process of life manifested by immanent
vital acts, whose perception constitutes the essential feature of
consciousness.

Unconscious phenomena, however, are so little related to the
ego that most people do not hesitate to deny their existence
outright. Nevertheless, Jung says, there is abundant evidence
showing that consciousness is far from covering the psyche in its
totality. Many things occur semi-consciously, and a great many
entirely unconsciously. The unconscious thus embraces the totality of all psychic phenomena that lack the quality of consciousness.[2] Hence we may say that the unconscious embraces the
totality of the life processes existing in man but not perceived by
knowledge, because knowledge is the necessary prerequisite
for consciousness.

Jung and Freud hold different conceptions of the unconscious; in fact, these differences led them to a final break. For
Jung, the unconscious is composed of two parts which should be
distinguished from one another: (1) One contains the forgotten
material, and the subliminal impressions and perceptions which
have little energy to reach consciousness. In addition, it also
contains all psychic contents incompatible with the conscious
attitude—elements which appear morally or intellectually inad-
missible, and are repressed on account of their incompatibility.
This is a more or less superficial layer of the unconscious, and
it closely corresponds to Freud's conception of it.[3] (2) There
is yet a deeper layer called impersonal, universal, collective, and
common to all men, even though it expresses itself through
personal consciousness. Its contents are not personal; they do

1. C. G. Jung, *The Collected Works of C. G. Jung,* Pantheon Books (New
York), V, 540. Cf. VIII, 137; VIII, 323: "The nature of consciousness is a
riddle whose solution I do not know. It is possible to say, however, that
anything psychic will take on the quality of consciousness if it comes into
association with the ego. If there is no such association it remains unconscious. . . . An object that happens to lie in the darkness has not ceased to
exist, it is probably no different from what it is when seen by the ego."
(*The Collected Works of Jung* shall be quoted as *Coll. Works*).
2. *Ibid.,* VIII, 133; IX,i, 76, 275.
3. *Ibid.,* VIII, 310–311; IX,i, 3–4, 116.

not belong to any individual alone, but to the whole of mankind. Some modes of behavior are the same everywhere, identical in all men. The collective unconscious is a common psyche of a suprapersonal kind whose contents are not acquired during the individual's life time.[4]

For Jung, consciousness and unconsciousness represent two stages in the process of man's evolution. Man evolves from animal, and consciousness from unconsciousness. Thus, the unconscious is, historically speaking, before consciousness and the mother of it: "Consciousness grows out of the unconscious psyche, which is older than it, and which goes on functioning together with it, and even in spite of it."[5] Just as the body has its evolutionary history and shows clear traces of the various evolutionary stages, Jung says, so too does the psyche. The collective unconscious is made up of two related although different contents, namely, archetypes and instincts.

I. *Archetypes*

The term *archetype,* Jung says, occurs as early as Philo-Judaeus with reference to the *Imago Dei* (God image) in man. Jung actually borrowed the idea of archetypes, however, from Saint Augustine, who speaks of "principle ideas" which are themselves not formed, but contained in the divine understanding. These principle ideas can be translated literally as archetypes.[6]

Jung uses several expressions to define archetypes: universal dispositions of the mind, a kind of readiness to produce over and

4. *Ibid.,* IX,i, 3–4, 186–187; VIII, 310–311.
5. *Ibid.,* IX,i, 281; Cf. V, 29: "Just as the body has its evolutionary history and shows clear traces of the various evolutionary stages, so too does the psyche."
6. *Ibid.,* IX,i, 4; VIII, 136. Mircea Eliade, in *Cosmos and History* (New York, 1959), viii-ix, writes: "In using the term archetype, I neglected to specify that I was not referring to the archetype described by Professor Jung. This was a regrettable error. . . . I need scarcely say that, for Professor Jung, the archetypes are structures of the collective unconscious. But in my book I nowhere touch upon the problems of depth psychology nor do I use the concept of the collective unconscious. As I have said, I use the term archetype, just as Eugenio d'Ors does, as a synonym for 'exemplary model' or 'paradigm.'"

over again the same and similar mythical ideas; the treasure of
the collective psyche, of collective ideas, of creativity; ways
of thinking, of feeling, and imagining found everywhere and at
all times independent of tradition; typical forms of behavior
which, once they become conscious, present themselves as ideas
and images; the forms, or riverbeds, along which the current
of psychic life has always flowed.[7]

Although these expressions are different, the idea underlying
them is always the same. The archetypes are typical and universal forms of apprehension which appear as primordial images
charged with great meaning and power, images that impart a
crucial influence upon our collective pattern of behavior, bringing us protection and salvation.

Existence of Archetypes—Jung has to prove the existence of
contents in the unconscious that fulfill the above-mentioned
definitions. Hence he has to show that certain psychic forms of
apprehension have always been found in man throughout the
ages. This can only be done if: (1) one observes the same thing
in different individuals; (2) others confirm that they have made
the same observations; and (3) the same or similar phenomena
can be shown to occur in the folklore of other peoples and races
and in the texts that have come down to us from earlier centuries. Jung's method, therefore, is historical. The collective
pattern of behavior proper to the archetypes presupposes a certain uniformity through the ages, demonstrated only by examining historical sources and comparing these sources with
observations on the pattern of behavior of contemporary man.
In other words, the old and new patterns of apprehension and
behavior have to show similarities and common characteristics.

How is it possible to prove this assumption? Since the collective unconscious contains material of a suprapersonal and
primitive nature, it is difficult to prove its existence by observing the behavior of normal individuals who will chiefly mani-

---

7. *Ibid.*, XI, 517, 519; XVI, 35; V, 228; XVI, 91; VIII, 227. Perhaps the
most complete definition given by Jung is the following: "In this 'deeper'
stratum we also find the a priori, inborn forms of intuition, namely the
archetypes of perception and apprehension, which are the necessary
determinants of all psychic processes."

fest the traits of their irreducible individuality. Jung, however, observes modern man and finds collective forms and ideas in the following phenomena.

1. Certain dreams. Dreams are spontaneous products of the unconscious. In order to show that dreams manifest a collective unconscious, one must look for motifs that could not possibly be known to the dreamer and still coincide with motifs known from historical sources. These dreams are valueless unless one can adduce convincing mythological parallels and the same functional meaning. For instance, Jung found in the dreams of pure Negroes living in the Southern United States motifs from Greek mythology; motifs absolutely unknown to the dreamers.[8] Where do these dreams come from?

In *Two Essays on Analytic Psychology* he relates the case of a woman patient with a mild hysterical neurosis caused by a father complex. In the course of the treatment, the patient transferred the father image to the doctor, but she was unable to cut off the transference. Then she had the following dream: "Her father (who in reality was of small stature) was standing with her on a hill that was covered with wheat-fields. She was quite tiny beside him, and he seemed to her like a giant. He lifted her up from the ground and held her in his arms, like a little child. The wind swept the wheat fields, and as the wheat swayed in the wind, he rocked her in his arms."[9]

Jung interprets the dream as a transpersonal dream, a vision of God. The dreamer swells the human person of the doctor to suprahuman proportions making him a gigantic primordial father who is the wind (a symbol of God), and in whose protecting arms the dreamer rests like an infant. The God-image of the dreamer, who was agnostic, corresponds to an archaic conception of God but not to a conscious idea of Him. Hence the unconscious seems to contain suprapersonal acquisitions and belongings. This material, which seems to appear free from the control of our will has to be impersonal, collective.[10]

8. *Ibid.*, IX,i, 48–53; VIII, 111.
9. *Ibid.*, VII, 129.
10. *Ibid.*, VII, 125–135; XVII, 116–117.

2. The second way of testing the existence of archetypes is a technique known as "active imagination," namely, a sequence of fantasies produced by deliberate concentration. There exists a correlation between dreams and fantasies; when the fantasies are made conscious the dreams become weaker and less frequent, which proves that they stem from the same source, the unconscious. The resultant sequence of fantasies relieves the unconscious and produces material rich in archetypal images.

3. Archetypal images are also found in the dreams of early childhood, from the third to the fifth year, and chiefly in the case of mental derangement, especially schizophrenics. Insane people frequently produce combinations of ideas and symbols that could never be accounted for by experiences of their individual lives, but only by recourse to the history of the human mind, to mythological thinking. The material of neurosis, Jung insists, is always understandable in human terms and is related to the personal life of the neurotic; neurosis presupposes individual fantasies, not a loss of reality. But the material appearing in psychosis is not understandable in personal terms; schizophrenia implies a loss of reality and a reactivation of archaic fantasies and thinking that cannot be derived from the conscious mind. However, we cannot suppose, Jung insists, that certain minds (psychotics) contain elements that do not exist at all in other minds. Mental disorders manifest material of a hidden but nonetheless general condition of man.[11]

In all these phenomena Jung finds a parallelism and similarity between the manifestation of contemporary and primitive man. The motifs and forms of the unconscious of the former, though spontaneously clothed with new dresses, are similar to the motifs and forms of mythologies of the latter, proving thus the existence of the permanent forms of apprehension and behavior through the ages that he calls archetypes.

Archetypes are crucial factors for the understanding of Jung's

11. *Ibid.*, IX,i, 278, 285; V, 140; VIII, 310–311. Frank de Greave, S.J., an anthropologist who worked in Africa, mentioned to me the following fact. Although the members of the tribe in which he worked were polytheists, those who were afflicted by schizophrenia were monotheists: a remarkable phenomenon.

philosophical structure of personality. "The more I have studied Jung's works," L. Stain says, "the more I have come to see that the essence of his greatness lies in his concept of archetypes, with their contrasting and complementary meaning."[12] And Igor Caruso writes, "Jung deserves credit for having shown that the most powerful formative forces of the soul manifest themselves in primitive images, which are common to all men (and not only to unfortunate neurotics!) namely archetypes. These are in no sense 'illusory,' but genuine functional capacities of the soul, which must be studied seriously."[13] It is therefore important to analyze Jung's arguments leading to the formulation of this hypothesis, as well as the semantics involved in his writings.

The deeper layer of the unconscious, Jung says, is suprapersonal, collective, universal, because its content is not acquired during the individual's lifetime, and is identical in all men. It was perhaps not a happy idea to call this content collective and universal, for all the "specific" properties of man are collective and universal insofar as they are partaken by all the individuals composing the human race. These specific properties, and not their individual marks (which are as such accidental) are what make intellectual knowledge and science possible. As Bertrand Russell put it: "The only difference must lie in just the essence of individuality which always eludes words and baffles description, but which, for that very reason, is irrelevant to science."[14] Therefore, the existence of a suprapersonal layer in the unconscious not only presupposes the manifestation of identical properties in all individuals, but it also presupposes the existence of primitive images, like heroes, gods, demons, dragons, monsters, spirits, etc., that usually appear in myths. "Such contents," Jung says, "are the 'mystical collective ideas' (*representations collectives*) of the primitive described by Lévy Bruhl. . . . He also shows that for the primitive, collective ideas

12. L. Stein, "Language and Archetypes," *Contact with Jung*, ed. Michael Fordham (London, 1963), p. 77.
13. Igor Caruso, *Existential Psychology* (New York, 1964), p. 101.
14. Bertrand Russell, *Introduction to Mathematical Philosophy* (London, 1960), p. 61.

also represent collective feelings. By virtue of this collective feeling-value, he also terms the representations collectives *'mystiques,'* since these representations are not merely intellectual, but also emotional."[15] Hence the value of Jung's discovery lies mainly in the appearance in modern man of archaic elements and primitive ideas. There seems to exist in the unconscious a natural tendency to produce again and again the same primordial ideas and images, namely, the archetypes.

Naturally, all historical proofs are in general hypothetical, which is what is to be expected here. The existence of archetypes is not a conclusion derived from psychological data. Like the majority of hypotheses concerning modern science, they are suggested by empirical observations, but not derived from them. Archetypes are—using the well-known expression of Einstein "free inventions"—free inventions of the mind of Jung, who later verified them in thousands of his patients. And yet, for a better understanding of this bold hypothesis it is significant to emphasize two facts. First, the usual manifestation of the archetypes occurs when man is placed in special psychological states, like dreams, schizophrenia, and active imagination. All these manifestations, however, presuppose a common denominator, namely, the diminution of the state of consciousness which is also the characteristic of primitive mentality. "Reduced intensity of consciousness and absence of concentration and attention, Janet's *abaissement du niveau mental,*" Jung says, "correspond pretty exactly to the primitive state of consciousness in which, we must suppose, myths were originally formed. It is therefore exceedingly probable that the mythological archetypes, too, made their appearance in much the same manner as the manifestations of archetypal structure among individuals today."[16] Hence both contemporary man in this special state, and archaic man share a common psychological attitude that enhances the revelation of the unconscious, which manifests itself into consciousness in a primitive way.

The archetypes, however, are not peculiar symptoms of

15. *Coll. Works,* VI, 530 *(Psychological Types,* trans. H. Godwin Baynes [London, 1926]).
16. *Ibid.,* IX,i, 155–156; Cf. IX,i, 119–120.

unusual or psychotic states. Psychotic states provide the occasion
for their appearance, but they are not the causes of their existence. Primordial thinking, Jung always protests, is neither psychotic nor infantile thinking, but the normal manifestation of
modern man under special conditions of consciousness.[17] Moreover, though the existence of archetypes is proved by recourse
to unusual states of consciousness, Jung insists that archetypes
can arise spontaneously at any time, at any place, and without
any outside influence.[18]

Second, the archetypes reveal themselves as clothed in modern
dress and they appear simultaneously with conscious material.
In practice it is arduous to sort out the contents belonging to
the archetypes from those belonging to the conscious mind, for
they are intimately interwoven. We must remember that
although consciousness and unconsciousness represent different
psychological functions, they are nevertheless manifestations of
a unique psyche. The same phenomenon is characteristic of
mythical thinking; the paradigm, the sacred story, appears
clothed in a variety of concrete forms, depending on the special
individual circumstances in which it emerges.

Archaic Man—In order to understand the nature of archetypes it is crucial to explore the psychology of primitive mentality, because man is still archaic, especially in his unconscious.
Hence it is natural if he shows in his behavior the trait of primitive thought: "Just as our bodies still retain vestiges of obsolete
functions in many of our organs, so our minds, which have

---

17. *Ibid.*, IX,i, 351: "The constellation of archetypal images and fantasies
is not in itself pathological. The pathological element only reveals itself
in the way the individual reacts to them and how he interprets them. The
characteristic feature of pathological reaction is, above all, *identification
with the archetype.*" In IX,i, 39, Jung says: "When, therefore, the analyst
penetrates the background of conscious phenomena, he discovers the same
archetypal figures that activate the deliriums of psychotics. Finally,
there is any amount of literature and historical evidence to prove that in
the case of these archetypes we are dealing with normal types of fantasy
that occur practically everywhere and not only with the monstrous products of insanity. The pathological element does not lie in the existence of
these ideas, but in the dissociation of consciousness that can no longer
control the unconscious." (See also VIII, 122; IX,i, 279; V, 28–29).
18. *Ibid.*, IX,i, 79.

apparently outgrown these archaic impulses, still bear the mark of the evolutionary stage we have traversed, and re-echo the dim bygone in dreams and fantasies."[19] The unconscious shows countless archaic traits.

The view is not new. Mircea Eliade blames Western philosophers for refusing to recognize the experience of primitive man as important. "Better yet," he says, "the cardinal problem of metaphysics could be renewed through a knowledge of archaic ontology."[20] According to Nietzsche, dreams carry us back to remote conditions of human culture.[21] And even Freud, who violently opposed the existence of Jung's collective unconscious, half admitted the archaic nature of dreams. Regarding myth, he says that it seems extremely probable that myths are distorted vestiges of the wish phantasies of whole nations, the age-long dreams of young humanity.[22]

Jung regards the archaic trait of human nature as most significant. Children go through a phase of archaic thinking and feeling, and there exists a layer, the unconscious, which behaves in the same fashion as does the archaic psyche productive of myth. The unconscious brings to our present the unknown psychic life belonging to the remote past. For our purpose, however, the outstanding property of archaic man is the property which Lévy Bruhl terms *participation mystique.* "For

19. *Ibid.,* V, 28. Mircea Eliade, in *Images and Symbols* (New York, 1961), pp. 34–45, says: "By directing attention to the survival of symbols and mythical themes in the psyche of modern man, by showing that the spontaneous rediscovery of the archetypes of archaic symbolism is a common occurrence in all human beings, irrespective of race and historical surroundings, depth psychology has freed the historian of religions of his last hesitations. We will give a few examples, in a moment, of this spontaneous rediscovery of archaic symbolism, and we shall see what these can teach a historian of religions."
20. Mircea Eliade, *Cosmos and History,* xii.
21. Friedrich Nietzsche, *Human All Too-Human,* trans. Helen Zimmern, *The Complete Works of Friedrich Nietzsche,* ed. Oscar Levy (New York, 1924), pp. 24–27: "This ancient element in human nature still manifests itself in our dreams, for it is the foundation upon which the higher reason has developed and still develops in every individual; the dream carries us back into remote conditions of human culture, and provides a ready means of understanding them better."
22. *Coll. Works,* V, 24.

primitive mentality," the French anthropologist says, "subject and objects are simultaneously thought and felt as homogeneous, that is to say, just as if they would share the same essence, or the same ensemble of qualities. . . . The true unity is not the individual, but the group."[23] This peculiar psychological state, Jung says, presupposes a special connection of the subject with the object to which it is bound by an immediate relation that he describes as a partial identity in mutual unconsciousness. When two persons have an unconscious relation to the same fact, they become in part identical, as often happens to children whenever they identify themselves with their parents. This property is natural and happens even now, although in rather more civilized form. Everything that is unconscious in ourselves we discover in our neighbor, and we treat him accordingly; what we combat in him is usually our own inferior side.[24]

Projection is the automatic process whereby a content unconscious to the subject transfers itself to an external object, so that it seems to belong to that object and not to the subject. Projection explains the dynamic of this partial identification, for one axiom pertaining to the psychology of the unconscious asserts that every relatively independent portion of the objective psyche has the character of personality—personality which is projected and personified upon external objects. And since everybody has complexes and independent unconscious factors, projection is a common psychic phenomenon. In primitive man, however, the mechanism of projection is even more common because his mind is yet undifferentiated and he lacks the ability to criticize himself through reflection. Hence, all his unconscious life is objectified and projected upon concrete external objects; for example, when a person is described as a leopard he supposes that he has the soul of a leopard. These identifications, brought about by projection, create a world in which man is completely contained psychologically as well as physically by the collective. Primitive man identified himself with nature and mankind; in the archaic world of primitives

23. Lévy Bruhl, *Bulletin de la Société Française de Philosophie* (Paris, 1929), vol. 29, pp. 105–139.
24. *Coll. Works*, X, 65; VI, 572; X, 37, 452.

everything has the soul of mankind, the collective unconscious, for the individual has yet no soul of his own.[25]

So much for Jung, but let us now inquire about the kind of identification corresponding to this psychological state. Victor White, in *God and the Unconscious,* after quoting the well-known Aristotelian aphorism *intelligibile in actu est intellectu in actu* goes on to say, "Subject and objects are not ultimate *a prioris,* they are conscious data which presuppose a preconscious identity, a *participation mystique* in the deepest sense."[26] Why? Because, according to Aristotle, actual knowledge is identical with its object, that is to say the subject by knowing becomes the object known in a mysterious way. Expressing the same idea, Aquinas says: "The perfection belonging to one thing is found in another. This is the perfection of a knower insofar as he knows; for something is known by a knower by reason of the fact that the thing known is, in some fashion, in the possession of the knower. Hence, it is said in *The Soul* that the soul is, 'in some manner, all things,' since its nature is such that it can know all things. In this way it is possible for the perfection of the entire universe to exist in one thing."[27]

It would be illusory, however, to believe that pure knowledge is capable of completely explaining the identification proper to primitives. Knowledge is required and yet is not enough, because emotions and the feeling of the supernatural play an essential role in primitive mentality. Hence emotions

25. *Ibid.,* X, 65–67.
26. Victor White, O.P., *God and the Unconscious* (Cleveland, 1965), p. 118.
27. Thomas Aquinas, *De Veritate,* q. 2, a. 2. Aristotle, *De Anima, The Works of Aristotle,* ed. W. D. Ross, trans. J. A. Smith (Oxford, 1931), 430 a, 20; 430 a, 14: "Mind is by virtue of becoming all things." The importance of consciousness and intellectual knowledge is pointed out by Jung's following words: "Man is indispensable for the completion of creation: in fact, he himself is the second creator of the world, who alone has given to the world its objective existence—without which, unheard, unseen, silently eating, giving birth, dying, heads nodding through hundreds of million of years, it would have gone on in the profoundest night of nonbeing down to its unknown end. Human consciousness created objective existence and meaning, and man found his indispensable place in the great process of being" (*Memories, Dreams, Reflections,* trans. Richard and Clara Winston [New York, 1963], p. 256).

and feelings make the mystical identification a reality. "Love implies a certain complacency of the lover for the thing loved. . . . Likeness, properly speaking, is the cause of love, for the very fact that men are alike having, as it were, one form, makes them to be, in a manner, one in that form. Hence the affection of one tends to the other, as being one with him; and he wishes good to him as to himself."[28] Thus, likeness, similarity, seems to underlie the mystic unity of primitives, because as their unconscious lacks differentiation it has to be everywhere and in everybody similar, alike. Therefore the unity of the collective unconscious, equally shared by everybody, produces a unity and complacency among the members of the tribe, and by projection also with nature. Upon this unity follows the partial identification of affections which is the essential trait of Lévy Bruhl's mystical participation. With Aristotle we can say that through knowledge man overcomes the limitation proper to his nature by sharing the perfection of other forms. But through love we overcome the division to which created nature is subjected.[29] Especially the primitive and the mystic feel the solidarity with mankind and nature, the former through the unity of the collective unconscious and the common strong feelings of the supernatural; the latter through the experimental knowledge of contemplation, which sees all the universe as the mirror of the perfections of God.

At the end of his life, Lévy Bruhl abandoned his views, and regarded the prelogical state of primitives as "an hypothesis inadequately founded"; primitives share the logic of our own. He also denied the existence of any law of participation. "Although there is not law," he says, "it is a fact that the primitive is often possessed by the feeling of participation of identity with nature and the supernatural, with which he enters in contact."[30]

28. Thomas Aquinas, *Summa Theol.*, trans. Fathers of the English Dominican Province, I–II, q. 27, aa. 1 and 3; *Ibid.*, q. 25, a. 2 ad 2: ". . . there is also an affective union, consisting in an aptitude or proportion, insofar as one thing, from the very fact of its having an aptitude for an inclination to another, partakes of it: and love betokens such a union. . . ."
29. Aristotle, *Post. Analit.*, II, ch. 6, 92 a, 20–25; Thomas Aquinas, *In Post. Analit.*, II, 1. 5, n. 455.
30. Lévy Bruhl, *Les Carnets de Lucien Lévy Bruhl* (Paris, 1949), pp. 77–78; Cf. pp. 60, 62.

And yet, in his writings Jung continuously borrows Lévy Bruhl's original standpoint. He does this, however, in such a personal fashion that it is difficult to say whether he expresses faithfully or not the views of the French anthropologist. Here is a sample: "We call it prelogical, because to us such an explanation seems absurdly illogical. But it seems so to us only because we start from assumptions wholly different from these of primitive man. . . . As a matter of fact, primitive man is no more logical or illogical than we are. Only his presuppositions are different, and that is what distinguishes him from us."[31] Here Jung seems to echo something that Lévy Bruhl wrote at the end of his life:

> In everything that concerns everyday experience, no essential difference is to be found between the mentality of primitives and our own. . . . Where complication arrives is in the matter of mystical experiences. How much is the extent of the difference which springs from the mystical orientation of the mentality of the primitive? Is there a logical rebound?. . . . It is here that the reflection of Einstein makes us reflect for ourselves. For he shows that the intelligibility of the sensible world as ordered and ruled by science is itself without meaning. Compared to the rational world of our sciences, the mythical world is unintelligible, imaginary, cannot be real. How can it happen that, irrational as it is, with its inconsistencies and absurdities, the primitive mentality seriously accepts it as real? In looking for the answer to this question we know that the intellibility of the rational world is itself unintelligible. Could it be that it is simply a difference of degree? A transfer from the unintelligibility of the detail to the world as it is in its totality?[32]

In other words, whether the prelogical state of primitives is true or not, it affects but little the general principles entailed in the theory of archetypes.

Myth and the Unconscious—For many anthropologists of the nineteenth century, myth was the science of primitive man. But

31. *Coll. Works,* X, 52.
32. Lévy Bruhl, *Les Carnets de Lucien Lévy Bruhl,* pp. 70–72.

not for many modern ones, or for Jung who asserts that primitive man is not interested in objective explanations of the obvious. Myth is mainly a psychic phenomenon that reveals the nature of the soul. "Myth explains to the bewildered human being what was going on in his unconscious and why he was held fast."[33]

Therefore a myth is a symbolic expression of the inner unconscious drama of the psyche which becomes accessible to man's consciousness by way of projection, as mirrored in the events of nature. The language of nature for primitive people is not the language of nature as such, but the language of an unconscious psychic event which is projected in natural events. The projection is fundamental, but unconscious; hence, as men were unaware of this automatic mechanism, it took thousands of years to detach it from the outer object. Man thought of everything except the psyche to explain the myth, for his failure to understand the mechanism of projection. The projection of the inner life of the psyche on physical events is the key for the understanding of myth.[34]

Primitives seldom think consciously nor do they invent myths, as moderns invent a physical theory. They simply experience them, and thoughts emerge spontaneously for myths convey vital messages to primitives. They are the psychic life of the archaic tribe, and since religion is connected with the revelation of the unconscious, a tribe mythology is its living religion whose loss, Jung says, is always and everywhere, even among the civilized, a moral catastrophe.[35]

How is a myth formed? The explanation of the formation of myth in archaic man is a most obscure phenomenon, and it would be too much to demand absolute cogency in the thought of Jung. There are objective and subjective conditions for myth formation. Subjective, because reduced intensity of con-

---

33. *Coll. Works,* V, 308. Also, Bronislaw Malinowski, *Magic, Science, and Religion* (New York, 1955), p. 108: "Myth . . . is not an explanation in satisfaction of a scientific interest, but a narrative resurrection of primeval reality."
34. *Coll. Works,* IX,i, 6–7.
35. *Ibid.,* IX,i, 154.

sciousness and absence of concentration and attention correspond to the primitive state of consciousness in which myths
were originated. Objective, insofar as the unconscious of primitive man possesses an irresistible urge to assimilate all outer
experiences to inner psychic events. As the body adapts itself
to environmental conditions, so the psyche must exhibit functional systems which correspond to regular events, and therefore a sort of parallel to regular physical occurrences. For
instance, the primitive man sees the rising and setting of the
sun: this is the objective happening. But the external observation must at the same time be a psychic happening, and the
daily course of the sun through the sky imprints itself in
the psyche in the form of an image from primordial time. The
sun in its course must represent the fate of a hero who, in
the last analysis, dwells nowhere but in the soul of man. The
myth contains the reflection of a physical process, not an
astronomical theory.[36]

Naturally, the Jungian theory of myth does not entail a
revival of Leibnitz's preestablished harmony between the external world and the cognitive powers. But it holds the principle
that natural events produce in the psyche, by means of subjective reactions, a distorted image of the physical happening that
when projected originates the myth. There exists a certain harmony between the physical event, the image produced by the
physical event, and the myth originated by the image.

But why is the physical happening distorted in the myth?
Partly on account of the strong emotional subjectivism of primordial man; partly on account of his identification with
nature and objects in the external world. What happens outside happens also inside and, naturally, for primitive mentality
emotions are more important than physics. Hence he registers
not the physical event, but the emotional fantasies aroused by
the physical event. For example, night for the archaic man
symbolizes snakes and the cold breath of spirits; morning, however, represents the birth of a beautiful god. In other words,
not the rain, storms, thunders, sun, and moon remain as images

36. *Ibid.*, IX,i, 156, 6; VIII, 153–154.

in the psyche, but the fantasies, the subjective reactions caused by the emotions they aroused.[37]

Thus Jung gives a psychological interpretation to myth whose implications he was compelled to study when he discovered mythical traces in contemporary man. Against the objective explanation of myth held by many anthropologists of the nineteenth century, he attempts a subjective-objective interpretation bold and original, though not free from criticism. He discovered the connection between the contents of the unconscious and myth,[38] emphasizing, as George Frazer does, the solidarity of the human psyche with the natural process of nature. With Eliade he stresses the essential necessity of projection.[39] Less clear and more problematic, however, is the double correspondence existing between physical and psychic occurrences; the physical event produces the psychical image which in its turn, through projection, originates the myth. Jung's theory may perhaps be correct; it seems, however, more plausible to ascribe the cause of myth not to the external event, but to the urge of basic inner needs inherent in human nature, needs that are expressed and solved in the history related in myths. Life, birth, death, resurrection, love, struggle, religion, evil, and survival are but a few basic human problems haunting man for millennia, basic even for primitives, who project them upon physical occurrences. The physical event does not seem to produce the myth, but the physical event provides the projection with the occasion for its appearance; thus, the coming of the sun provides the occasion for the birth of a hero who dwells nowhere but in the soul of man. As Eliade says, "Symbols cannot be reflections of cosmic rhythms as *natural phenomena,* for a symbol always reveals something *more* than the aspect of cosmic life it is thought

37. *Ibid.,* VIII, 154–155.
38. Lévy Bruhl, *Les Carnets de Lucien Lévy Bruhl,* p. 199: "Parente intime de reve et du myth." Jung, *Memories, Dreams, Reflections,* p. 131: "As early as 1909 I realized that I could not treat latent psychosis if I did not understand their symbolism. It was then that I began to study mythology."
39. Mircea Eliade, *Myth and Reality* (New York, 1963), p. 185.

to represent."[40] The symbols arise, from the beginning, as a creation of the unconscious psyche, not as a reflection of a cosmic event.

Since archaic man relates and subordinates all causality to spirits, gods, and the supernatural, myths by their very nature are sacred histories explaining the work of gods upon the cosmos and man. Jung considers myth as the living religion of primitive man, in agreement with Lévy Bruhl and modern anthropologists. "Myths," Eliade says, "describe the various and sometimes dramatic breakthrough of the sacred (or the 'supernatural') into the world. . . . The myth is regarded as a sacred history and hence a 'true history,' because it always deals with *realities*."[41]

Origin of Archetypes—Jung's writings do not always distinguish clearly between myth and archetypes. Perhaps the distinction may lie in the concepts of act and potency, whole and part, and cause and effect. Archetypes are a kind of readiness to produce over and over again the same or similar mythical ideas. Thus, archetypes are only potencies that when actualized bring forth the same mythical idea. Archetypes and myths are also like whole and parts, because myth seems to be only a partial expression of the content of archetypes since archetypes manifest themselves in forms not always equivalent to myth, as in fairy tales, dreams, and the product of psychotic activity. Finally, myths and archetypes are like causes and effects, because the existence of archetypes depends on myth: "What we do find . . . is the myth of the sun-hero in all its countless modifications. It is this myth, and not the physical process, that forms the sun archetype."[42] Thus archetypes are originated as a consequence of the subjective fantasies or ideas aroused by myths; archetypes are recurrent impressions made by subjective reactions. On the other hand, once the archetype is formed, it possesses a kind of

40. Mircea Eliade, *Images and Symbols*, p. 176.
41. Mircea Eliade, *Myth and Reality*, p. 6. Lévy Bruhl, *op. cit.*, p. 81: "Les myths son l'histoire sainte de societes primitives." B. Malinowski, *op. cit.*, p. 108: "Myth . . . is a narative resurrection of primeval reality, told in satisfaction of deep religious wants, moral cravings, social submissions, assertions, even practical requirements. . . . Myth is thus a vital ingredient of human civilization."
42. *Coll. Works*, VII, 68.

readiness to produce over and over again the same or similar mythical ideas.[43]

In spite of Jung's explanation, the relation of myth and archetypes is not yet clear. It is the myth which forms the archetype, and at the same time, it is the archetype which produces mythical ideas. Is it a vicious circle? Not likely, because for Jung, the subjective fantasies of myths are the causes of archetypes. But once the archetype is formed, it is endowed with a kind of readiness to arouse the same mythical ideas which were the cause of its formation, a familiar psychological process. Habits and dispositions are formed in the same way; repetition of acts forms the habit, but once the habit exists it is inclined to produce the very acts that were the cause of its existence: "Not only are archetypes, apparently, impressions of over-repeated typical experiences, but, at the same time, they behave empirically like agents that tend towards the repetition of the same experiences."[44]

The origin of archetypes is also related to history, for they are explained by assuming them to be the deposit of constantly repeated experiences of humanity. Experiences of thousands of years of adaptation and existence have been engraved in our psychic constitution as forms without content. Not every experience, however, produces these forms, but the mental processes of our ancestors traced them.[45] Hence Jung regards the archetypes as the historical background of the psyche and, as such, they contained in a concentrated way the entire succession of engrams (imprints) which for time immemorial have determined the psychic structure as it now exists and is inherited with the brain structure. Thus the investigation of the unconscious yields recognizable traces of the archetype structure which coincides with the myth motif, because the creative substratum is everywhere the same human psyche and the same brain, which, with minor variations, functions everywhere in an identical way.[46]

But no such engrams have been found in the brain, and Jung

43. *Ibid.*, VII, 68–69.
44. *Ibid.*, VII, 69.
45. *Ibid.*, VII, 68–69; VI, 272; VIII, 53–54; IX,i, 48.
46. *Ibid.*, VI, 211; VIII, 170; V, xxix, 390.

himself realizes that the repetition of experiences does not totally clear the enigma: "Naturally, this assumption," he says, "only pushes the problem further back without solving it."[47] Moreover, although Jung discovered reminders of Greek mythology in the dreams of pure American Negroes, he also reports the experience with European immigrants whose dreams were similar not to European mythologies, but to those of American Indians, which shows the importance of soil and weather in the psychology of peoples. But Jung never denies the significance of these elements. On the contrary, he regards them as vital elements in the making of our mental structure. "Just as, in the process of evolution, the mind has been molded by earthly conditions, so the same process repeats itself under our eyes today. It is not difficult to tell a Spanish Jew from a North American Jew, a German Jew from a Russia Jew. . . . Our contact with the unconscious chains us to earth, and makes it hard for us to move. . . . He who is rooted in the soil endures."[48]

Jung, pressed by criticism, gradually modified his hypothesis on the origin of archetypes and says: "These images are 'primordial' images insofar as they are peculiar to whole species, and if they ever 'originated' their origin must have coincided at least with the beginning of the species."[49] This is probably true, and equivalent to saying that they were not originated by recurrent experiences. He also confesses that, "whether the archetypes ever 'originated' at all is a metaphysical question and therefore unanswerable."[50]

The origin of archetypes is shrouded in mystery, but it is of great importance to emphasize and make clear that the validity of the existence of archetypes is totally independent of the knowledge of their origin. They are like migrant birds; we clearly see them, although we do not know where they come from.

Properties of Archetypes—Archetypes are not innate ideas by means of which we know, as in Plato's theory of knowledge. They are inborn dispositions to produce parallel images, ideas

47. *Ibid.*, VII, 69.
48. *Ibid.*, X, 45, 49.
49. *Ibid.*, IX,i, 78; Cf. XI, 89.
50. *Ibid.*, IX,i, 101.

in the Platonic sense that influence our thoughts, feelings, and actions. In his first work, Jung called the archetypes "dominants," that is, *types*. Some types of situations and types of figures repeat frequently, and Jung calls these "motifs." They emerge often in dreams, like for example the shadow, the wise old man, the mother, the anima, etc. These "motifs" are prominent archetypes and crucial factors in Jung's process of individuation.[51]

Archetypes are typical, universal, uniform, and regular modes of apprehension which manifest themselves everywhere in identical fashion, not as concrete forms but as forms without content, representing merely the possibilities of a certain type of perception and action. The typical form of apprehension of archetypes is not a pure intellectual apprehension of external objects, as is the activity of the speculative intellect productive of science. Nor is it the apprehension proper to the practical intellect, prerequisite for the appetite that being blind needs the presentation of objects by the cognitive power which directs the action and judges the value of its operation. Archetypes gaze inward, and their apprehension falls upon the inner primordial images that are directly connected with myth. The archetype represents the authentic element of what Jung calls the *spiritus rector* which apprehends the internal psychic world, not the nature of external objects or the value of them.[52]

Although archetypes are factors composing the collective unconscious, they are nevertheless camouflaged in modern attire and interwoven with concrete elements of the individual psyche. Archetypes are forms without content, and their pre-existent traces are filled out by individual experiences. Hence although the archetypes always manifest themselves in identical fashion, their concrete expression, filtered through individual consciousness, may assume great diversity. Personal life actualizes the potentialities of archetypes because they possess an invariable nucleus of meaning, but always in principle, never as regards their concrete manifestation. For instance, the specific

51. *Ibid.*, V, 158, 301; IX,i, 75, 183; XI, 519.
52. *Ibid.*, VIII, 137–138, 206.

appearance of the mother image into consciousness at any given time cannot be deduced from the mother archetype alone but it depends on the conscious and concrete experiences with mothers, and also upon innumerable other factors.[53]

Archetypes are not intellectual modes of apprehension of the external world. But as primordial images, they underlie all thinking and have considerable influence on scientific ideas, religion, philosophy, and ethics. For example, the idea of the principle of conservation of energy, discovered by Robert Mayer is archetypal, according to Jung. It is connected with the idea of power, an idea which has been stamped in the human brain for centuries. Only certain conditions are needed for its appearance, and these were evidently fulfilled in the case of Robert Mayer. The ideas of atoms and ether are also primitive intuitions, according to Jung. Wolfgang Pauli, Nobel laureate and one of the leading physicists of the century, ascribes to archetypal ideas the root of Kepler's scientific theories.[54] The archetypes seem also to have influence in all states of the mind requiring intuition, creative imagination, fantasy, artistic elaboration, and the inner experiences of the mystic.

However, in spite of the support of such an outstanding physicist as Pauli, very few scientists and philosophers will accept without reservations Jung's astonishing interpretation. The discovery of the principles of modern physics, and of science in general as well, presupposes a painstaking, slow, and reflective intellectual elaboration. These principles, the history of science teaches, never appear abruptly, as archetypes do, but only after a long period of meditation. When Newton was asked how he came to make the discovery of gravitation, he replied. "I keep the subject constantly before me, and I wait until the first glimmer of light begins to dawn slowly and gradually, and changes into full light and clarity."[55]

53. *Ibid.*, V, 64; VIII, 3, 110; IX,i, 80.
54. *Ibid.*, XI, 289; VII, 68; VIII, 158, 137 fn.
55. Quoted by Pierre Duhem, *The Aim and Structure of Physical Theory* (Princeton, 1954), pp. 256–257. Naturally, the discovery of modern scientific theories presupposes a certain amount of intuition and creative imagination. But these two factors are conscious and reflective, not unconscious.

The archetypes cannot be known directly because they are unconscious. But they reveal themselves and are made visible in the products of fantasy where they find their specific and concrete application. Archetypes are inherited dispositions of the mind to produce parallel fantasy images which are only indirectly related to external objects. They depend much upon the unconscious fantasy activity and appear more or less abruptly as visions, dreams, and sudden intuitions. The image is like a concentrated symbolic expression of the total psychic situation; it never takes the place of reality, and as a rule it lacks all projection in space. Images are visual, primordial, and collective, proper to the mentality of primitives. They show similarities with familiar mythologic motives, and they are usually connected to the sacred.[56]

Besides images there are also ideas which owe their origin to images because they constitute, as it were, their maternal soil. Ideas are abstract elaborations of the intellect, distinguished from images which are concrete manifestations of fantasy. They are imparted with creative force, vitality, and operation; they also condition feelings.[57]

The contents of the archetypes emerge into consciousness in the form of tendencies or definite ways of looking at things. These subjective tendencies are stronger than the objective influence of the external world, on account of their psychic value which is higher. Hence they superimpose themselves upon all external impressions, for the inner world is more valuable than external realities. When the archetypes are revealed in dreams, fantasies, or in life, their influence either exercises a numinous or fascinating effect, or impels to action. These effects are so strong as to produce extensive alterations in the subject, such as religious conversions, suggestions, and even schizophrenia. In the case of religious phenomena, characterized by the numinous, the subject is gripped by the unconscious as though by an instinct. Where does this power of archetypes come from? Jung answers: from the feeling of being a part of the whole.[58]

56. *Coll. Works*, IX,i, 78; V, 158; VI, 554–555.
57. *Ibid.*, VI, 547–550.
58. *Ibid.*, VI, 476; VII, 69; V, 158, 178.

The archetypes are not obscure corners of the mind, but the mighty deposit of ancestral experiences accumulated over millions of years. They are the echo of prehistoric happenings to which each century adds an infinitesimal amount of variation and differentiation. The archetypes bring to contemporary man the mind of our ancestors, their mode of thinking, feeling, and experiencing life. They are the unwritten history of mankind from time unrecorded, making the past to be present. Rational formulas, Jung continuously insists, may satisfy the present, the immediate past, but never the experience of man as a whole. We think in term of years, the unconscious thinks and lives in term of millennia.[59]

That the archetypes bring forth to the present individual the mind of our ancestors is probably correct, as dreams, schizophrenia, and other observed phenomena reveal. More problematic is the share we are supposed to possess of the wisdom of archaic man, which we inherit with the archetypes. Where does the wisdom of archaic man lie? Why do archetypes think in terms of millennia? There exists, indeed, a natural wisdom in the process of evolution and adaptation of man to environmental circumstances. Primitives living in the jungle know the science of survival, of hunting, fishing, and of justice. Even more, they possess a mythical wisdom in order to explain and solve the basic human riddles, and they have a healthy psychological attitude toward certain family and tribal problems, as their initiations, for example, indicate. But they are often the victims of nature rather than its masters. They live in terror of magical influences which may cross the path of their lives at any moment; magic is the science of the jungle, and fear the state of mind of primitives. Probably the best wisdom we can learn from the primitives lies in the unselfish approach to the problems of the tribe, their religious attitude, and their stoic acceptance of suffering which, in their case, is an inexorable law they know to be part of their lives. In other words, we go back once more to the disputed origin of archetypes. The wisdom, might, and value of archetypes are not necessarily linked

59. *Ibid.*, VIII, 376; XI, 168.

to the archaic activity of primitives nor to their wisdom. They would rather depend on the intrinsic nature and properties of man, especially those properties connected to religion and other spiritual values.

The archetypes dispose of a whole world of images whose boundless range yields in nothing to the claims of the world of external realities. But insofar as archetypes go, they are as many as there are "typical situations in life," since they typify the most frequently and intensely used functions of the human soul. Therefore, the most ordinary events with immediate realities, like husband, wife, father, mother, child, hero, danger, birth, death, and resurrection, etc., emerge as an exalted group of archetypes endowed with tremendous power. The archetypes are, besides, the supreme regulating principles of religion and political life. Some of them are "dominant," like the anima, animus, wise old man, witch, shadow, earthmother, and so forth. Others are the "organizing dominants," usually with the function of combining and unifying several archetypes, as the self, the circle, and the quaternity.[60]

II. *Instincts*

Instincts are psychological factors pertaining to the collective unconscious. Thomas Reid defines them saying: "By instinct, I mean a natural impulse to certain actions, without having any end in view, without deliberation and without any concep-

---

60. *Ibid.,* IX,i, 48; VIII, 156; VI, 211. Regarding the images of archetypes, Jung says: "Like the sea itself, the unconscious yields an endless and self-replenishing abundance of living creatures, a wealth beyond our fathoming. We may long have known the meaning, effects, and characteristics of unconscious contents without ever having fathomed their depths and potentialities, for they are capable of infinite variation and can never be depotentiated" (XVI, 177). Jolande Jacobi, *The Psychology of C. G. Jung* (New Haven, 1954), pp. 61–64: "The number of archetypes is relatively limited for it corresponds to the possibilities of typical fundamental experiences, such as humans have had since the beginning of time. Their significance lies, precisely, on that 'primal experience,' which they represent and mediate. . . . The sum of the archetypes signifies thus the sum of all latent potentialities of the human phyche."

tion of what we do."[61] Jung finds this definition insufficient; for him the uniformity of the phenomenon and the regularity of its recurrence form the characteristic trait of instincts. Instincts are "typical modes of action, and wherever we meet uniform and regularly recurring modes of action and reaction we are dealing with instincts, no matter whether it is associated with a conscious motive or not."[62] Instincts are collective, universal, and regularly occurring phenomena whose energy is unconscious. They manifest themselves as natural impulses toward certain activities, expressed as patterns of biological behavior. They are motivating forms of psychic events which pursue their inherent goals long before there is any consciousness. In other words, for Jung, instincts are psychic elements, free from the control of the conscious mind and endowed with a natural inclination towards the objects fitting for them. This idea reminds us of the following words of Aquinas: "The natural appetite is that inclination which each thing has, of its own nature, for something; wherefore by its natural appetite each power desires something suitable to itself. . . . "[63]

Instincts and archetypes are different psychological factors making up the collective unconscious. They are different because instincts are modes of existence and archetypes are modes of apprehension; instincts are natural impulses expressed as typical and regular modes of action and reaction while archetypes are dominants which emerge into consciousness as ideas and images.[64] And yet while instincts and archetypes are different, they are not independent; they are, on the contrary, intimately related, for the archetypes are the images of instincts themselves. Archetypes are the patterns of instinctual behavior; that is to say, the forms and categories that regulate the instincts. The image is the instinct's perception of itself; the self portrait of the instinct in exactly the same way as consciousness is the inward perception of the objective life process. The image of

61. *Coll. Works*, VIII, 130.
62. *Ibid.*, VIII, 135. See also: VIII, 200–201, 118, 115, 158; VI, 565; IX,i, 43–44.
63. Thomas Aquinas, *Summa Theol.*, I–II, q. 78, a. 1 ad 3. Cf. I, q. 80, a. 1.
64. *Coll Works*, VIII, 133–135, 217–218; VI, 476.

archetypes is the bridge unifying instincts and archetypes.[65]

However, this connection is not always clear in Jung's own writings. For example, he quotes Freud in the following passage: "An instinct can never become an object of consciousness—only the idea that represents the instinct can. Even in the unconscious, moreover, an instinct cannot be represented otherwise than by an idea." Jung criticizes the second part of the sentence saying: "Exactly *who* has the idea of the instinct in the unconscious state? For unconscious ideation is a *contradiction in adjecto*."[66] Ideas are elaborations of the conscious mind exclusively; hence an unconscious idea is an impossibility. But Jung seems to fall into the same difficulty. He says: "Just as the conscious apprehension gives our actions form and direction, so unconscious apprehension through the archetype determines the form and direction of instinct."[67] The riddle is obvious, because an "unconscious apprehension" seems almost as impossible to understand as an unconscious ideation. The only possible ideation of the unconscious is realized by means of images—the conscious symbol of archetypes—and the corresponding ideas abstracted from them. This is perhaps Jung's own interpretation, for he says: "There are, in fact, no amorphous instincts, as every instinct bears in itself the pattern of its situation. Always it fulfills an image and the image has fixed qualities. Such an image is an *a priori* type. . . . The images of archetypes are these *a priori* instinct types which provide the occasion and the pattern for man's activities, insofar as he functions instinctively. . . . We may say that the image represents the *meaning* of the instinct."[68]

By relating archetypes and instincts Jung is aware of a thorny problem: the connection between the dynamism of the unconscious and its corresponding apprehension of objects. The unconscious is not a static factor but, on the contrary, a vital power which manifests its activity through the operation of instincts. Hence, there will be as many instincts as there are

65. *Ibid.*, IX,i, 44; VIII, 137, 158.
66. *Ibid.*, VIII, 200 fn.
67. *Ibid.*, VIII, 137.
68. *Ibid.*, VIII, 201.

different kinds of operations. And yet, how is it possible to know the different kinds of operations if they are unconscious? The originality of Jung's ideas lies mainly in the consideration of archetypes as the patterns of instinctual behavior, as the images or self-portraits of instincts. Thus the archetypes specify and distinguish the different kinds of instincts because to every regular and uniform form of activity there corresponds a regular and uniform form of apprehension. The diversity of instincts reveals their nature to consciousness through the appearance of different kinds of symbolic images that are like the goal of the instinctual activity. "Instincts," Jung says, "have two main aspects: on the one hand, that of dynamism and compulsion, and on the other, specific meaning and intention."[69] And further: "Instincts are highly conservative and of extreme antiquity as regards both their dynamism and their form. Their form, when represented to the mind, appears as an image which expresses the nature of the instinctive impulse visually and concretely, like a picture. . . . Instinct is anything but a blind and indefinite impulse, since it proves to be attuned and adapted to a definite external situation. This latter circumstance gives it its specific and irreducible form. . . . its form is age-old, that is to say, *archetypal*."[70]

Are instinctual human activities independent of knowledge? Is apprehension equivalent to knowledge? Instincts are by definition unconscious, but the cognitive power perceives their activities, as is obvious when a being endures pangs of hunger or deep loneliness.[71] But this does not answer our question directly. It is manifest, however, that in most cases the instinctual reaction underlying motion seems to be always in correspondence with specific human needs already known by a previous cognitive apprehension. This is clear in the case of the five instincts which Jung mentions, namely, hunger, sex, drive to activity, reflection, and creativity, whose objects are presented to the instinct by the intellect or senses. Sensitive and intellectual

69. *Ibid.*, X, 287.
70. *Ibid.*, X, 282.
71. Although the appetite as such is unconscious, it can be known by analysis of its acts. For example, Aquinas explains how the will can be known by means of the intellect: *Summa Theol.*, I, q. 87, a. 4, ad 2.

knowledge is required for the instinctual activity which belongs to man, inasmuch as he is sensitive and rational. But knowledge does not seem required for other activities, because from every form follows a natural inclination. And as Aquinas says, "In those things that lack knowledge that form is found to be inclined always towards one thing fitting to it." Although in these cases he adds, "Even natural love, which is in all things, is caused by a kind of knowledge, not indeed existing in natural things themselves, but in Him who created their nature."[72] The activity of any instinct totally deprived of knowledge seems unintelligible.

Do instincts need primordial images as their self portrait? Does instinctual human activity depend on the apprehension of archaic patterns? The continuous activity of instincts, seemingly independent of any archaic connotation, appears to deny such necessity. No primordial image is required for a hungry man or a person in love. Appropriated concrete existing objects are sufficient to orient their activities.

Nobody would deny such observations, but these obvious facts have no bearing on the existence of archetypes because, as we explained above, archetypes are interwoven with individual elements. Consequently, the regularity and uniformity of instinctual behavior are explained in terms of the regular apprehension of archetypes; their concrete actualization, however, is explained by the individual external beings which fill their potentialities. Primordial images will probably appear whenever there is a slackening of consciousness, as in dreams or other circumstances. For example, Eliade relates the following contemporary event: "When the Congo became independent in 1960, in some villages their inhabitants tore the roofs off their huts to give passage to the gold coins that their ancestors were to rain down. . . . Even the orgiastic excesses had a meaning, for, according to the myth, from the dawn of the New Age all women would belong to all men."[73] The myth of the

72. Thomas Aquinas, *Summa Theol.,* I–II, q. 27, a. 2 ad 3. The complexity of human inclinations can be seen in *Summa Theol.,* I–II, q. 94, a. 2.
73. Mircea Eliade, *Myth and Reality,* p. 3. In *Cosmos and History* he says: "Marriage and the collective orgy echo mythical prototypes; they are repeated because they were consecrated in the beginning by gods, ancestors, or heroes" (p. 4).

destruction of the world, followed by a new creation and the establishment of the golden age, underlies these primordial activities. Furthermore, there are unmistakable traits of myth in the behavior of contemporary man, as will be shown later. Hence, as evident in these examples, primordial images and concrete external objects are not mutually opposed, but rather complementary.

Archetypes and instincts, however, do not always behave in the way explained above. When the archetypes appear in the form of spirit, Jung says, the relation between archetype and instinct follows a different course. Then archetypes and instincts are the most opposite imaginable, as can be seen when one compares a man who is ruled by his instinctual drive with a man who is seized by the spirit. But they subsist side by side as reflection in our mind of the opposition that underlies all psychic energy. Psychic energy flows as a consequence of the opposition between instinct and spirit. However, the question of whether a process is to be described as spiritual or as instinctual remains shrouded in obscurity. A poorly developed archetype will see in the instinctual drives the source of all reality. Conversely, a consciousness that finds itself in opposition to the instinct can—in consequence of the enormous influence exerted by the archetype—subordinate instinct to spirit.[74]

The connection existing between the archetype of the spirit and instincts reminds us of the interwoven world of the will and lower passions. Their corresponding objects appear on occasions as opposite, and since the control of the will over the passions is far from being absolute, struggle and hardship ensues as a natural sequel. For Jung, however, opposition and polarity are prerequisites of energy; the greater the opposition the greater the flow of energy. But this seems to contradict the facts of psychological observation. More energy is available in a man whose passions are subdued to the will than in a man unable to control them, although it is also evident that no human growth is possible without struggle, fight, and even failures.

74. *Coll. Works,* VIII, 206–207.

II

Jung's Process of Individuation

As a psychologist Jung is mainly concerned with a purely intellectual analysis of the structure and dynamics of human personality. But Jung is not only a psychologist, he is also a psychiatrist, a therapist interested in the welfare of his patients and
in the growth of their personalities. Psychology, he says, culminates of necessity in a development process which is peculiar
of the psyche; a development of man to the limits corresponding to his nature, occurring only when the person becomes a
psychological individual, a separated indivisible unity, a whole.
Becoming a whole is the answer to the great question of our
day: How can consciousness, our most recent acquisition which
is bounded ahead, be integrated with the oldest, the unconscious, which has lagged behind? individuation, therefore, is a
synthetic human phenomenon which follows the natural course
of life; consciousness must confront the unconscious, and a
balance between their opposition must be found. And since,
according to Jung, the unconscious is the root of religious experience and the dwelling of the God-image, individuation is "the
life in God," for man is obviously not a whole without God.[1]

Difficulties—Individuation is an exceedingly difficult task; it
always involves a conflict of duties and claims, the claims of
consciousness against those of unconsciousness, the solution of
which requires us to understand that our "counter will," the
unconscious, is also an aspect of God's will. It is an heroic and

1. C. G. Jung in H. L. Philp, *Jung and the Problem of Evil* (New York,
1959), p. 225. *Coll. Works,* VIII, 223; IX,i, 275, 330; VII, 171. "Individuation . . . is a process of differentiation, having for its goal the development
of the individual personality" (VI, 561).

often tragic task comparable to the torture of initiation; not merely a punishment, however, but the indispensable means which leads man toward his destiny. Hence, it involves suffering, and every step forward along the path of individuation is achieved only at the cost of intense spiritual suffering, a passion of the ego for the violence done to it by the self.[2]

People naturally prefer not to ponder upon how much fear and sorrow fall to the lot of man, for suffering is disagreeable. But suffering and pain are not only the traits of neurosis, they have also a positive significance and life demands for its fulfillment a balance between joy and sorrow. Victor E. Frankl, against the pleasure principle made absolute, writes: "Lack of success is not equivalent to meaninglessness; to suffer for a condition that ought not to be is an 'essential and significant' part of human life."[3] For Jung also, the Christian doctrine of the value of suffering is of profound therapeutic significance. The principle aim of psychotherapy, he says, is not to transport the patient to an impossible state of happiness, but to help him to acquire steadfastness and philosophical patience in the face of suffering. Either we fall into the false suffering of a neurosis, or we experience the genuine suffering necessary to achieve maturity.[4]

Moreover, individuation is dangerous, with danger rooted in the tremendous power of the archetypes that consciousness must assimilate. When we are dealing with the unconscious we have to be cautious, for consciousness is like a fertile field exposed to a raging torrent by the bursting of a dam. If the consciousness of man is weak, the unconscious swallows the ego and a pathological inflation may ensue, which is dangerous because

2. Coll. Works, XI, 156–157, 272, 198.
3. Victor E. Frankl, in Igor Caruso, Existential Psychology, p. 73. V. Frankl, Man's Search for Meaning (New York, 1968), trans. Ilse Lash, p. 106: "If there is a meaning in life at all, then there must be a meaning in suffering. Suffering is an ineradicable part of life, even as fate and death. Without suffering and death human life cannot be complete. The way in which a man accepts his fate and all the sufferings it entails, the way in which he takes up his cross, gives him ample opportunity—even under the most difficult circumstances—to add a deeper meaning to his life."
4. Coll. Works, XVI, 81.

it presupposes the identification of consciousness with the collective contents of the unconscious. This is equivalent to the
loss of an individual's soul, to a state of God-almightiness.
Even primitive man knows this danger and protects himself
against it by religious and magical practices. This is why the
medicine man, Jung says, has always been a priest; he is the
savior of the soul as well as the body, and religions are systems
for the healing of psychic illness.[5]

There are passive elements in the unconscious which may be
stirred up as soon as we begin to look inside; elements which,
if not well known and controlled, may occasion neurosis and
even psychosis. On the other hand, the suppression of the
unconscious is also dangerous, for the unconscious is life, and
if it is suppressed, life turns against us in the form of neurosis.
These difficulties make it almost impossible to explore the
unconscious alone; only the analyst can take us into this for-
bidden territory to the regions of the inner inferno. Nor is
every analyst capable of this tremendous task. Therefore the
doctor himself should be analyzed first: "The analyst is blind
to the attitude of his patients," Jung says, "to the extent that
he does not see himself and his own unconscious problems. For
this reason I maintain that a doctor must himself be analyzed
before he practices analysis."[6] Individuation is not possible
without the mutual transformation of patient and doctor. In

5. *Ibid.*, XI, 344; VII, 140, 144.
6. *Ibid.*, IV, 235. Cf. XVI, 8; IV, 198. "I have seen many cases where the
patient assimilated the doctor in defiance of all theory and of the latter's
professional intentions—generally, though not always, to the disadvantage
of the doctor. The stage of transformation is grounded on these facts, but
it took more than twenty years of wide practical experience for them to be
clearly recognized. Freud himself has admitted their importance and has
therefore seconded my demand for the analysis of the analyst. What does
this demand mean? Nothing less than the doctor is as much 'in the analysis'
as the patient. He is equally a part of the psychic process of treatment and
therefore equally exposed to the transforming influence." Jacques Maritain, "Freudianism and Psychoanalysis—A Thomist View" in *Freud and
The 20th Century* (New York, 1957), ed. Benjamin Nelson, pp. 239–240:
"It is generally the case of having to choose one good doctor out of a
thousand; in this instance it is a case of having to choose one good psycho-
analyst out of ten thousand. . . ."

the process, the stronger and more stable personality will decide the final issue.

Archetypes of the Collective Unconscious—In individuation conscious and unconscious factors have equal rights. Therefore open conflict and collaboration are the essential requisites of human growth. The solution of the problems afflicting man, however, stems from the unconscious, because as a consequence of the self-defense mechanism of man, it stands in a compensatory relation to the conscious mind. The unconscious contains all those elements that are necessary for the self-regulation of the psyche as a whole, namely, the archetypes, which are instinctive defense mechanisms that automatically intervene when danger is great. Hence, although the unconscious is dangerous and powerful, it also contains all the elements that can effectively correct the one-sideness of the conscious mind if the elements that are there are made conscious, i.e., understood and integrated into it as realities.[7]

Dangers and sufferings, therefore, are never solved exclusively by what the rational man thinks of himself; only the suprahuman revealed truth of the irrational archetypes shows him the way out of his distress. The archetypes intervene automatically, and their coming into action is represented in the fantasy by helpful images which are imprinted on the human psyche. Thus, it is only through the revelation of the unconscious that individuation and integration are possible. This revelation manifests itself in different forms. Through dreams, active imagination, drawings, and pictures the forgotten psychic past comes into light and symbols appear. We go back into paths trodden from time immemorial, whose milestones, Jung says, are religions. For modern man too, religions—especially Christianity and Buddhism—are healing systems for psychological illness. Man is never helped in his sufferings by what he thinks of for himself; only suprahuman revealed truth lifts him out of this distress.[8]

Symbolism—Ernst Cassirer thought of man as a "symbol-

7. *Coll. Works,* VII, 108, 175–176; IX,i, 289; XI, 345.
8. *Ibid.,* XI, 344, 299; IX,i, 350.

making creature," and Jung speaks of the "image-making power of the human psyche." Symbolism is inherent to all peoples and cultures and extends to art, religion, science, literature, language, and to almost every single human activity. The unconscious is also revealed always in the form of symbols. And since individuation is an irrational life process which expresses itself in definite symbols, the knowledge of these symbols is indispensable; it is through them that the harmonization and union of the contents of conscious and unconscious are realized. Out of these symbols, new situations emerge, leading man towards wholeness.[9]

Saint Augustine defines the sign as "that which over and above the impression it produces on the senses, brings to the mind something other than itself."[10] Signs are instruments of knowledge and communication; the sign reminds us of the thing it signifies; it is a means of reaching to that thing or of communicating ideas or images to others. For example, a natural sign like smoke brings to mind the idea of fire; and through language, which is a conventional sign, we are able to convey our thoughts to our fellowmen.

And yet, a symbol is for Jung much more than a sign; symbols are a natural manifestation of the unconscious, of its nature, life, motions, and laws. Through them, therefore, we are able to grasp, although only partially, the contents of our objective psyche. The symbol is not a sign standing for a known fact, but an anthropomorphic expression of something suprahuman and only partly conceivable. Symbols are images of contents which for the most part transcend consciousness and bring to the mind a sense of mystery. They are the highest possible expression for something divined but not yet totally known even to the observer; something which imparts in us a life-giving stimulating effect to our thinking as well as to our feelings. The symbol is alive as long as it is pregnant with meaning. Its nature is neither concrete nor abstract, neither rational nor

9. *Ibid.*, XI, 289.
10. Saint Augustine, *De Doctrina Christiana: Signum est quod praeter speciem quam ingerit sensibus, facit aliquid in cogitationem venire.*

irrational, neither real nor unreal, neither hidden nor manifest; it is always both.[11]

The unfolding of the process of individuation expresses itself in symbols of an irrational nature. But symbols are poly-valent; they possess many meanings, and Jung believes in the multiple significance of symbolic contents, as Eliade and Saint Augustine do. Hence, when the symbol appears, ordinary con-scious knowledge is not sufficient; a knowledge of the history of religious symbolism, philosophy, and myth is necessary if we wish to interpret the message that a symbol brings to us from the unconscious. In the process of individuation, the important symbols express man's primary intuition of his relation to the world and God. In addition, according to Jung, the help which medieval alchemy affords us in understanding the symbols of the individuation process is of utmost importance, for the alchemists were not trying to discover the philosopher's stone but were projecting into matter the processes and motions of their unconscious towards individuation.[12]

Process of Individuation—There are two aspects in the pro-cess of individuation: (1) Dispositive, or the process of divest-ing the soul of the wrappings of a false individuation called *persona,* and of protecting man against the suggestive power of primordial images. (2) Perfective, or the process of making as fully conscious as possible the cluster of unconscious contents and of synthetizing them with consciousness through the act of

11. *Coll. Works,* XI, 207; V, 207; VI, 604; XII, 270–271. "It is necessary to have the magic of the symbol which contains those primitive analogies that speak to the unconscious. The unconscious can be reached and expressed only by symbols, which is the reason why the process of individu-ation can never do without the symbol. The symbol is the primitive expression of the unconscious, but at the same time it is also an idea cor-responding to the highest intuition produced by consciousness."

12. *Ibid.,* XVI, 102; IX,i, 287; XVI, 8. Saint Augustine, in *Confessions,* Bks. 9,7 and 13,31, says that the serpent can be the symbol of evil and of wisdom. Mircea Eliade, *The Two and the One* (London, 1965), p. 203: "An essential characteristic of religious symbolism is its multivalence, its capacity to express simultaneously several meanings the unity between which is not evident in the plane of immediate experience." See also Ernst Cassirer, *An Essay on Man* (New Haven, 1944), p. 68.

recognition. To achieve this goal we must make the fullest possible use of the healing factor of compensation.[13]

Because the unconscious cannot be swallowed up or ignored, the assimilation of the unconscious and the development of the personality are not achieved without differentiation. Differentiation is the way of determining which elements belong to consciousness and unconsciousness, respectively. A partial or blurred differentiation leads to an immediate melting away of the individual in the collective; therefore, the conscious processes must be clearly separated from the unconscious ones, and the latter then observed objectively. Only this knowledge leads to the possibility of an accommodation with the unconscious followed by a further attempt at synthesis.[14]

Since differentiation is a cognitive activity, it requires previous knowledge of the symbols appearing in dreams, active imagination, and other manifestations of the unconscious. The archetypes, however, are not integrated by pure rational means (for they are autonomous complexes) but by recourse to a dialectic method, often in dialogue form, carried out between the ego and the unconscious in order to come to terms with the archetypes. First we must understand the meaning of the fantasies produced, then we must experience them to the full, which demands not only perception, discussion, and passivity, but above all active participation. The patient complies with this demand if he conducts himself in reality as the fantasy and dreams are suggesting that he behave. To face the demands of the unconscious often requires moral strength and fortitude, and in these it becomes clear how much the growth of man is a moral problem.[15]

The solution of moral difficulties depends on the ethical qualities of the individual and on the power of symbols as well. Not only are the symbols pregnant with meaning, they also contain healing characteristics, power, and the ability to transform the libido from the unconscious to consciousness, from the

13. *Coll. Works*, VII, 109–110, 171; IX,i, 40.
14. *Ibid.*, IX,i, 180–181; VII, 204.
15. *Ibid.*, IX,i, 40; VII, 204.

material to the spiritual, from lower into higher form, and vice versa. The symbol works by suggestion, carries conviction, and at the same time expresses the content of that conviction. That is why the symbolic apparatus inherent in religion and philosophy is of the greatest importance. The vitality of a religion, Jung says, depends on the vitality of its symbols: "When I see how China (and soon India) will lose her old culture under the impact of materialistic rationalism, I grow afraid that the Christian West will succumb to the same malady, simply because the old symbolic language is no longer understood and people cannot see any more where and how it applies."[16] God approaches man in the form of symbols.[17]

As individuation proceeds to its goal, man undergoes a change of personality; in Jung's term, a "rebirth," which naturally does not presuppose the alteration of the original disposition, but a transformation of man's general attitude. The natural transformation processes announce themselves mainly in dreams which exhibit symbols of rebirth, for it is in them that the union of conscious and unconscious is consummated: "Out of the union emerge new situations and new conscious attitudes. I have therefore called the union the 'transcendent function.' This rounding out of personality into a whole may well be the goal of any psychotherapy that claims to be more than a mere cure of symptoms."[18] At this stage, the center of personality

16. C. G. Jung, in H. L. Philp, *Jung and the Problem of Evil*, p. 254. Cf. *Coll. Works*, IX,i, p. 289.
17. C. G. Jung, in H. L. Philp, *Jung and the Problem of Evil*, p. 226; *Coll. Works*, V, 225–226, 232; XI, 503. Ira Progoff, *Jung's Psychology and Its Social Meaning* (New York, 1953), p. 231: "The psychic process which Jung describes is, then, a symptom of transition in the fundamental values of any period of history. . . . Jung interprets all of these signs that the traditional symbols of Western civilization are ceasing to be operative, that they are becoming less and less able to hold together the personality of the Western individual, and that therefore new symbols soon come to the fore."
18. *Coll. Works*, IX,i, 289. Cf. IX,i, 180–181, 276; VII, 217. Saint Augustine, *Divine Providence and the Problem of Evil*, Bk. 2, ch. 18, 48: "It is oneness that I seek, it is oneness that I love. . . ." Bk. I, ch. 2, 3: "In like manner, the soul spreading out from itself is battered by a kind of immensity and worn out in the quality of a beggar, because its nature forces it to seek everywhere that which is one, and the multitude does not permit it to find unity." For a philosophical explanation of man's unity see Thomas Aquinas, *Summa Theol.*, I, q. 76, a. 1.

has been shifted from the ego to the self; man has really attained the goal he was striving for, the fulfillment of his own specific nature, namely, unity and wholeness.

Individuation assumes the greatest imaginable variety of forms depending on different individuals and on the variety of cultures to which they belong. The only common factor is the emergence of a certain definite number of archetypes which appear in connection with the different steps of the process. The conscious mind must come to terms with the figure of the unknown woman (anima), the unknown man (shadow), the wise old man (mana-personality), and the symbol of the self. This process is summarized in this dream of a ten-year-old girl. "Once in a dream I saw an animal that had lots of horns. It spiked up other little animals with them. It wriggled like a snake and that was how it lived. Then a blue fog came out of all four corners, and it stopped eating. Then God came, but there were really four Gods in the four corners. Then the animal died, and all the animals it had eaten came out alive again."[19]

I. *The Shadow*

The process of individuation invariably starts when the patient becomes conscious of the shadow. Everybody "carries" a shadow because not everything in man is perfect and good. The shadow signifies the negative side of our personality, the sum of those unpleasant qualities we have to hide together with insufficiently developed functions. The shadow is the inferior personality made up of everything that will not fit in with the laws and regulations of conscious life. It is a darkness which hides influential autonomous factors, usually a negative feeling value; the hidden, repressed, and guilt-laden personality. The shadow, however, is not necessarily evil, but inferior and un-adapted, not wholly bad. Furthermore, since all the archetypes develop good and bad effects, the shadow does not consist only of morally reprehensible tendencies, but it also displays a number of good qualities such as normal instincts, appropriate

19. *Coll. Works*, IX,i, 353. Cf. VII, 108; XII, 89; IX,ii, 156.

reactions, realistic insights, and creative impulses.[20]

The shadow represents first and foremost the contents of the personal unconscious, but not exclusively. Besides the personal shadow—easy to detect, and relatively evil—there is also the archetype of the shadow. When the archetype of the shadow appears, Jung says, it is a rare and shattering experience for man to gaze into the face of absolute evil. The shadow has a most frequent disturbance in the ego, not only on account of its own effects, but also because the contents of the personal unconscious (the shadow) merge indistinguishably with the archetypal contents of the collective unconscious and drag the latter with them when the shadow is brought into consciousness. This may exert an uncanny influence on the conscious mind, even of the most cold-blooded rationalist.[21]

Jung believes in the evolution of man from animals; thus the shadow is that hidden and inferior part of the personality whose ultimate ramifications reach back into the realm of our animal ancestors, and it comprises the whole historical aspect of the unconscious. Hence, we carry with us the primitive and inferior with its drives and emotions, the lowest level of which is indistinguishable from animal instincts.[22]

Nothing that is autonomous in the psyche is impersonal or neutral; all autonomous psychic factors have the character of personality. Hence, the shadow appears in the consciousness either in projection upon suitable external objects, or as personified. Everything that the subject refuses to acknowledge about himself is personified, such as the inferior traits of character and other incompatible tendencies. The shadow personifies in dreams in the form of symbols, as for example, a black snake, and it also has been portrayed by poets and writers, e.g., the Faust-Mephistopheles relationship, and E. A. Hoffman's *The Devil Elixir*. When the contents of the personal shadow are interwoven with the archetypal contents of the collective unconscious, then the personification may assume grotesque and horrible forms in dreams and fantasies, so that even the most

20. *Ibid.*, IX,ii, 266, 28; XI, 197, 76–78; VII, 65 fn.
21. *Ibid.*, XII, 32; IX,ii, 8–10.
22. *Ibid.*, IX,ii, 33, 266; XI, 76.

hard-boiled rationalist is not immune from shattering night-mares and, haunting fears. The psychological elucidation of these images, which cannot be ignored, leads into the depths of religious phenomenology.[23] The shadow appears also in projection as when we burden our neighbors with the faults we obviously have ourselves. The unconscious does the projection and the projection changes the world into a replica of one's own unknown face, which isolates the subject from his environment.[24]

The shadow possesses an emotional nature, a kind of autonomous possessive quality and, as such, it is incapable of moral judgment. For this reason, the shadow poses a moral problem that challenges the whole ego-personality, for no one becomes conscious of the shadow without considerable effort. This problem is as important, Jung says, as that of sin in the Church, because to become conscious of its presence involves the recognition of the dark aspect of our personality as present and real. The ego is endowed with the power of moral judgment, and is aware of evil and the subsequent possibility of repentence and redemption. The therapist, Jung explains, has to deal with people who were confronted with the black shadow, and he knows—less by religious training and education than from instinct and experience—that in evil there is something very like Saint Augustine's *felix culpa*. But the doctor must not weigh whether a thing is for or against the Church, but whether it is for or against life and death; there is no evil that in the last analysis cannot produce good, Jung asserts.[25]

Although we are told not to be all gold, the meeting with the shadow is far from easy. In the abstract we know that we are not perfect, but in the concrete a moral effort is required to recognize that we are less good than we imagine ourselves to be. Usually the educated man tries to repress the inferior man and forces the latter into revolt. The more he represses his shadow, the worse; the less conscious a man is of his shadow, the blacker and denser the shadow becomes. A man who is possessed by the shadow is always standing in his own dark light and falling

23. *Ibid.*, XII, 32; IX,i, 284–285, 322; X, 42.
24. *Ibid.*, XII, 29; IX,ii, 9–10.
25. *Ibid.*, XII, 29–31; IX,ii, 8–9.

into his own trap.[26] For this reason, Jolande Jacobi says, "We
see persons gradually or suddenly afflicted with sterility who try
convulsively, with an awful exertion of will, far beyond their
power, to hold themselves 'on top,' and who can confess their
own weaknesses neither to themselves, nor to others. . . . We
see how it is difficult or impossible for these persons to get
through their own feelings, to enter into a genuine relation, or
to do a piece of living work."[27]

Self-knowledge is, therefore, the first requisite to encounter
the shadow, which is the most accessible element of the unconscious because its nature can be inferred from contents of the
personal unconscious. But although psychologically speaking
the contents of the personal unconscious can be discovered
easily, a considerable moral effort is required to face this archetype, for we do not face self-scrutiny without resistance, and
only after much painstaking work extending over a long period
of time.[28] Recognition of the shadow leads to the modesty we
need in order to acknowledge imperfection. A modest man
knows that whatever is wrong in the world is in himself, and
if he only learns to deal with his own shadow he has done something for the world. Failure to recognize the archetype, Jung
says, has brought white man and the whole world to the brink
of destruction. For instance, convinced of their own rectitude
the Nazis committed crimes of unprecedented scale; Hitler
represented the shadow to an overwhelming degree, and since
Germany was prey to mass psychology, it fell for him. The first
condition for moral health is therefore humility; recognition
of the shadow is a reason for it, for genuine fear of the abys-
mal depths of man. This recognition is important because our
dark side is not harmless; it brings the archaic psyche, the whole

26. *Ibid.*, XI, 76; IX,ii, 8; IX,i, 123.
27. Jolande Jacobi, *op. cit.*, p. 147.
28. *Coll. Works*, IX,ii, 8. Thomas Aquinas, *Summa Theol.*, II–II, q. 60, a.
3: "As Tully says, suspicion denotes evil thinking based on light indications, and this is due to three reasons. First, from a man being evil in himself, and from this very fact, as though conscious of his own wickedness, he
is prone to think evil of others according to Eccles. X: 3. The fool when
he walketh in the way, whereas he himself is a fool, esteemeth all men
fools. . . ."

world of archetypes, into direct contact with the conscious world and mind. The shadow lurks behind every neurotic dissociation, and can only be annexed to consciousness if the corresponding unconscious contents are made conscious. Consequently, it is imperative to discover our shadow, because insofar as it is conscious there is always a possibility of correction; if repressed, there is no possibility at all, and, on the contrary, it is liable to burst forth suddenly in a moment of awareness, upsetting the ego and breeding neurosis.[29]

Hence, the integration of the shadow not only presupposes the knowledge of its existence but also requires the solution of the moral and emotional problems connected with it. We must admit the tendencies bound up with the shadow and allow them some measure of realization, tempered with the necessary criticism. Individuation always involves resistances, usually bound up with projections and personifications which are not recognized as such: "The cause of emotion appears to lie, beyond all possibility of doubt, in the *other person*. No matter how obvious it may be to the neutral observer that it is a matter of projections, there is little hope that the subject will perceive this himself. He must be convinced that he throws a very large shadow before he is willing to withdraw his emotionally-toned projections from their objects."[30]

Confession is a therapeutical necessity in confronting our shadow, our sins, and our guilt. A secret shared with several persons is as beneficial as a merely private secret is destructive; the latter, Jung says, works like a burden of guilt, cutting off

---

29. *Coll. Works*, XI, 76, 198, 83; XII, 29; X, 301, 222–223. "The tide that rose in the unconscious after the first World War was reflected in individual dreams, in the form of collective, mythological symbols which expressed primitivity, violence, cruelty: in short, all the powers of darkness. When such symbols occur in a large number of individuals and are understood, they begin to draw these individuals together as if by magnetic force, and thus a mob is formed. . . . I had observed the German revolution in the test tube of the individual, so to speak, and I was fully aware of the immense dangers involved when such people crowd together. But I did not know at the time whether there were enough of them in Germany to make a general explosion inevitable" (X, 220).
30. *Ibid.*, IX,ii, 9. Cf. XI, 198; X, 287. See also A.A.A. Terruwe, *The Neurosis in the Light of Rational Psychology* (New York, 1960).

the unfortunate possessor from communion with his fellows. But if we are conscious of what we are concealing, the harm done is decidedly less than if we do not know what we are repressing. In this case, the hidden content is kept secret even from ourselves, hence, generally speaking, an unconscious secret is more injurious than a conscious one. All personal secrets, therefore, have the effect of sin or guilt, whether or not they are, from the standpoint of popular morality, wrongly secrets. Through confession, we throw ourselves into the arms of humanity again, freed at last from the burden of moral exile.[31]

Not only unrevealed secrets are harmful, however, for we are also loaded with emotions, and inhibited emotions have the same effect that unrevealed secrets do. Saint Augustine, in his *Confessions*, tells how at the death of Monica, his mother, a huge wave of sorrow flooded his heart ready to flow outwardly in tears; yet, at the same time, under the forceful command of his mind, he repressed their flow until they were dry. "But I know," he says, "I was suppressing my heart, and I suffered still another sorrow at my sorrow, and was afflicted with a two-fold grief." Only when he let the tears flow, did his soul find rest: "It was a relief to weep on Thy sight about her and for her, about myself and for myself. I gave free course to the tears which I was still restraining, permitting them to flow as fully as they wished, spreading them out as a pillow for my heart. It rested on them. . . . I wept for my mother during a

---

31. *Coll. Works*, XVI, 57–59. "Experience shows that religion is, at the very least, a psychic fact that has existed from time immemorial and expresses itself in a thousand different forms. Protestant theology, strangely deluded, calls this view 'psychologism,' and in so doing robs itself of the most effective means of combating man's insecurity—the confessional, which the Catholic Church has wisely appropriated to the benefit of mankind" (X, 549). It is convenient, however, to make a distinction between the sacrament of penance and psychoanalytic confession. The main difference lies in the fact that the sacramental confession deals with sins which belong necessarily to the conscious sphere alone; there is not such a thing as an unconscious sin in the moral sense of the word. Psychoanalysis, however, deals chiefly with problems which belong to the unconscious realm. But there are also similarities between both spheres. See Victor White, O.P., *God and the Unconscious*, pp. 178–188.

little part of an hour, the mother who had wept over me for many years that I might live before Thy eyes."[32]

Nature abhors a vacuum and when an emotion, unconnected with any religious view, is withheld, it is just as disturbing in its effects as the unconscious secret, and just as guilt-laden. This explains the extraordinary significance of genuine confession— a truth that was probably known to all the initiation rites and mystery cults of the ancient world. There is a saying from the Greek mysteries: "Give up what thou hast, and then thou will receive." The goal of the cathartic method is full confession— not merely the intellectual recognition of the facts with the mind, but the confirmation by the heart and actual release of suppressed emotions.[33]

The shadow has to be assimilated, Jung says, but he makes this important distinction: "Repression is a sort of half-conscious and half-hearted letting go of things, a dropping of hot cakes or a reviling of grapes which hang too high, or a looking the other way in order not to become conscious of one's desires. Freud discovered that repression is one of the main mechanisms in the making of a neurosis. Suppression amounts to a conscious moral choice, but repression is a rather immoral 'penchant' for getting rid of disagreeable decisions. Suppression may cause worry, conflict and suffering, but never causes a neurosis. Neurosis is always a substitute for legitimate suffering."[34] A neurosis implies an intensification of the shadow, and to cure it, he insists, the suppression of our dark personality is as little a remedy as beheading would be for a headache. The question is no longer how we can get rid of our shadow, but rather how we can live with our dark side without becoming dark ourselves. Shadow and consciousness have to live together,

---

32. Saint Augustine, *Confessions*, Bk. 9, ch. 12. Victor Frankl, *op. cit.* "There was plenty of suffering for us to get through. . . . But there was no need to be ashamed of tears, for tears bore witness that a man had the greatest of courage, the courage to suffer. Only very few realized that. Shamefacedly some confessed occasionally that they had wept, like the comrade who answered my question of how he had gotten over his edema, by confessing, 'I have wept it out of my system.' "
33. *Coll. Works*, XVI, 59; XVI, 68.
34. *Ibid.*, XI, 75.

even in an admittedly precarious unity, for opposition and polarity are sources of psychic energy; hence we do not suppose to repress the shadow, for then it becomes a hidden source of neurosis. Nor is it wise to suppress it, for it is a part of human personality. Overcoming evil, Jung says, is an impossibility; evil is as positive a factor as good is.[35]

The assimilation of the shadow, however, does not merely require that the shadow and evil become conscious; the awareness of the existence of our dark personality simply brings into action the civil war that was latent. Freud, despite his insights, overlooked the fact that no man has yet been able single-handedly to hold his own against the power of darkness, the unconscious. The spontaneous revelation of the source of life only marks the beginning of progress towards a new synthesis, that is to say, the contents of the shadow are complemented by the spiritual contents of the unconscious, the archetypes.[36] Hence, the integration of the shadow, our masculine partner, is merely the first stage in the analytic process. In individuation the shadow is an important factor, but the body which casts it

---

35. *Ibid.*, XI, 75–78; XVI, 236; X, 467; XII, 168; *Jung and the Problem of Evil*, p. 18. Saint Thérèse of Lisieux relates the following dream: "I dreamt one night that I went for a walk alone in the garden, and when I got to the bottom of the steps that led up to it, I stopped overcome with fright. In front of me, quite close to the tunnel one had to go through there was a barrel of lime; and on it I saw two horrible little demons, dancing about with a surprising quickness of movement. . . . All of a sudden their flashing eyes fell on me, and thereupon, apparently much more frightened of me than I was of them, they jumped down the window, looking anxiously to see if I was still there, and finding that I went on watching them they ran to and fro as if in desperation" (*Autobiography of St. Therese of Lisieux* [New York, 1958], trans. Ronald Knox, p. 52).

In Jungian terms this dream would probably be interpreted in terms of certain relationship between consciousness and the shadow. This poses the crucial and thorny problem of the relation between theology and psychology. Thérèse's own interpretation is very simple: "There was nothing very extraordinary, to be sure, about this dream of mine; but I suppose God allowed me to remember it for a special purpose. He wanted me to see that the soul, when in a state of grace, has nothing to fear from the spirits of evil; they are cowards, so cowardly that they run away at a glance from a child" (*Ibid.*).

36. *Coll. Works,* XI, 344–346.

is even more significant, and women always stand where men's shadows fall. The integration of the anima, our feminine factor, follows logically the assimilation of the shadow.[37]

II. *The Anima*

No man is entirely masculine, Jung says; he has always something of the feminine in him. Very masculine men have carefully guarded and hidden a soft emotional life, often incorrectly described as "feminine." There are three main feminine characteristics in man: (1) The first derives from mother and wife, and from early childhood it exerts a definite influence in man. (2) In addition, there are traits which, although hidden because of ideas prevailing in Western society, are still very real, and presumably the consequence of the presence of a minority of female genes in man's body. (3) Finally, there is the archetype of the anima, that is, an a priori archaic factor endowed with properties characteristic of a feminine personality.[38]

Jung calls this archetype "the anima" from the Greek *anemos*, wind, spirit. Anima among primitives is the soul, the principle of living beings, the magic breath of life, or flame. The archetype of the anima, however, must not be confused with the Christian idea of soul as *anima rationalis,* or any other philosophical conception. She is rather the *feminine* or *chthonic* part of the soul; not an abstract concept, but only an empirical elaboration which Jung describes in terms of his specific phenomenology. The nature of the anima shows itself not merely in the personal or social sphere, but in phenomena of world-wide proportions. Therefore, to say anything valuable about the concept of anima it is imperative to know the universal significance of it in the psychology of primitives, in mythology, in comparative religion, and in the history of literature.[39]

37. *Ibid.,* IX,i, 22; X, 113; IX,i, 270.
38. *Ibid.,* VII, 203, 163, 199.
39. *Ibid.,* IX,i, 25, 28–29; IX,ii, 13, 19. Jung gives full explanation of the following dream: "I am in a great Gothic cathedral. At the altar stands a priest. I stand before him with my friend, holding in my hand a little

Jung defended the origin of archetypes as the repetition of ancestral experiences. The anima is the deposit, as it were, of all ancestral experiences of men with women. Consequently, the anima is archaic and clings even now to the ways of early humanity. She likes to appear in historical dress, especially Grecian and Egyptian; in antiquity she was symbolized as a goddess and witch; in medieval man as Queen of Heaven and Mother Church; in modern times, the anima is evident in certain literary works especially in novels such as Rider Haggard's *She,* and in Pierre Benoit's *L'atlantide.*[40]

The psychological implications of Jung's ideas on the anima can hardly be overestimated because Western civilization is one-sided. In her remarkable essay *Male and Female,* Margaret Mead shows, through the analysis of a diversity of cultures, how artificial the roles ascribed by them to men and women are, and the dangers of limiting the scope of sexes—which impares the normal development of personality instead of enhancing it. Through history the more complex activities have been defined and redefined; the role of men and women depends upon tradition and culture and is never a well-defined activity. The fear of effeminacy, for example, is one of the principal sources of resistance to religion, as H. C. Rumke points out in *The Psychology of Unbelief,* effeminacy being associated with passivity and weakness. Hence, the widespread idea that religion is unmanly, or an affair of women.[41] On the other hand, women do not participate actively in official worship: "There are societies," Margaret Mead says, "that wished to achieve the full beauty of a chorus which spanned the possibilities of the human voice, but in linking religion and music together also wished to ban women, as unsuited for an active role in the church, from the choir. Boys' voices provide an apparently good substitute, so

---

Japanese ivory figure, with the feeling that it is going to be baptized. Suddenly an elderly woman appears, takes the fraternity ring from my friend's finger, and puts it on her own. My friend is afraid that this may bind him in some way. But at the same moment there is a sound of wonderful organ music" (VII, 105). The elderly woman is the anima.

40. *Ibid.,* IX,i, 29; VII, 207.
41. H. C. Rumke, *The Psychology of Unbelief* (1952), pp. 47f.

also do eunuchs, and so in the end we have music modelled on a perfect orchestration of men and women's voices but at the price of the exclusion of women and the castration of men."[42]

There exists a collective image of a woman in man, Jung says, with the help of which he apprehends the nature of women. Consequently, in marriages the anima plays an active part because man tries to win the woman who best corresponds to his unconscious femininity, a woman who can receive the projection of his soul. "We see," Jolande Jacobi says, "the man who blindly falls victim to a certain type of woman—how often one sees precisely highly cultivated intellectuals abandon themselves helplessly to hussies because their feminine, emotional side is wholly undifferentiated . . . or the woman who, apparently incomprehensibly, falls for an adventurer or swindler and cannot get loose from him. The character of our soul-image, the anima or animus of our dreams, is the natural measure of our internal psychological situation. It deserves very special consideration in the way of self-knowledge."[43]

It is difficult for a man to distinguish himself from the anima, for she is invisible. The anima, however, exists, and it is important to recognize this distinction for a man cannot identify himself to an autonomous complex. In fact, it is even right to treat the anima as an autonomous personality and address personal questions to her. Thus it is urgent to objectify her effects and try to understand the contents underlying these effects.[44] The anima personifies the unconscious spontaneously in dreams, visions, and fantasies; and many other more effects can also be made conscious through active imagination. The anima appears in a great variety of forms, for although all the archetypes want life, this one especially does, which is the archetype of life itself. She wants life, either good or bad, the beautiful and pleasant as well as the ugly and evil. Consequently, she can be symbolized as an angel of light and as a serpent of paradise, as a siren, water nymph, grace, daughter,

42. Margaret Mead, *Male and Female* (New York, 1960), p. 277.
43. Jolande Jacobi, *op. cit.,* pp. 151–152. Jung, *Coll. Works,* VII, pp. 187–188.
44. *Coll. Works,* VII, 203, 163, 199.

and succubus who infatuates young men and sucks the life from them. She also shows a certain affinity with animals, like tigers, snakes, and birds.[45]

The anima does not merely personify herself in dreams, visions, and fantasies. As an autonomous complex she is also unconsciously projected upon external objects, usually on the opposite sex, giving rise to magic and complicated relationships. And since the anima is both good and bad, the contents which she projects will appear as expressions of this double manifestation of her nature, sometimes as a heavenly goddess, sometimes as the infernal deity. The anima is initially projected upon mothers who are always the first bearers of the soul-image; then it is projected upon those women who arouse the man's feelings, whether in a positive or a negative sense. Later, in the form of the mother-image, she is transformed to the wife. Consequently in many instances, as soon as the man of Western society marries, he becomes childish, sentimental, or tyrannical, always preoccupied with the prestige of his masculinity. Under the cloak of the ideally exclusive marriage he is really seeking his mother's protection, thereby giving his wife illegitimate authority over him. Actually it is not the mother, but the projection of the anima that is the factor disturbing most marriages, because their feminine side is wholly undifferentiated.[46]

Man's consciousness, Jung says, is towards the general; his activities are consequently business, state, and nation. His unconscious anima, in contrast, and in healthy compensatory activity, is unipersonal, monogamous. On the other side, women's consciousness is centered in the family, husband, and children; namely, towards unity. Their unconscious, the animus, however, tends towards plurality; the animus is polygamous and polytheist, it does not appear as one person, but as a plurality of persons. The animus is like an assembly of fathers or dignitaries of some kind who lay down *ex cathedra* judgments; the animus likes God-like men and addicts. These marks are impor-

45. *Ibid.*, IX,i, 25–29, 13; IX,ii, 13, 19.
46. *Ibid.*, VII, 195–196; IX,ii, 13–14, 19; VII, 27.

tant facts for understanding and interpreting the projection of anima and animus.[47]

The image of the parents is the one that should be projected least because it is conscious, while projection is an automatic unconscious activity. In reality, Jung says, it is obviously the parent-image which seems to be projected most frequently, as seen plainly in cases of transference, where the mother-image or the father-image is projected on the analyst. But since the projection is never conscious, we must therefore assume that above and over these images, highly emotional contents are still bound up with the parental images and need to be made conscious. These are the archetypes and the religious ideas associated with them and with the parental images. For example, the divine syzygy, the male and female pair of deities, is not simply a single idealization of the parents or other couples; myth has always expressed the idea of the divine syzygy, the divine pair, or the idea of the hermaphroditic nature of the creator. In other words, against Freud's ideas on religion, Jung does not identify God and parental images; they are different, even though it is a fact of psychological experience that theistic ideas are associated with parental images, and we are not conscious of them.[48]

The anima is the archetype of life itself, and thereby the archetype which best sums up all the statements of the unconscious. The anima is the life behind consciousness, and the a priori element underlying moods, reactions, impulses, and everything that is spontaneous in psychic life. She is not a shallow creature but a breath of eternity, and she likes the beautiful and the ugly, the good life and the bad life. The realm of the anima is the realm of gods, everything that she touches is numinous, dangerous, taboo, magical; she possesses a secret knowl-

47. *Ibid.,* VII, 206–208; IX,ii, 268.
48. *Ibid.,* IX,i, 59–63; IX,ii, 21. The relation between parents and God is a natural one. For example, it was easy for St. Thérèse of Lisieux, who says: "I simply cannot explain how fond I was of Papa; everything about him filled me with admiration," to have a similar love for the Father in Heaven. Mircea Eliade, in *Images and Symbols,* p. 23 fn., criticizes, from the point of view of history of religion, the two basic hypotheses of Freud concerning the origin of religion.

edge or hidden wisdom. As part of her life the emotions, too, are affected by the anima, making men touchy, irritable, irrational, moody, jealous, and vain. She is endowed with considerable power of fascination and possession, unleashes terrors, plays tricks, happy and unhappy delusions, causes ecstasies, and outbursts of affection. For example, Jung explains, when a highly respected professor in his seventies abandons his family and runs off with a young red-headed actress, we know that the gods have claimed another victim. This is the manner in which demonic power reveals itself to us.[49]

The animus, however, produces opinions that are invariably collective. If the woman happens to be pretty, these animus opinions have for the man something rather touching and childlike about them which makes him adopt a benevolent manner. But if competence is expected of a woman, then her animus opinions irritate the man to death because they are based on nothing but opinion for opinion's sake. "Unfortunately I am always right," one of these creatures once confessed to Jung. A woman possessed by the animus is always in danger of losing her femininity. On the other hand, the animus is also procreative being in the sense that the inner masculine side of woman brings forth creative seeds which have the power to fertilize the feminine side of man. This would be the *femme inspiratrice*.[50] The assimilation of the anima requires the overcoming of social demands and traditions. Society expects man to play a role in life, and the acquisition of personal prestige is usually the common aim of our actions—as against the authentic aim of individuation. Collective thinking and collective effort are easier than individual thinking and individual effort. The collective, nevertheless, cannot take the place of the individual. Jung calls this attitude of man towards society *persona*, which means the mask worn in antiquity by an actor signifying the role played. Here is a mask that feigns individuality and tries to make others believe that one is an individual; yet it is not true individuality but simply a mask we wear to

49. *Coll. Works,* IX,i, 26–30, 70, 270.
50. *Ibid.,* VII, 206–208.

play a social role. Moreover, imitation makes things worse. Man possesses a capacity which is of great possible value for collective purpose but most pernicious for individuation, and this is the faculty of imitation. It is not the law, Jung asserts, that makes the social order; it is imitation. People are content to ape some outstanding personality, characteristic, or activity, thus achieving an outward distinction which gives the feeling of having accomplished something.[51]

The construction of the collective persona presupposes a concession to the external world, a genuine self-sacrifice which drives the ego into identification with the mask, making people believe they are what they pretend to be. But man pays a heavy toll for this identification in the form of irritability, bad moods, uncontrolled emotions, phobias, compulsive ideas, and vices. The socially "strong man" is often a mere child in his private life because he has repressed everything individual for the benefit of the social. The persona, the ideal picture of a man, is inwardly compensated by feminine weakness; as the individual outwardly plays the strong man, he becomes inwardly a woman, the anima. Hence, it is the anima that reacts and compensates the persona by playing a decisive role in stripping off the mask of the mere social; the gradual strengthening of the anima simultaneously parallels the gradual weakening of the persona.[52]

The assimilation of the anima by the conscious mind is a task far from simple, for it is difficult to gain insight into her: (1) There is no moral education in that respect: man knows the existence of a shadow, but Western mentality represses any feminine trait of man's personality. (2) It seems natural for men to have irrational moods and for women to express irrational opinions; consequently, these manifestations of the anima are not recognized as such. (3) The anima is by projec-

---

51. *Ibid.*, VII, 151–153, 155–156, 148. Jung gives the following definition of persona: "The persona is a complicated system of relations between individual consciousness and society, fittingly enough a kind of mask, designed on the one hand to make a definite impression upon others, and on the other, to conceal the true nature of the individual" (VII, 190).

52. *Ibid.*, VII, 191–193. In VI, 594, Jung gives an account of the compensatory function of the anima with respect to consciousness.

tion outside the territory of man, and, besides, the projection is so strong that it fills the ego personality with an unshakable feeling of rightness. (4) Finally, since much of the knowledge regarding the anima depends on historical sources, perfect knowledge of her phenomenology is the property of only a few specialists. The nonscholar has to content himself with grasping few traits of her complex personality.[53]

The integration of the anima into consciousness follows a triple process: *objectification, differentiation* of the ego from the contents of the anima, and *separation* of consciousness from mana-personality.

The first step in integrating the archetype is what Jung calls the *objectification* of the anima. Since the things of the inner world influence us all the more powerfully for being unconscious, it is essential for individuation to objectify the effects of the anima. The more personally the anima is taken, the better, because the ego has to get the right idea of the power and factors ruling the "other world," the world of the unconscious. The "other side" has to be given the opportunity for perceptive psychic activity, and fragments of the anima come to the surface in the form of thoughts and pictures in moments of great affectivity. Then a dialectic encounter can follow since, as explained before, it is quite right to treat the anima as an autonomous personality and to address questions to her.[54]

The second step is the differentiation of the ego from the contents of the anima. The anima is not a substitute for the mother but a numinous archetype which, when it is integrated, constitutes Eros. But archetypes are often camouflaged under modern attire, and it is arduous to differentiate the contents belonging to the anima. Without differentiation, however, there is no procedure to distinguish the contents pertaining to the ego from those contents pertaining to the anima. Differentiation not only presupposes knowledge of symbolism for interpreting fantasies, dreams, and images produced by the anima; it also presupposes experiencing them to the full in an active way, the way suggested by these fantasies and dreams. For

53. *Ibid.*, IX,ii, 16–17, 29.
54. *Ibid.*, VII, 199–200, 201–203.

instance, one of Jung's patients had the following fantasy:
"He sees his fiancée running down the road towards the river. It
is winter, and the river is frozen. She runs out on the ice, and
he follows her. She goes right out and then the ice breaks, a
dark fissure appears, and he is afraid she is going to jump in.
And this is what happens: she jumps into the crack, and he
watches her sadly."[55] The conscious attitude of this patient was
one-sidedly intellectual and the fantasy is warning him of the
necessity of giving a hearing to the unconscious. His fiancée
is a symbol for his anima, and the fantasy expresses the fact that
without any hindrance on his part, his anima is disappearing
again into the unconscious. The fantasy demands not passivity
but active participation; he should never remain idle spectator
while his fiancée tries to drown herself; he should leap up
and stop her. In this way he should have won a victory over his
one-sided intellectualism, thus asserting the validity of the irrational standpoint of the unconscious.[56]

The dissolution of projection is extremely difficult, especially
when the anima is projected on the mother, because the mother
is real and the archetype hidden. As explained previously this
separation has been symbolically expressed in all primitive cultures by the rites of initiation which sometimes are cruel but
nevertheless of high therapeutic value because they express the
severance of the adult from childhood. The child is protected
by the father against the dangers of the external world; by the
mother against the dangers that threaten from the darkness of
the psyche. In the puberty rites the initiate receives instruction
about the things "of the other side," so that he is put in position to dispense with the mother's protection and to cross the
threshold to adulthood.[57]

The withdrawal of the protection of the anima is not exempt
from dangers, for the energy bound up in the projection is now
at the disposal of the unconscious, and as a result the anima
may overpower the ego. Whoever is afraid of the inner world,
Jung says, needs support; that is why primitive man out of

55. *Ibid.*, VII, 211–213; Cf. IX,ii, 13; VII, 204, 213.
56. *Ibid.*, VII, 211–217.
57. *Ibid.*, VII, 195; IX,ii, 18.

deep psychological necessity begot religious instruction and embodied it in a magician or priest. Religious dogmas and ritual are like dams and walls which help to channel the libido. The history of comparative religion shows that the manifestation of the unconscious in the form of religion is still valid for those who can go back to it. The symbols of old religions did not drop from the blue but were born from the soul that dwells within us. And now, its power can burst upon us, with annihilated force, in the guise of mass suggestions against which the individual is defenseless. "The anima, the 'feminine principle' in the psyche," Victor White says, "is activated by religion. What Saint Augustine called 'that part of the soul which is, as it were, an image or type of woman in every soul,' is that which is able to express the religious attitude of the creature towards God. It is that which, Saint Augustine explains, was tempted in Eve and which consents as maiden, bride, and mother in Mary and the Church. Although religion is willing activity of the ego, the activity of the ego and the will is here precisely that of consent to the subordination of the anima to the Divinity."[58] Hence to the degree that the patient takes active part and uses the help provided by religion and other factors, the anima and animus gradually disappear as dangerous elements. But when the unconscious contents are not realized they give rise to a negative activity and personification, that is to say, to the autonomous activity of the animus and anima. Psychic activity then develops, states of possession ranging in degree from moods to psychosis. The unknown "someone" has taken mastery over our conscious mind.[59]

The third step is the separation of consciousness from mana-personality. The goal of individuation in this phase is the conquest of the anima as an autonomous complex and her transformation into a function of the relationship between the conscious and unconscious. When the anima is conquered, the ego which has conquered her is invested with the properties of the anima, with her numinous power, that is to say, with mana-personality. The making conscious of the anima enables us to

58. Victor White, O.P., *Soul and Psyche* (London, 1960), p. 198.
59. *Coll. Works*, VII, 220.

gain knowledge of the contrasexual element of our psyche, and once she is incorporated into our conscious orientation our personality is broadened: "In the second half of life," Jolande Jacobi says, "the goal is above all the psychic *coniunctio,* a union with the contrasexual within one's own inner world and with its image-bearer in the outer, in order that the 'spiritual child' may be born."[60] These words seem like an echo of Saint Augustine:

> The text begins by expounding the creation of woman, and her creation is said to be for the help of the man, that by spiritual copulation she might bring forth spiritual offspring, that is to say the good works of divine praise; while he rules, she obeys: he is governed by wisdom, she by the man. The head of the man is Christ, and the man is the head of the woman (1 Cor. XI:3). And so it is said, "It is not good to be alone." . . . Woman is created as an example of this reality, whom the order of things subjects to man. And that which more evidently appears in two people, that is the male and female, even can be considered in one person—so that the appetite of the soul, by which the members of the body are set in action, has an interior sense as subject to the virile principle and by just law imposes design on its helper, as the man should rule the woman and not allow her to dominate the man—for when that happens, the result is a perverse and wretched household.[61]

The numinous experience of the assimilation of the anima is not exempt from dangers, nor does it close the process of individuation. Behind the anima's mana lurks a new archetype which is the main source of her power and numinosity. Jung calls this archetype the "wise old man," and the process now enters a new state. Individuation is yet on the way.

III. *The Wise Old Man*

Although the anima may be a chaotic urge to life, something meaningful clings to her, a secret knowledge or hidden wisdom

60. Jolande Jacobi, *op. cit.,* 162.
61. Saint Augustine, *De Genesi contra Manich.,* II, xi, 28, 205–206.

which contrasts with her irrational nature. The anima and life are meaningless insofar as they offer no interpretation. And yet, Jung explains, in all chaos there is a cosmos, in all disorder a secret order, in all caprices a fixed law. It is just the most unexpected, the most chaotic thing which reveals a deeper meaning, and the more this meaning is recognized the more the anima loses her compulsive character, for everything that operates is grounded in its opposite. There exists an archetype that rests hidden behind the meaningful nonsense played out by the anima; this is the archetype of meaning or the wise old man. The wise old man is like the father of the soul, and the anima stands in the relationship of daughter to it.[62]

As the anima represents the feminine personality of man, so the wise old man represents the archetype of the father or the archetype of the spirit for it symbolizes the spiritual character factor—not the conscious but the unconscious one. The archetype of the spirit appears in situations in which insight, understanding, good advice, determination, and planning are needed, but cannot be mastered on one's own resources. The archetype compensates this state of spiritual deficiency by contents designated to fill the gap. The wise old man means reflection, knowledge, insight, wisdom, and cleverness. He also represents moral qualities which manifest the spiritual character of this archetype, such as good will and the readiness to help. On the other hand, he also manifests the ambivalent character of his nature and is capable of working for either good or evil, which decision depends upon man's own free will.[63]

The wise old man personifies itself in dreams and visionary meditation. It first appears in the father—being a personification of meaning and spirit in its procreative sense—as well as in the guise of a magician, doctor, teacher, professor, grandfather, or any person possessing authority. The archetype also rises into consciousness as mana-personality—a dominant of the

62. *Coll. Works*, IX, 30–31, 35. Jolande Jacobi, *op. cit.*, p. 164: "Its counterpart in the process of individuation of the woman is the 'Magna Mater,' the great earth-mother, which represents the cold and objective truth of nature."
63. *Coll. Works*, XII, 118; IX,i, 215–216, 222, 253, 34–35.

collective unconscious with the idea of the "extraordinary potent"—which personifies in the form of hero, chief, medicine man, saint, ruler of men and spirits, and the friend of God. Historically the mana-personality evolves into the hero and God-like being, whose earthly form is the priest. As evil, the archetype appears in dreams as the wicked magician, usually dressed in black, who from sheer egoism does evil for evil's sake. Finally, in the fairy tales the wise old man personifies in the form of animals, such as wolf, bear, or lion.[64]

With the conquest of the anima, the ego is freed from two collectivities: the personal collectivity (persona) and the unconscious collectivity (anima). The ego has integrated the anima and becomes itself a mana-personality; but the problem is not solved yet, and a new danger arises from the unconscious. The masculine collective, corresponding to the father-image emerges now from obscurity personified as a friend of God, a man of authority, or a magician possessing great power, attracting the mana to himself. Thus he becomes a superman, a demi-God, and individuation now requires the solving of the conflict between the ego and the magician.[65]

The differentiation of the ego from the mana-personality is indispensable for separating the contents belonging to each and to make conscious those which are specific to the mana. This presupposes for the man the second and real liberation from the father; for the woman the real liberation from the mother. The result is true individuation and rebirth as is symbolically expressed, for example, in the Christian sacrament of baptism; baptism severs man from the carnal parent and recreates him *in novam infantiam* into the condition of immortality and spiritual childhood.[66]

64. *Ibid.*, IX,i, 230–231, 215–216; VII, 226; V, 332.
65. *Ibid.*, VII, 225–228.
66. *Ibid.*, VII, 233. Jolande Jacobi writes these mysterious words: "To venture a somewhat daring formula one might say: the man is materialized spirit, the woman matter impregnated with spirit; consequently, the man is essentially determined by the spirit, the woman by matter" (*The Psychology of C. G. Jung*, p. 165). Saint Augustine says: "Such is the meaning of the great sacrament of baptism which is solemnized among us: that those who attain to this grace die to sin, just as we say He died to sin, in that

The dissolution of mana-personality has to be achieved through its conscious assimilation. But how? The problem arises because the mana is a being of superior wisdom and superior will; therefore, by making these contents conscious, we know and want more than other people. This is the problem, Jung asserts, of Christ, Paul, and all spiritual men. Nietzsche, though in the wrong way, tried to solve it through the master man and supreme sage who knows neither God nor evil. With Nietzsche man stands alone, as he did, godless and worldless, away from creatures and God—a neurotic and unnatural solution which at last led him to his death. Then the problem is, what can and must we do? The integration of the mana-personality through conscious assimilation of its contents leads us back to ourselves as an actual living "something" poised between two world pictures and their discerned potentialities. This "something" is a virtual center that claims everything. Jung calls this center the self. The self is, therefore, the new archetype which will finally solve the problem of individuation.[67]

IV. *The Self*

The archetype of the self is the most important element composing the unconscious, and it is the goal of the psychotherapeutic process. The self is an expression of human wholeness, of the totality of man; that is to say, of both his conscious and unconscious contents. To achieve wholeness in man, as in the deity, the opposites are canceled out; good and evil, conscious and unconscious, masculine and feminine, dark and light, are raised to a synthesis symbolically expressed by the *coniunctio oppositorum*.[68]

He died to the flesh, that is, to the likeness of sin; and that they live through being reborn of the font (whatever may be the age of the body) just as He lived again from the tomb" (*Enchiridium*, ch. 13, 42). We have to point out, however, this distinction: rebirth in the Jungian sense means a pure natural transformation; rebirth in the Augustinian sense means a supernatural transformation.

67. *Coll. Works,* VII, 235–236.
68. *Ibid.,* V, 138; XII, 25–27; XI, 82.

The idea of the self, Jung concedes, has not been scientifically proven; it is rather a useful hypothesis which has been verified by empirical and historical facts. However, he only proposed the idea of the self after mature consideration and careful appraisal including many years of painstaking psychological research. (1) Historically Jung discovered the self in the East as a purely spiritual idea symbolically represented in the mandalas, the symbols of contemplation. In Western philosophy this archetype stands for a totality, comprising conscious and unconscious phenomena. In mythology and comparative religion the self represents totality, and is an expression of monotheism. In this case it is historically symbolized by quaternities, circles, mandalas, and trinities. These symbols are authenticated as God-images. (2) Human wholeness as such is nothing but an abstract idea. It is, nevertheless, empirical insofar as it is anticipated by the psyche in the form of spontaneous and autonomous symbols of unity and totality, such as circles and quaternities, which appear in patients—usually educated people—determined by archetypal ideas unknown to them. The unconscious produces motif symbols and ideas that the conscious mind grasps only with difficulty. But these symbols and ideas, however, play a crucial role in individuation. (3) Psychologically, Jung says, the symbol of the self cannot be distinguished from the God-image; the two ideas are of the same nature; the God-image is the self, although this idea is shocking to the European mentality. As a psychological phenomenon this archetype represents the union of the conscious and unconscious and it stands for the psychic totality. Thus formulated it is a psychological concept.[69]

The self represents the innermost recesses of the unconscious and is so far removed from the conscious mind that it can only be partially symbolized by human figures. The other part of it has to be expressed by objective abstract symbols. The human figures are father, son, daughter, mother, queen, God, and goddess. The abstract symbols are the dragon, snake, elephant, lion worm, etc. Plant symbols are generally flowers: the lotus and rose. The geometrical figures are the circle, the sphere, the

69. *Ibid.,* IX,ii, 268, 31, 34; XI, 307, 502, 580, 469; IX,i, 335, 369; V, 368.

square, the quaternity, the clock, the firmament, and so forth.[70]

The archetype of the self is intimately connected with its symbols, especially with the symbol of the mandala. Found by Jung in the East as symbols of contemplation, mandalas are birth places, vessels of birth in the most literal sense, lotus flowers in which Buddha comes to life.[71] In India mandalas are circles, and in Tibetan Buddhism they are instruments of prayer, usually containing three circles. In patients the mandalas seem to be free creations of fantasy, but determined by certain archetypal ideas unknown to their creators, and expressions of a peculiar attitude that Jung calls religious. Mandalas are symbols of order, most of which have a magic and intuitive irrational character. They transform chaos into cosmos, rearranging the personality and finding a new center. Mandalas principally appear in connection with chaotic states of disorientation and have the purpose of reducing the confusion to order by expressing balance and wholeness, even in cases in which this is not the conscious intention of the patient.[72] Here is an example of a dream: "I was trying to decipher an embroidery pattern. My sister knew how. I asked her if she had made an elaborate hemstitched handkerchief. She said, 'No, but I know how it was done.' Then I saw it with the threads drawn, but the work not yet done. One must go around and around the square until near the center, then go in circles."[73] The dreamer herself had no idea of what was going on in her, namely, the beginning of a new orientation, nor would she have understood it consciously.

If the motif of the mandala is archetypal, it ought to be a

70. *Ibid.*, IX,i, 187.
71. *Ibid.*, IX,i, 355, 130.
72. *Ibid.*, IX,i, 360, 362. Cf. IX,ii, 31; XI, 81. Igor Caruso reports the following case: "A woman patient produces seven paper cuttings in the form of a mask, one on top of another, and fastened with a paper clip; they represent—behind the impressive but mysterious social mask or 'persona'—the secret layers of her personality. Each of these little drawings affords manifold opportunities for interpretation. With them, a larger explanatory drawing which represents the patient's renunciation of the masklike 'persona' and the beginning of an integration of the secret layers into the heart or 'self' of the personality—the same heart that has already appeared as a mandala" (*op. cit.*, p. 199).
73. *Coll. Works,* IX,i, 362.

collective phenomenon and theoretically should appear in everyone. In practice, however, it is only found in distinct form in relatively few cases, though this does not prevent it from functioning as a concealed pole around which everything ultimately revolves. But every carrier, Jung says, is charged with an individual destiny and only the realization of this can make life meaningful.[74]

Mircea Eliade says, "Perhaps the most important function of religious symbolism—especially important because of the role it will play in later philosophical speculations—is its capacity for expressing paradoxical situations or certain patterns of ultimate reality that can be expressed in no other way."[75] The self is an example of this, for it stands for the conjunction of opposites. Naturally, the conjunction, Jung explains, can only be understood as a paradox; that is to say, a statement about something indescribable and transcendental. The self is both definite enough to indicate the sum of human wholeness, and indefinite enough to express the indescribable nature of this wholeness. It combines uniqueness and eternity, the individual with the universal; it is both male and female, old and yet a child. And though it is a true *complexio oppositorum*, this does not mean that it is anything like a contradiction in itself. In the self good and evil are indeed closer than identical twins; the truth about the self, the baffling union of good and evil, Jung asserts, comes out concretely in the paradox that although sin is the gravest and most pernicious thing existing, it is still not so serious that it cannot be disposed of with "probabilist" arguments.[76]

---

74. *Ibid.*, XII, 212.
75. Mircea Eliade, *The Two and the One*, pp. 205–206. For Nicholas of Cusa, the *coincidentia oppositorum* was God's best definition. Not so for Thomas Aquinas or St. Augustine. *Summa Theol.*, I, q. 13, a. 11: "This name 'He who is,' is most properly applied to God, for three reasons. . . ." Saint Augustine, *De Trinit.*, V, ch. 1.
76. *Coll. Works*, XII, 21; IX,ii, 267, 225, 68–69. Probabilism is defined as "the system of moral theology based on the principle that, if the licitness or illicitness of an action is in doubt, it is lawful to follow a solidly probable opinion favoring liberty, even though the opposing opinion, favoring the law, be more probable" (*The Oxford Dictionary of the Christian Church* [Oxford, 1957], p. 1108).

The self symbolizes the goal of human growth, the wholeness of man. Jung found in his patients an irrational drive towards this wholeness, even though the psychological development of the self is, in Jung's own words, obscure. "These processes are all so mysterious, that it remains questionable whether human understanding is a suitable instrument to grasp and express them. Not without reason does alchemy describe itself as art, feeling rightly that it has to do with formative processes that can be grasped only in experience but can merely be hinted at intellectually."[77] Hence, we should not expect a full philosophical analysis of the emerging of the archetypes, but only a few sketches drawn out from the experience he had with his patients.

The self requires a shifting of man's psychological center: the center of gravity goes from the ego to the self, from man to God; the ego disappears in the self and man in God.[78] This is the result of a change of attitude, a transformation of personality.

During this transformation . . . one has to expose oneself to the animal impulses of the unconscious, without identifying oneself with them and without running away. Identification would mean that one live out his bestial impulses without restraint; running away, that one repressed them. What is demanded here, however, is something quite different, namely, to make them conscious and to recognize their reality, whereupon they automatically lose their dangerousness. . . . One must stay with the unconscious, and the process which began by self observation must be lived through in all its developments and joined on to consciousness with as much understanding as possible. This naturally often implies an almost unbearable tension because of the unparalleled incommensurability between conscious life and the process in the unconscious, which latter can be experienced only in one's inmost feelings and may nowhere touch the visible surface of life.[79]

The self is present in everybody a priori, eternally present,

77. C. G. Jung, *Integration of Personality,* p. 166.
78. *Coll. Works,* XI, 581.
79. C. G. Jung, *Integration of Personality,* p. 153.

and beyond individual birth and death, but, as a rule, in an unconscious condition. It is, nevertheless, a definite experience of later life when this fact becomes conscious, and because of the tremendous difficulties entailed in individuation, in practice occurs only in a few. And rightly so, since it is impossible to reach this goal without first enduring the agony of the previous death. "Baptism endows the individual with a living soul," Jung says. "I do not mean that the baptismal rite in itself does this, by a unique and magical act. I mean that the idea of baptism lifts man out of his archaic identification with the world and transforms him into a being who stands above it. The fact that mankind has risen to the level of this idea is baptism in the deepest sense, for it means the birth of the spiritual man who transcends nature."[80]

The greatest and most important problems, Jung believes, are basically all insoluble; and they are so because they express the polarity immanent in every self-regulating system. The problems are not solved, but only transcended, a transcendence which is revealed as a raising of the level of consciousness, as a deepening of personality.[81] "If we succeed in making the self into a new center of gravity of the individual, then a personality arises from there that, so to speak, suffers only in the lower levels but in the upper is peculiarly detached from every sorrowful and joyful event alike."[82] At this point, all opposites are united in the self, which does not signify that man is then perfect but complete, because the self also includes evil; a completion which is not achieved without a great deal of hardship due to the tension between the ego and the self:

> The realization of the self . . . leads to a fundamental conflict, to a real suspension between opposites . . . and to an approximate state of wholeness that lacks perfection. To strive after

80. *Coll. Works,* X, 67; XII, 211–212. *Jung and the Problem of Evil,* p. 233.
81. *Coll. Works,* XIII, 15.
82. *Ibid.,* XIII, 45–46. St. Teresa of Avila, *The Interior Castle* (New York, 1921), trans., Benedictines of Stanbrook, "Seventh Mansion," ch. 2, n. 14: "This 'center of the soul' or 'spirit' is so hard to describe or even to believe in, that I think my inability to explain my meaning saves your being tempted to disbelieve me; it is difficult to understand how there can be crosses and sufferings and yet peace in the soul."

completion in this sense is not only legitimate but is inborn in man as a peculiarity which provides civilization with one of its strongest roots. This striving is so powerful, even, that it can turn into a passion that draws everything into its service. . . . The individual may strive after perfection ("Be you therefore perfect [τελειοι] as also your heavenly Father is perfect") but must suffer from the opposite of his intentions for the sake of his completeness. "I find a law, that, when I would do good, evil is present with me."[83]

Jung is logical and faithful to his principles until the end; all the pairs of opposites are transcended in a final synthesis symbolically signified by the archetype of the self.

As previously explained with the other archetypes, the self cannot be integrated without discrimination, separation, opposition, and discussion. It needs the withdrawal of the external projections in order to wake up the self inside, which entails the usual danger of inflation. If the ego is assimilated by the self the result is a psychic catastrophe; the image of wholeness remains then in the unconscious, sharing its archaic nature and the space-time continuum characteristic of it. Patience, attention, accurate observation, and objective self criticism are valuable on the intellectual side for solving this inflation. If the self becomes assimilated by the ego, the result is similar inflation but of a different sort. In the first case reality must be protected against the archaic dream state; in the second, room must be made for the archaic at the expense of the world of consciousness. We have to listen to the inner authority, let us call it "counter will," and reach a balance; the irrational forces yearning for wholeness, as opposed to the ego's claims. But from the tension of opposites unity and wholeness is born, and its symbols cannot any longer be distinguished from the *imago Dei*.[84] "Self realization, in regard to oneself, means the possibility of anchoring oneself in that which is eternal and indestructible, in the primal nature of the objective psyche. By this the individual places himself again in the eternal streams

---

83. *Coll. Works*, IX,ii, 69.
84. *Ibid.*, IX,ii, 23–35. *Jung and the Problem of Evil*, pp. 228, 233.

in which birth and death are only stations along the way and the meaning of life no longer lies in the ego."[85]

The whole process of individuation is summarized in this remarkable dream of a young woman totally unacquainted with the literature of the subject:

> I came to the bank of a broad, flowing river. I couldn't see much at first, only water, earth, and rock. I threw the pages with my notes on them into the water, with the feeling that I was giving something back to the river. Immediately afterwards I had a fishing rod in my hand. I sat down on a rock and started fishing. Still I saw nothing but water, earth, and rock. Suddenly a big fish bit. He had a silver belly and a golden back. As I drew him to land, the whole landscape became alive: the rock emerged like primeval foundation of the earth, grass and flowers sprang up, and the bushes expanded into a great forest. A gust of wind blew and set everything in motion. Then, suddenly, I heard behind me the voice of Mr. X (an older man whom she knew only from photographs and from hearsay, but who seems to have been some kind of authority for her). He said, quietly but distinctly: "The patient ones in the innermost realm are given the fish, the food of the deep." At this moment a circle ran round me, part of it touching the water. Then I heard the voice again: "The brave ones in the second realm may be given victory, for there the battle is fought." Immediately another circle ran round me, this time touching the other bank. The sun rose over the horizon. I heard the voice, speaking as if out of the distance: "The third and the fourth realms come, similarly enlarged, out of the other two. But the fourth realm"—and here the voice paused for a moment, as if deliberating—"the fourth realm joins on the first. It is the highest and lowest at once, for the highest and the lowest come together. They are at bottom one." Here the dreamer awoke with a roaring in her ears.

85. Jolande Jacobi, *op. cit.*, p. 202; *Coll. Works*, XII, 211: "It is therefore probable that we are dealing with an a priori 'type,' an archetype which is inherent in the collective unconscious and thus beyond individual birth and death. The archetype is, so to speak, an eternal presence, and it is only a question of whether it is perceived by consciousness or not."

The details of the dream may be commented on as follows: the bank of the river represents the threshold, so to speak, to the unconscious. Fishing is an intuitive attempt to catch unconscious contents (fishes). Silver and gold, in alchemical parlance, signify feminine and masculine, the hermaphrodite aspect of the fish, indicating that it is a *complexio opposi-torum*. The older man is a personification of the "wise old man." We know already that the fish is a "miraculous food," the eucharistic food of the τελειοι. The first circle that touches the water illustrates the partial integration of the unconscious. The battle is the conflict of opposites, may be between unconsciousness and the shadow. The second circle touches the "other bank," where the union of opposites takes place. . . . The fourth realm, stressed by a weighty pause, is the One that adds to the three and makes all four into unity. The circles naturally produce a mandala, the outermost circle paradoxically coinciding with the center, and recalling the old image for God. "God is a circle whose center is every-where and the circumference nowhere." The motif of the first coinciding with the fourth was expressed long ago in the axiom of Maria: "One becomes two, two becomes three, and out of the third comes the One as the fourth."[86]

Is Jung's process of individuation a new philosophy, a new religion, a new approach to life? We would say that the process of individuation is Jung's attempt to pose and solve the difficul-ties and puzzles endangering modern man. Jung looks with gloom at the panorama of Europe when he writes:

If metaphysical ideas no longer have a fascinating effect as before, this is not due to any lack of primitivity in the Euro-pean psyche, but simply to the fact that erstwhile symbols no longer express what is now welling up from the uncon-scious as the end result of the development of Christian consciousness through the centuries. This end-result is a true *antinimon pneuma,* a false spirit of arrogance, hysteria, wooly-mindedness, criminal amorality, and doctrinaire fanaticism, a purveyor of shoddy spiritual goods, spurious art, philo-sophical stutterings, and Utopian humbug, fit only to be fed

86. *Coll. Works,* IX,ii, 151–153.

wholesale to the mass man of today. That is what the post-Christian spirit looks like.[87]

Jung offers individuation as the means to change this state of affairs.

87. *Ibid.*, IX,ii, 35.

III

Religion and Individuation

Freud, considered a genius by scientists, is generally rejected in religious circles because of his materialistic view of man. The popularity of Jung among religious people on the other hand, cannot be denied. According to many, Jung is the modern psychologist who has restored the religious factor in man, setting up the long-awaited bridge between psychology and religion. Not everybody, however, shares such an optimistic viewpoint.[1] So let us try a synthetic study of Jung's own writings which shall help us to elucidate the problem and to understand better the process of individuation, for religion and individuation are intimately interwoven.

Philosophical Background

Jung's ideas on religion and God cannot be understood without the knowledge of some of his philosophical principles. The most important principle for understanding Jung's conception of analytic psychology is the principle of opposites. According to Jung, the root of psychological drives lies in a double polarity which constitutes the quintessence of life. "Old Heraclitus, who was indeed a very great sage, discovered the most marvelous of all psychological laws: the regulative function of opposites. He called it *enantiodromia*, a running contrarywise,

1. Edward Glover, *Freud or Jung?* (New York, 1957), p. 163: "Jung's system is fundamentally irreligious. Nobody is to care whether God exists, Jung the least of all." Cyril Connelly, *Ibid.*, p. 7: "I am alarmed at the popularity of Jung's ideas on the Catholic Church." H. L. Philp, *Jung and the Problem of Evil,* xi: "After many years of psychological study . . . I find too much sectarianism and often too much dogmatism. . . . I have been disappointed in my search."

by which he meant that sooner or later everything runs into its opposite."[2] The tension between the two opposites is the source of energy and the greater the tension of opposites the greater the energy that comes from them. Energy is crucial in Jung's system and there is no energy without the tension of the opposites. The opposites are the key to the dynamics of human personality.

If polarity and opposition are universal laws, then nothing can exist without its opposite. Therefore, "every psychological extreme secretly contains its own opposite or stands in some sort of intimate and essential relation to it."[3] As a consequence of this polarity everything in nature is found in natural pairs, a prerequisite for polarity and opposition. For instance, good and evil, masculine and feminine, death and life, conscious and unconscious, anima and persona, ego and shadow, and so forth.

The opposites are compensatory of each other; that is to say, one opposite compensates the deficiencies of the other opposite, thus balancing the complex elements of human personality. The compensatory function of the opposites is an expression of man's self-defense mechanism; for example, extroversion compensates introversion, the unconscious compensates the conscious mind, the ego compensates the anima, and vice versa. Compensation also exists in the realm of ethics where evil compensates the good and good the evil. The compensatory function of the opposites is automatic, free from the arbitrary control of our will.

Opposition and duality play an important role in the development of human personality. Duality is not a luxury but a prerequisite of growth, and needs to be preserved by all means. In the last stage of the process of development however, duality and opposition are harmonized and integrated into a higher synthesis. It is unity and wholeness, the goal of man, and this goal is intimately connected with religious content, and symbolically expressed by the archetype of the self.

The law of evolution is also a universal law of nature; the

2. *Coll. Works,* VII, 71.
3. *Ibid.,* V, 375. Cf. IX,i, 96.

whole cosmos is evolving towards consciousness, which is the remote goal of everything existing.

Existence of Religious Factors

Does a religious factor exist in man? For Jung the existence of a religious factor in man is not an a priori principle. It is rather an empirical conclusion derived from the examination of countless patients who came to him for help. "The soul," he says, "possesses by nature a religious function. . . . But were it not a fact of experience that supreme values reside in the soul, psychology would not interest me in the least, for the soul would then be nothing but miserable vapor. I know, however, from hundredfold experience that it is nothing of the sort, but on the contrary contains the equivalent of everything that has been formulated in dogma and a good deal more. . . . I did not attribute religious function to the soul. I merely produced the facts which prove that the soul is *naturaliter religiosa*, i.e., possesses a religious function."[4]

The manifestations of the religious function in man are so extraordinary and unusual, and its properties are so different from those of other human functions, that there is no possibility of reducing religion to any other human activity. The spiritual appears in the psyche as a drive, indeed a true passion. It is not derivative from another drive but a principle *sui generis*, namely the indispensable primitive power in the world of drives. "Since religion is incontestably one of the earliest and most universal expressions of the human mind, it is obvious that any psychology which touches upon the psychological structure of human personality cannot avoid taking note of the fact that religion is not only a sociological and historical phenomenon, but also something of considerable personal concern to a great number of individuals."[5]

And it is this superior force of religion which has at all times constrained men to ponder the inconceivable and even to

4. *Ibid.*, XII, 12–13.
5. *Ibid.*, XI, 5.

impose the greatest suffering upon themselves in order to achieve the goals required by the holy. Religion, Jung says, is as real as hunger and the fear of death; it is the strongest and most original of all man's spiritual activities, although it is also the activity which more than even sexuality or social adaptation is thwarted in modern man.[6]

Nature of Religion

Religion is directly connected with the contents of the collective unconscious. But how is it possible to know these contents? These contents are known through revelation. This is not the Christian revelation which presupposes the manifestation of a transcendent God existing outside man and the universe. No, the Jungian revelation is a personal and unique phenomenon which everybody can experience if properly disposed. This unique experience manifests the secrets hidden in the unconscious, because "revelation is an 'unveiling' of the depths of the human soul first and foremost, a 'laying bare'; hence it is an essentially psychological event, though this does not, of course, tell us what else it might be."[7] In other words, "religion is a careful and scrupulous observation of what Rudolf Otto aptly termed the numinosum, that is, a dynamic agency or effect not caused by an arbitrary act of the will. On the contrary, it seizes and controls the human subject who is rather its victim than its creator."[8] Religious experience is so powerful that it pro-

6. *Ibid.,* X, 155; VII, 237; XI, 104–105: "Religious experience is absolute; it cannot be disputed . . . and the one who has it possesses a great treasure, a thing that has become for him a source of life, meaning and beauty, and that has given a new splendor to the world and to mankind."

7. *Ibid.,* XI, 74. Thomas Aquinas, *De Verit.,* q. 12, a. 12: "Revelation . . . a kind of clouded awareness mixed up with darkness." Cardinal Newman, *Newman's Idea of a University* (London, 1912), p. 223: "Revelation is all in all the doctrine; the apostles its sole depository; the inferential method its sole instrument; and ecclesiastical authority, its sole sanction."

8. *Coll. Works,* XI, 7. Rudolf Otto, *The Idea of the Holy* (Oxford, 1943), p. 12: "Numinosum, its nature is such that grips or stirs the human mind with this and that determinate affective state. . . . If we do so we shall find we are dealing with something for which there is only one appropriate expression, *mysterium tremendum.* The feeling of it may at times come

duces deep psychological effects, even transformations of human
personalities and alteration of consciousness.[9]

The root of religion is revelation, so the nature of religion—
and, as a consequence, of God—will depend, psychologically
speaking, on the nature of the contents of the collective unconscious which erupts into consciousness as revelation opens the
treasures stored in the depths of the human psyche. The collective unconscious reveals itself as full of power, with a sense of
mystery and strong feelings. This kind of human experience
Jung calls religious experience, and the factors producing this
experience are the archetypes of the collective unconscious.
The contents and ideas appearing in consciousness are Gods:
"Gods are personifications of the collective unconscious, for
they reveal themselves to us through the unconscious activity
of the psyche."[10]

Causes of Religious Experience

Which are the religious factors producing that special state
of mind called the numinous? To answer this question, pure
empirical observations are insufficient. We have to cross the
threshold of Jung's working hypotheses: the factors producing
the experience of the numinous are the archetypes of the
collective unconscious.

Religion has always been an important factor in human
behavior. Therefore the archetypes, which store ancestral experiences, have to contain "the whole spiritual heritage of mankind's evolution, born anew in the brain of every individual."[11]
And since religion is universal and underlies all events, the his-

---

sweeping like a gentle tide, pervading the mind with a tranquil mood of
deepest worship." He says again: "Revelation does not mean a mere passing over into the intelligible and comprehensible. Something may be
profoundly and intimately known in feeling for the bliss it brings or the
agitation it produces, and yet the understanding may find no concept for
it" (p. 135).
9. *Coll. Works,* XI, 8; XI, 7, 312
10. *Ibid.,* XI, 163.
11. *Ibid.,* VIII, 158.

tory of religion in its wide sense is a treasure house of archetypal forms. Especially important is the archetype of the self.

Religious experience follows the general rules governing the
activities of the unconscious. The contents of the unconscious
erupt into consciousness generally in the second half of life,
that is to say, over thirty-five. At that time the unconscious
spontaneously invades consciousness, and since consciousness
and unconsciousness are the extreme of a dual polarity, religion
appears as compensatory of consciousness. The great religions,
Jung says, confirm the existence of a compensatory ordering
factor which is independent of the ego, and whose nature
transcends consciousness.[12]

The contents of the collective unconscious appear in the
beginning as autonomous complexes independent of the control of the mind and of the arbitrary power of the will. They
are dangerous because, in addition to being autonomous, they
are automatically projected upon external objects which absorb
part of their energy. The process and techniques leading to the
differentiation and assimilation of these contents by the conscious mind constitute the most important steps towards individuation. And since the archetypes of religion are the most
important archetypes, religion and individuation are interwoven. Therefore the analysis of dogmas and Gods is always
simultaneously parallel with the steps of the process of
individuation.

Contents of Religion

Psychologically speaking, Jung identifies God with the contents of the collective unconscious. And since man is in continuous evolution, these contents, though essentially always the
same—because they are collective—appear, however, in different ways according to the degree of consciousness of man and
the concrete circumstances in which man finds himself. Since
these contents are collective they have little to do with the ego
and much to do with the archetypes; since they are experienced,
their connection to passions and feelings is intimate.

12. *Ibid.,* XI, 294; XI, 488; IX,ii, 125.

In primitive man the contents of the archetypes appear as myths; myth is a process of the unconscious. Consequently, since the contents of religion are identified with the contents of the unconscious, myth is no more than a living religion; its ritual is magic.[13] Although myth is archaic, it is nevertheless connected with the process of individuation of primitives, and the ritualistic performances carried out for the purpose of producing the effect of the numinous were the prerogative of the medicine man, such as invocations, taboos, sacrifices, and incantation. Therefore, myth is the religion of primitive man, and since man's evolution towards consciousness is a slow process, the contents of religion in modern man are underlined by mythical contents. Myth is therefore the crux for understanding religion. For instance, Jung calls Christ the living myth of our culture, asserting that the myths of Near and Middle East underline Christian dogmas,[14] and that the history of dogmas goes back into the grey mist of neolithic prehistory. They were ancient mysteries protecting man against the uncanny things that live in the depths of the psyche. From myth to religion, Jung says, there is only one step.[15]

As man evolves, dogma appears as the substitute of myth; dogmas stem from myths and presuppose a slow evolution of them. In dogmas the contents of myth are replaced by new Gods who appear as the expression of the psyche, as the hero appears sometimes in myth. The ritual of dogmas is not, as in myth, the prerogative of the medicine man, but "of physicians, prophets and priests; finally, at the civilized age, of philosophy and religion."[16]

Dogma, Jung says, expresses an irrational whole by means of imagery and reflects the spontaneous and autonomous activity of the objective psyche, the unconscious. Dogmas are not only expressions of the contents of the archetypes, but also of their dynamic autonomous activity; they symbolize the motions of the libido. Dogmas are imbued with emotional

13. *Ibid.,* IX,i, 154.
14. *Ibid.,* IX,ii, 179.
15. *Ibid.,* XI, 300; IX,i, 12.
16. *Ibid.,* XI, 294.

values and express the soul more completely than scientific theories because they last for centuries, as against the dialectical nature of scientific theories.[17]

Since the existence of the collective unconscious is a psychological hypothesis and dogmas are symbolic expressions of the contents of the unconscious, dogmas are intimately related to psychology. Hence, for Jung, the Catholic way of life is completely a psychological problem, and Catholic dogmas are psychological expressions of Catholic man: "Almost the entire life of the collective unconscious has been channelled into dogmatic archetypal ideas and flows along like a well controlled stream in the symbolism of creed and ritual. It manifests itself in the inwardness of the Catholic psyche."[18] Therefore, since the archetypes of the collective unconscious can be shown empirically to be equivalents of religious dogmas, the better these dogmas express the unconscious, the better they are, the longer they last, and the greater the possibility of success: "The dogmatically formulated truths of the Christian Church express, almost perfectly, the nature of the psychic experience, and this matchless knowledge is set forth in grand symbolical images. The unconscious thus possess a natural affinity with the spiritual values of the Church, particularly in their dogmatic form, which owes its special character to centuries of theological controversy—absurd as this seemed in the eyes of later generations—and to the passionate efforts of many great men."[19] In conclusion, Jung says, we may say that Christianity has come to stay because it fits in with the existing archetypal pattern.[20]

Moreover, dogmas are healing systems for the ills of the soul because they control the terrific emotional values of the unconscious. In this sense dogmas protect man against the uncanny things that live in the depths of the soul: "This was the purpose of rite and dogma; they were dams and walls to keep back

17. *Ibid.*, XI, 46; XI, 45–46.
18. *Ibid.*, IX,i, 12.
19. *Ibid.*, XVI, 193.
20. *Ibid.*, IX,i, 14; XII, 17.

the dangers of the unconscious, the 'perils of the soul.' "[21] Dogmas, therefore, canalize the libido, the energy of the unconscious, protecting man from the power stored in the psyche.

What happens, then, in a religion without dogma? Jung warns of the dangers of this kind of religion, referring especially to Protestants. Protestantism, having no dogmas, lacked the protecting walls, and therefore the energy liberated went into the channels of curiosity and science. Many Protestants abandoned dogmas to embrace science but, he says, in this way Europe became the mother of dragons that devoured the greater part of the earth.[22] Jung, the psychologist, sees in history the influence of the healing factor of dogmas when he says: "Christianity was accepted as a means to escape from the brutality and unconsciousness of the ancient world. As soon as we discard it, the old brutality returns in force, as has been made overwhelmingly clear by contemporary events. This is not a step forwards, but a long step backwards into the past. . . . Who throws Christianity overboard and with it the whole basis of morality, is bound to be confronted with the age-old problem of brutality. We have had bitter experience of what happens when a whole nation finds the moral mask too stupid to keep up. The beast breaks loose, and a frenzy of demoralization sweeps over the civilized world."[23]

The absence of religion produces natural psychic disturbances. The conscious mind may ignore its presence, but the factors are there in the unconscious, and the more the ego tries to repress them, the greater the disturbance and the greater the autonomy and power of the complexes of the collective unconscious. Religion is, in this sense, a form of psychic therapy and one of the greatest helps in the psychological process of adaptation. Hence, since the existence of religion is a psychological need in man, whenever the spirit of God is excluded from human consideration an unconscious substitute takes place. The energy of the unconscious free of the protecting

21. *Ibid.*, IX,i, 22.
22. *Ibid.*, XI, 47; IX,i, 22.
23. *Ibid.*, V, 230.

walls of dogmas finds its outlet in communism, Hitlerism, fascism, etc., the modern dragon that threatens to devour the earth. Our fearsome gods have only changed their names: they now rhyme with *ism*.[24]

Even more, as will be explained later, Jung asserts that many neuroses are never cured unless the religious factor is restored: "During the last thirty years, people from all civilized countries have passed through my hands. . . . among all my patients in the second half of life—that is to say, over thirty-five—there has not been one whose problem in the last resort was not that of finding a religious outlook on life. It is safe to say that every one of them fell ill because he had lost what the living religions of every age have given to their followers, and none of them has been really healed who did not regain his religious outlook."[25] Furthermore, he says that "side by side with the decline of religious life, the neuroses grow noticeably more frequent. . . . We are living in a period of the greatest restlessness, nervous tension, confusion, and disorientation of outlook."[26] Jung sees in psychic sufferings the symptoms of a wrong attitude coming from the total personality. Even the moral viewpoint is a real factor with which psychology must reckon. General conceptions of a spiritual nature are indispensable constituents of psychic life.[27]

Dogmas are valuable insofar as they are rooted in religious experience. Experience, and not faith, is their starting point. This experience is at least in part irrational, and if dogmas become too external and void of experience, then they are completely obsolete, no more than relics of the past. The rational mind has to keep in touch with the unconscious, and according to the nature of the unconscious, so the experience and formula-

24. *Ibid.*, VII, 202–203; X, 190. Jung says: "Religious ideas, as history shows, are charged with an extremely suggestive emotional power. Among them I naturally reckon all *representations collectives*, everything that we have learned from history of religion, and anything that has an *ism* attached to it. The latter is only a modern variant of the denominational religions" (IX,i, 61).
25. *Ibid.*, XI, 334.
26. *Ibid.*, XI, 335–336.
27. *Ibid.*, VIII, 355–356; XI, 330–336.

tion of dogmas must be. Here Jung departs from Christianity because, according to the theory of opposites, evil is a factor as important as good, and since the unconscious contains both good and evil, dogmas cannot dispense with it. Therefore, a formulation of dogmas which is rooted only in good is incomplete and does not do justice to the whole nature of archetypes. In consequence, the gods who appear in consciousness cannot only be good, since "evil needs to be pondered just as much as good, for good and evil are ultimately nothing but ideal extensions and abstractions of doing, and both belong to the chiaroscuro of life. In the last resort there is no good that cannot produce evil and no evil that cannot produce good."[28] The gods of the collective unconscious are dualistic, and the Church has become detached from the world of nature because Christianity has dispensed with the dark part of God, Satan.

To attain full individuation in the Jungian sense it is necessary to withdraw the external projection which dogmas presuppose: "It (individuation) can only happen when you withdraw your projections from the *outward* historical or metaphysical Christ and thus *wake up* Christ within. . . . The self (or Christ) cannot become conscious and real without the withdrawal of external projections."[29] Faith, in the Christian sense, entails both the existence of a transcendent God and of an historical Christ. But since an exclusively religious projection may rob the soul of its values, and since dogmas express the contents of the collective unconscious, in the last resort the contents belong to the unconscious, not to external Gods in which they are projected. The withdrawal of the projection is a natural consequence of his views: "Jung rescues religion from dogma," Joseph L. Henderson says, "he shows me how to withdraw the mistaken projection."[30] In the end Jung gets rid

28. *Ibid.*, XII, 31; XII, 35, 15.
29. C. G. Jung, in H. L. Philp, *Jung and the Problem of Evil*, p. 233. *Coll. Works*, XIII, 53: "The *imitatio Christi* has this disadvantage: in the long run we worship as a divine example a man who embodied the deepest meaning of life, and then, out of sheer imitation, we forget to make real our own deepest meaning—self-realization."
30. Joseph L. Henderson, "C. G. Jung: A Personal Evaluation," in *Contact with Jung* (London, 1963), ed. by Michael Fordham, p. 222.

of any external connotation, although the withdrawal of the projection is dangerous and is recommended only for a few and just at the end of the process of individuation. Otherwise the withdrawal would entail the danger of inflation, the feeling of God-almightiness.

Myths and dogmas are not only expressions of the contents of the unconscious, but of what, perhaps, is more important: its motions and life. "Myths and dogmas are self-portraits of the movement of the libido. Thus the sun, the snake, the fire, the horse are its symbols."[31] For instance, the course of the sun in myth is an expression of the movement of the libido; the sun's nocturnal journey means the repression of libido; the sun's journey across the heavens means progression of the libido. Therefore, on the Christian level dogmas are symbolic expressions of the life of the unconscious of the Christian man. For instance, the mystery of the Eucharist, Jung says, transforms the soul of the empirical man into his totality, symbolically expressed by Christ. The Mass is, in this sense, the rite of the individuation process. The humanity of Christ symbolizes the ego; his divinity, the unconscious. The Mass therefore expresses symbolically the union of the conscious and the unconscious in the process of individuation. In archaic man the numinous experience of the individuation process was the perogative of shamans and medicine men; they experienced sickness, torture, and regeneration. These experiences in the Christian man, at a higher level, "imply the idea of being made whole through sacrifice, of being changed by transubstantiation and exalted to the pneumatic man—in a word, of apotheosis. The Mass is the summation and quintessence of a development which began many thousands of years ago."[32]

31. Hans Schaer, *Religion and the Cure of Souls in Jung's Psychology* (London, 1951), p. 71.
32. *Coll. Works*, XI, 294; XI, 273. Jung says: "A living example of the mystery drama representing the permanence as well as the transformation of life is the Mass. If we observe the congregation during this rite we note all degrees of participation, from mere indifferent attention to the profoundest emotion. The group of men standing about the exit, who are obviously engaged in every sort of worldly conversation, crossing themselves and genuflecting in a purely mechanical way—even they, despite their

Jung describes the life of the unconscious in the language of dogmas. He says that although his writings sound as if they were a sort of theological speculation, it is in reality modern man's perplexity expressed in symbolic terms. For instance, when using the term "crucifixion" or "sacrifice of the cross," one should understand "realization of the four functions" or "wholeness."[33] Jung finds in the writings of the alchemists the best manifestation of his ideas. The alchemists were not chemists but mystics who through the unconscious projection into matter of the contents of the archetypes were expressing in that way the motions of their psyche towards individuation.

Gods

Jung is agnostic with respect to the existence of a transcendent God. To me, he says, the question whether God exists at all or not is futile. It is futile because his metaphysical attitude is essentially Kantian: "Epistemological criticism proves the impossibility of knowing God but the psyche comes forward with the assertion of the experience of God. God is a psychic fact of immediate experience."[34] This is a cornerstone for understanding Jung. The whole idea of God is based on experience, not on the hypothesis of the existence of a transcendent and personal Deity, which he consider unattainable.

Jung does not totally exclude metaphysical truths nor deny the possibility of something real underlying the religious experience, especially in his last years. In practice, however, he ignores them as useless, and even as "actual impediments on

---

inattention, participate in the sacral action by their mere presence in this place where grace abounds. The Mass is an extramundane and extratemporal act in which Christ is sacrificed and then resurrected in the transformed substance; and this rite of his sacrificial death is not a repetition of the historical event but the original, unique, and eternal act. The experience of the Mass is therefore a participation in the transcendence of life, which overcomes all bounds of space and time. It is a moment of eternity in time" (IX,i, 117–118).
33. C. G. Jung, in H. L. Philp, *Jung and the Problem of Evil*, p. 245.
34. *Coll. Works*, VIII, 328.

the road to wider development,"[35] especially if these truths have lost touch with personal experience. Existence for him is synonymous with experience. Existence of God is therefore synonymous with experience of God. God is an object of personal experience.

The God of Jung is inside, and he calls a systematic blindness the prejudice that God is outside man. God is inside, because, psychologically speaking, the God-image is a complex of ideas of an archetypal nature representing a certain sum of energy which appears in projection.[36] The soul must contain in itself the faculty of relation to God, i.e., a correspondence, and this correspondence is, in psychological terms, the archetype of the God-image. What is, therefore, God? The soul's deepest and closest intimacies is precisely what God is.

If God lies in the deepest and closest intimacies of the soul, his properties will reflect—at least psychologically speaking— the properties of the unconscious where he lies. The properties of God have to be imbued with anthropomorphic traits, the qualities of the unconscious. For instance, since man is continuously evolving, God is also evolving, and appears in different ways.[37] The metamorphosis of the gods is parallel to the metamorphosis of man.

The evolution of God and man are mutually interwoven. Hence, creation has also to manifest this characteristic, because "all creation *ex nihilo* is God's and consists in nothing but God, with the result that man, like the rest of the creation, is simply God concrete. . . . It was only quite late that we realized that God is Reality itself and therefore—last but not least— man. This realization is a millennial process."[38] Thus Jung's

---

35. *Ibid.,* IX,ii, 34. Cf. V, 231; VII, 233 fn.
36. *Ibid.,* V, 56; XI, 58, 10–11.
37. *Ibid.,* XI, 84. Jung says: "Eternal truth needs a human language that alters with the spirit of the times. The primordial images undergo ceaseless transformation and yet remain ever the same, but only a new form can be understood anew" (XVI, 195). Jolande Jacobi, *Complex, Archetype, Symbol in the Psychology of C. G. Jung* (New York, 1959). "The metamorphosis of the Gods in our outward worlds is inexhaustible, and never ceases" (p. 118).
38. *Coll. Works,* XI, 402.

conception of creation has nothing in common with that of Christians. Creation for him implies the gradual acquisition of consciousness of the universe, especially of God and man. Why? Because the purpose of creation is connected with the transformation of God; the encounter of the creator with the creature changes the creator. The purpose of creation is the necessity of a greater consciousness in God. This is clear in the Book of Job.

Yahweh is the God of the Jews, but a God without consciousness. How is this to be proved? Because of his encounter with Job. Job sees through the injustice done to him the duality and imperfections of Yahweh. Job possesses a superior knowledge of God which God himself does not possess. He realizes God's inner antinomy and, to his horror, he discovers that Yahweh is in a certain respect less than human. This explains the behavior of Yahweh, the behavior of an unconscious being who cannot be judged morally. Yahweh is amoral, jealous, irritable, good and evil, but he is not responsible for his actions, for he is too unconscious to be moral; morality presupposes consciousness.[39]

What happened after God's encounter with Job? Here are Jung's own words:

> The victory of the vanquished and oppressed is obvious; Job stands morally higher than Yahweh. In this respect the creature has surpassed the creator. . . . Job's superiority cannot be shrugged off. Hence a situation arises in which real reflection is needed. That is why Sophia steps in. She reinforces the much needed self-reflection and thus makes possible Yahwehs' decision to become man. . . . Job is morally superior to him and therefore he has to catch up and become human himself. . . . Yahweh must become man precisely because he has done man a wrong. He, the guardian of justice, knows that every wrong must be expiated, and Wisdom knows that moral law is above even him. Because his creature has surpassed him he must regenerate himself.[40]

39. *Ibid.*, XI, 372; XI, 367–383, 428.
40. *Ibid.*, XI, 404–405.

Job possesses greater consciousness than Yahweh and therefore, psychologically speaking, the incarnation of God is a necessity in order to obtain, through suffering in his human nature, a greater consciousness. The gods of Jung evolve from unconsciousness to consciousness. The incarnation of God is the crux for his understanding and, therefore, the Book of Job is for Jung what Genesis and the fall of Adam is for Christians; Christ did not come to deliver mankind from evil; when God becomes man it means nothing less than a world-shaking transformation of God.[41] Therein lies the Copernican revolution of Jung's ideas on God.

Trinity

Jung's ideas on the Trinity are not an intellectual explanation of the dogma. On the contrary, he says that as a metaphysical truth the Trinity remains inaccessible to him, and has never contributed in the slightest to his belief or to his understanding. Jung, however, always cautious, does not deny the possibility of metaphysical truths that may underlie this archetypal statement.

Jung explores the New Testament and says that there is not a single passage where the Trinity is formulated in an intellectually comprehensible manner: "Logic, and the like, shows that, despite all the mental exertion of the Councils and of scholastic theology, they [theologians] failed to bequeath to posterity an intellectual understanding of the dogma that would lend the slightest support to belief in it. There remained only submission to faith and renunciation to one's own desire to understand."[42] This in a sense is true, because "by definition," no human mind can understand the mystery of the Trinity. This does not mean that the mystery is contradictory or false, but simply beyond the scope of human comprehension and for this reason an object of faith; faith and comprehension cannot be given simultaneously in the same intellect.

41. *Ibid.*, XI, 401.
42. *Ibid.*, XI, 153.

How does Jung explain the Trinity? As usual, by resorting
to the unconscious: "Although they (trinitarian formulae) are
no evidence for the Trinity in the New Testament, they nevertheless occur and, like the three divine Persons, are clear indications of an active archetype operating beneath the surface and
throwing up triadic formulations."[43] Thus the existence of the
Trinity is proved through the numinous revelation of the archetypes of the collective unconscious which project their contents
in triads. That is to say, man's conceptions of God are organized
into triads and trinities. Since trinities and quaternities symbols occur frequently in dreams, folklore, myth, and other manifestations of the unconscious, from them Jung concludes that
the idea of the Trinity is based on something that can be experienced and must, therefore, have a meaning. This explains
the wide gulf between the Christian approach and dogmatic
definition of the Trinity on the one hand, and Jung's psychological view of the mystery on the other.

Following the theory of evolution Jung relates the apparition
of the Trinity with a gradual development of consciousness in
man. On the archaic level there is not Trinity, but only unity,
so the Trinity entails a gradual unfolding of the archetype in
man's consciousness, or rather, its absorption into the pattern of
ideas transmitted by the cultures of antiquity.[44] This culture
is not merely Christian culture, but goes back four thousand
years, and the development of the Christian idea of the Trinity
unconsciously reproduced the archetype of the *homoousia*
which first appeared in Egyptian theology, though the Egyptian
model cannot be considered the archetype of the Christian
idea. Thus the archetypes of the unconscious follow a slow process of transformation. Their objective content, expressed in
projection, depends both on the state of evolution of the collective unconscious and on the ideas and culture in which the
contents of the archetype appear. Jung points out that nobody

43. *Ibid.*, XI, 139. Cf. XI, 200.
44. *Ibid.*, XI, 140; XI, 151: "Thus the history of the Trinity presents itself
as the gradual crystallization of an archetype that moulds the anthropomorphic conceptions of father and son, of life, and of different persons into an
archetypal and numinous *figure*, The Most Holy Three-in-One."

can doubt the manifest superiority of the Christian revelation over its pagan precursors.[45]

How, then, is explained psychologically the appearance of the symbol of the Trinity? Although Jung's reasoning is obscure, nevertheless it is possible to synthesize his ideas. The Father represents the state of culture lacking reflection; this kind of consciousness sees everything as one, the Father. To probe it, Jung tells how he had the occasion for observing this phenomenon in a tribe of Negroes in Mount Elgin, in Africa; they believe that the creator had made everything good and beautiful. For primitive people, man, the world, and God form a whole (oneness), a unity unclouded by criticism. This is the world of the Father.[46]

But a reflective consciousness, like that of Job, is puzzled by the duality of God's creation, not in agreement with this unity. The Christianity symbolized by the Son, therefore, forces the individual to reflect and to judge the Father by his works:

> The famous question about the origin of evil does not yet exist in a patriarchal age. . . . The world of the Father typifies an age which is characterized by a pristine oneness with the whole of Nature, no matter whether this oneness be beautiful or ugly or awe-inspiring. But once the question is asked: "Whence come the evil, why is the world so bad and imperfect, why are there diseases and other horrors, why must man suffer?"—then reflection has already begun to judge the

45. *Ibid.*, XI, 137; XI, 148. Again Jung says: "For the Trinity is undoubtedly a higher form of God-concept than mere unity, since it corresponds to a level of reflection on which man has become more conscious" (XI, 136). And stressing a similar idea he says: "Nobody can doubt the manifold superiority of the Christian revelation over its pagan precursors, for which reason it is distinctly superfluous today to insist on the unheralded and unhistorical character of the Gospels, seeing that they swarm with historical and psychological assumptions of very ancient origin" (XI, 137).

46. *Ibid.*, XI, 133–134. "Generally speaking, the father denotes the early state of consciousness when one was still a child, still dependent on a definite, ready-made pattern of existence which is habitual and has the character of law. It is a passive, unreflected condition, a mere awareness of what is given, without intellectual or moral judgment" (XI, 181). "The world of the father typifies an age which is characterized by a pristine oneness with the whole of Nature" (XI, 134).

Father by his manifest works, and straight-way one is conscious of a doubt, which is itself the symptom of a split in
the original unity. One comes to the conclusion that creation
is imperfect—nay more, that the Creator has not done his
job properly, that the goodness and almightiness of the Father
cannot be the sole principle of the cosmos. Hence the One
has to be supplemented by the Other, with the result that
the world of the Father is fundamentally altered and is super-
seded by the world of the Son.[47]

Once again we see the gradual manifestation of God's duality
and the struggle of Him on his road to consciousness. The Son
has to incarnate.

But the world of the Father and the Son is incomplete
because the incarnation of the Son is not continuous. Here
lies the necessity of the Holy Spirit. The Holy Spirit appears
as a continuation of the incarnation of God who is indwelling
in the empirical man through the Holy Spirit. As man gains
consciousness, making the unconscious content conscious, God,
who dwells in man also gains consciousness with the help of
empirical man. The Holy Spirit represents the final and complete stage in the evolution of God and the divine drama
towards consciousness.

To summarize, the collective unconscious evolves both
through centuries and individually in man in order to obtain
consciousness. But in the Christian man the unconscious
obtains consciousness in a way symbolically represented by the
Trinitarian formula. The Trinity, Jung says, is a revelation
not only of God but also of man.

47. *Ibid.*, XI, 134. Cf. "The picture changes when the accent shifts to the
son. . . . Legitimate detachment from the father has been effected. Legitimate detachment consists in conscious differentiation from the father and
from the habitus represented by him. This requires a certain amount of
knowledge of one's own individuality, which cannot be acquired without
moral discrimination and cannot be held to unless one has understood its
meaning. Habit can only be replaced by a mode of life consciously chosen
and acquired. The Christianity symbolized by the 'Son' therefore forces
the individual to discriminate and to reflect, as was noticeably the case
with those Church Fathers who laid such emphasis on knowledge as opposed to necessity and ignorance" (XI, 181).

Quaternity

The Trinity is not a complete expression of the process of the unconscious. "Whereas the Christian symbolism is a Trinity, the formula presented by the unconscious is a quaternity." The missing element in the Christian formula is the devil: "The dogmatic aspect of the evil is absent from Trinity and leads to a more or less awkward existence on its own as the devil."[48]

In terms of creation the necessity of the evil factor appears in the poisonous quality of the *prima materia*. Matter, Jung says, is not included in the Trinity formula; but since the material world is real and, as such, an intrinsic part of the divine *actus purus,* then the devil is there.[49] In other words, if everything real is part of God and matter is real, it has to be included in God. Accordingly, this situation gives rise to a quaternity, for the devil cannot be destroyed; he is eternal, he is the fourth. There is no total creation without the dark side, the devil; there is no principle of individuation without the dark side, the shadow. Once again we see the working power of opposites, the tension of opposites that makes energy possible.

The quaternity formula includes Lucifer as the dark side of God. But on different occasions Jung speaks of a quaternity as including a feminine factor. The symbol of the Trinity is exclusively masculine in character. The fourth element was the earth, or the body, and they were symbolized by the Virgin. In this way the feminine element is added to the Trinity, thereby producing the quaternity.[50]

The number *four* is for Jung a magic number. He sees quaternities everywhere. The quaternity is the religious symbol not only of Catholicism but of many other religions. In Catholicism, however, the fourth element is Mary "because the Three are the *Summum Bonum,* and the devil is the principle and personification of evil. In a Catholic quaternity, the fourth would be the Mother who is 99 percent divine. The

48. *Ibid.,* XI, 59.
49. *Ibid.,* IX,i, 195.
50. *Ibid.,* XI, 62–63; XI, 196–198.

devil does not count, being μὴ ὄν, an empty shadow owing to the *privatio boni,* in which the Bonum is equal to οὐσια."⁵¹ Catholics dispense with the devil because, according to Saint Augustine, evil has no positive entity and Mary is almost divine. Hence a Catholic quaternity includes the feminine element.

Jung gives special importance to the dogma of the Assumption. He sees the force of nature behind the pontifical definition, and in God and Mary a cautious approach to the solution of opposites. But he warns Catholics, who say that the quaternity is without a shadow, that the devil is there. Psychologically speaking the feminine part of the quaternity is the symbol of the archetype of the anima, our feminine figure of the unconscious. "She would be a matrix of the quaternity, a Θεοτόκος or *Mater Dei.*"⁵²

If the psychological quaternity appears sometimes as the devil, the dark element, and at other times as the feminine element, namely Mary or Sophia, then it seems that the quaternity would make a quinary. To this obvious objection Jung answers: "The quaternity is a hypothetical structure, depicting wholeness. It is not a logical concept, but an empirical fact. The quinarious or quinio (e.g., in the form of 4 + 1, i.e., quincunx) does occur as a symbol of wholeness (e.g., in China and occasionally in alchemy) but relatively rarely. Otherwise the quinio is not a symbol of wholeness, quite the contrary (e.g., the five-rayed star of the Soviets or of the U.S.A.). The latter is rather the chaotic *prima materia.*"⁵³ We are unable to interpret this mysterious answer.

51. C. G. Jung, in H. L. Philp, *Jung and the Problem of Evil,* p. 216.
52. *Coll. Works,* XI, 63. Jung says: "It was interesting to note that, among the many articles published in the Catholic and Protestant press on the declaration of the dogma of the Assumption, there was not one, so far as I could see, which laid anything like the proper movement and the psychological need behind it" (XI, 461). Although the psychological need is not the reason for the declaration of the dogma of the Assumption, it is interesting to note that the "feeling" of the Christian people has a bearing on the development of the Christian dogma, especially regarding the dogmas concerning Mary. See, Marin Sola, O.P., in his well-known book, *La Evolución Homogenea del Dogma Católico* (Madrid, 1952), pp. 405–407.
53. C. G. Jung, in H. L. Philp, *Jung and the Problem of Evil,* p. 216.

Christ

The history, nature, and concrete life of Christ is for Jung of little importance. Why? Because Jung's approach to Christ is psychological, neither theological nor metaphysical. Jung sees in the person of the Redeemer a "collective" figure fulfilling the expectations of the unconscious of the people who lived at that time. So the question of who Christ really was is irrelevant. Christ personifies the collective expectations of the unconscious because he lived the concrete, personal life which in all essential features had at the same time archetypal character. Since the archetypes of the collective unconscious are not personal, but universal, the life of Christ symbolizes the eternal life of the species, and thus what happens in the life of Christ happens always and everywhere.[54] Here lies the central idea of Jung's approach to Christ; the life of Christ is a perfect expression of the needs of the archetypes of the unconscious.

Consequently, in the Gospels, myths, legends, and factual reports are interwoven into a whole; that is to say, what is archetypal and what is individual. Hence, Jung says, the Gospels would immediately lose their character of wholeness if one tried to separate the individual from the archetypal. Christ, as an expression of the unconscious, is a myth "because he is still living myth of our culture. He is our culture hero, who, regardless of his historical existence, embodies the myth of the Divine Primordial Man, the mystic Adam."[55] Indeed, Christ is himself God, and as such he occupies the center of the Christian mandala; he is the leader of the flock, his body is bread to be eaten, and his blood wine to be drunk. Christ is also human, thus he is the hero born without sin, more complete and more perfect than the natural man. He is therefore the Anthropos.[56]

Jung asks two questions: (1) What was in man that was stirred up by the Christian message? (2) What was the answer Christ gave to man?

54. *Coll. Works,* XI, 88–89.
55. *Ibid.,* IX,ii, 36. Cf. XI, 89.
56. *Ibid.,* XI, 155.

1. What the Christian message stirred up was the archetype of the self in the soul of every man, with the result that the concrete Rabbi Jesus was rapidly assimilated by the archetype because Christ realized the idea of totality in which the opposites are united. Historically, the self is identified with the God-image and, accordingly, is identified with Christ because Christ represents a divine or heavenly king, a glorified man, a son of God unspotted by sin, and the first Adam before the Fall, when Adam was still a pure image of God; hence Christ, like the self, represents a totality.[57] The connection between Christ and the self, the self and the God-image, and the myths symbolizing this God-image, is summarized in the following important words:

> Since he (the hero of more than human stature) is psychologically an archetype of the self, his divinity only confirms that the self is numinous, a sort of god, or having some share in the divine nature. In this mythologem may lie the root of the argument in favor of *homoousia*. For psychology it makes a vast difference whether the self is to be considered "of the same nature" as the Father, or merely "of similar nature." The decision in favor of *homoousia* was of great psychological importance, for it asserted that Christ is of the same nature as God. But Christ, from the point of view of psychology and comparative religion, is a typical manifestation of the self. For psychology, the self is an *imago Dei* and cannot be distinguished from it empirically; the two ideas are therefore of the same nature. The hero is the protagonist of God's transformation in man; he corresponds to what I call "mana personality."[58]

Hence psychologically speaking, the "more than human properties" of the mythological hero confirm the divine nature of the self. But Christ is a perfect symbol of the archetype of the self because Christ symbolizes the hero's attributes: a divine Father, hazardous birth, precocious development, miracles, death, choir of angels, shepherds, etc. Therefore, it was Christ's

57. *Ibid.,* IX,ii, 37; XI, 156.
58. *Ibid.,* V, 391–392.

attributes which make him an embodiment of the self. He stirred up the archetype of the self because Christ expresses better than anything else the contents of this archetype. "He became the collective figure whom the unconscious of his contemporaries expected to appear."[59] The self of man responded to the Christian message.

2. What was the answer Christ gave to that which was stirred up by the Christian message? The answer is individuation in man; incarnation in Christ. Since in psychological terms Christ and the self are identical, everything that happens to Christ is happening to man. The process of individuation presupposes a long and painful road towards wholeness and rebirth. Individuation involves suffering, a passion of the ego from the violence of the self. The humanity of Christ represents the ego; his divinity, the self; thus as a consequence of the integration of consciousness and unconsciousness, the ego enters the divine realm where it participates in God's suffering. The cause of suffering is the same in both; for man it means individuation and wholeness; for God it means incarnation and consciousness.

Jung sees in the life of Christ projections of the inner life of the unconscious. For example, he says: "The three days descent into hell during death describes the sinking of the vanished value into the unconscious, where, by conquering the power of darkness, it establishes new order, and then rises up to heaven again, that is, attains, supreme clarity of consciousness."[60] But if the life of Christ does not represent perfectly the inner life of the unconscious, then the answer given by the Christian message is good but not perfect. This is Jung's contention, and his ideas are connected with two things; the process of individuation and the necessity of evil for duality.

1. The process of individuation: Jung, as explained before, is careful to make a sharp distinction between wholeness and perfection. The goal of individuation is not perfection but wholeness. Although it is natural to seek perfection, the archetype, however, fulfills itself only in completeness. "I find then

59. *Ibid.*, XI, 154–155; IX,ii, 181.
60. *Ibid.*, XI, 90.

a law, that, when I would do good, evil is present with me."[61] This is an unusual idea; the ego may look for perfection, as in the Christian attitude, but the self looks for completeness. Completeness and not perfection is the supreme human goal.

2. The necessity of evil for duality. In a sense, this is a consequence of the first, because without integration of evil there is no totality, and the figure of Christ is not totality for he lacks the nocturnal side of the psyche's nature, the darkness of the spirit, and he is also without sin.[62] Therefore, although the attributes of Christ make him out as an embodiment of the self, looked at from the psychological angle, Jung says, he corresponds to only one-half of the archetype. According to the metaphysical doctrine of *privatio boni* wholeness seems guaranteed in Christ. But in the plan of empirical psychology one must take evil rather more substantially; there it is simply the opposite of good. Jung is amazed when a Protestant theologian had even the temerity to assert that God can only be good. Thus, Christ can only lead to perfection, not to wholeness.

Jung finds the psychic complement of Christ in the doctrine of the two sons of God, Satan and Christ. In consequence, the coming of the Antichrist is not just a prophetic prediction, but an inexorable psychological law. Hence if Christ is half the archetype, namely the light side, "the other half appears in the Antichrist, which is just as much a manifestation of the self, except that he consists of its dark aspect."[63] Psychologically, the Antichrist corresponds to the shadow of the self, the dark side of human personality.

The coming of the Antichrist is related to the conception of Yahweh. Yahweh was a totality including both good and evil, that is, Satan and Christ as his two sons. In the Book of Job, the devil was still on good terms with Yahweh and Christ. At the time of Christ's incarnation, however, Satan became detached from Yahweh, fell from heaven and was hidden not in hell, but in matter. Since the incarnation presupposes a world-

---

61. *Ibid.*, IX,ii, 69. Jung quotes St. Paul, Rom. 7: 21.
62. *Ibid.*, IX,i, 157.
63. *Ibid.*, IX,ii, 44. Cf. IX,ii, 41, 46.

shaking transformation of God, the incarnation of the dark side is logical, and "nothing less than the counterstroke of the devil provoked by God's incarnation; for the devil attains this true stature as the adversary of Christ, and hence of God, only after the rise of Christianity."[64]

Jung's ideas on God as a duality are logical. The primitive God, Yahweh, lacked consciousness; the incarnation is the solution to acquire it. But since Christ and Satan are both parts of God, it is natural to expect a double incarnation, the incarnation of the light side represented by Christ, and the incarnation of the dark side represented by Satan who is to become the Antichrist.

For Jung, the solution of individuation lies not in the Gospels but in the Apocalypse. Saint John's consciousness was Christian, his unconscious collective. His ego was identified with the Gospel of love, and, consequently, the imitation of Christ creates a shadow in St. John's unconsciousness. His consciousness sees only the light side of God, and, as expected, a tremendous *enantiodromy* takes place that John himself could not understand and failed to see. The unconscious compensates for the one-sided attitude of consciousness, and the opposite collide in his visions. His visions are not personal, but collective and a consequence of an unusual tension between consciousness and unconsciousness.[65] What St. John sees is "the power of destruction and vengeance"; his visions are, therefore, the visions of the dark side of God missing in the Christian message and symbolized as "monsters with horns, the sun-moon child," etc. Like Job he saw the fierce and terrible side of Yahweh. The missing quaternity is restored, and the God of St. John is both perfect and imperfect, a duality. "God has a terrible double aspect; a sea of grace is met by a seething lake of fire, and the light of love glows with a fierce dark heat of which it is said—it burns but gives no light. That is the eternal, as distinct from the temporal, Gospel: *one must love God but must fear him.*"[66]

64. *Ibid.,* IX,ii, 42. Cf. XI, 401.
65. *Ibid.,* XI, 444; XI, 443.
66. *Ibid.,* XI, 450–451.

The Holy Ghost

In Jung's process of individuation the role played by the
third Person of the Trinity is even more relevant than Christ's.
More important than the individual event of the incarnation
of Christ is what happens after his death, namely, the collective
indwelling of the Holy Ghost, the seizure of the individual by
the spirit. Although the third Person of the Trinity is eternal,
He appears empirically in this world only when Christ had left
the earthly stage, bestowing man with the power to do great
works. The Son came from the Father, and common to both is
the living activity of the Holy Ghost, who according to the
Christian doctrine, is breathed forth, spirited by both the Father
and the Son.[67]

The Holy Ghost, Jung says, cannot be logically derived from
the Father and Son relationship. Father, Mother, and Son seems
more reasonable and natural relationship than Father, Son, and
Holy Ghost. But this is not a question of natural situation or
a logical conclusion, for the Holy Ghost, as the breath of Father
and Son, can only be understood as an idea introduced by a
process of human reflection: in some mysterious and unexpected way an important mental process, peculiar to man, has
been imported into the revelation of this Person.[68]

Thus Jung goes beyond the logical difficulties of the process
to introduce us into the realm of psychology because the psychological human factor of reflection explains the Holy Ghost
as the breath common to Father, Son, and man. It is not the
product of conscious reflection but unconscious, that is to say
the act by which an unconscious content erupts into consciousness. A similar view is known in Egypt: "Through reflection,
'life' and its 'soul' are abstracted from Nature and endowed
with a separate existence. Father and Son are united in the
same soul, or, according to the ancient Egyptian view, in the
same procreative force, Ka-mutef. Ka-mutef is exactly the same
hypostatization of an attribute as the breath or 'spiration' of the

67. *Ibid.,* XI, 135, 58.
68. *Ibid.,* XI, 158–160.

Godhead."[69] Hence, when the "revelation," i.e., the content manifested by the unconscious reflection, is hypostatized, projected, and personified, it then becomes the third Person of the Trinity: "God becomes manifest in the human act of Reflection."[70]

The appearance of the Holy Ghost requires two factors. First, the procreative "spirit" of God, the spirit of life left behind for man's service to activate the dynamism of the unconscious. This is the spirit that the Son has received from the Father and by which He himself was begotten; this same spirit the Son will transmit to his children, the ordinary man. "Not only is he the life common to Father and Son, he is also the Paraclete whom the Son left behind him, to procreate in man and bring forth works of divine parentage."[71]

This is yet obscure semantics. In Jungian psychological terms, the archetype of the spirit is behind the revelation of the Holy Ghost. This archetype is the quintessence of the life of the mind, just as the "living being" is the quintessence of the life of the body. The spirit is ambivalent, dark and light, good and evil, independent and inscrutable, mediator and uniter of opposites, superior to consciousness and capable of giving vital expression to those psychic potentialities that lie beyond the reach of the ego-consciousness. The archetype of the spirit underlies the process of unconscious reflection of the Holy Ghost. "Psychologically, the spirit manifests itself as a personal being, sometimes with visionary clarity; in Christian dogma it is actually the third Person of the Trinity."[72]

Secondly, the appearance of the Holy Ghost requires the psychological element upon which the activity of the spirit falls: the archetype of the self. Since the symbols of the self cannot be distinguished from God-images, the emergence of the self into consciousness—what Jung calls the unconscious reflection—carries a symbol pregnant with religious meaning. In

69. *Ibid.*, XI, 158–159, 158 fn.
70. *Ibid.*, XI, 161.
71. *Ibid.*, XI, 159.
72. *Ibid.* VIII, 335.

other terms, the reflection necessary for the existence of the
Holy Ghost is equivalent to the revelation into consciousness
of the archetype of the self. Therefore, through the descent of
the Holy Ghost, that is to say, through the indwelling, the self
of man enters into a relationship of unity with the substance
of God which is followed by the revelation of its content, the
God-image as uniter of opposites: "Just as the Holy Ghost is
a legacy left to man so, conversely, the concept of the Holy
Ghost is something begotten by man and bears the stamp of
its human progenitor."[73] The Holy Ghost is the expression of
an imponderable psychic event, a revelation not only of God
but at the same time of man.

Wholeness is psychologically achieved in man by the revelation of the self which unites all the conscious and unconscious
elements of the individual. And since good and evil are essential elements making up man, good and evil and all the rest
of the opposites are united in the self, attaining thus a higher
synthesis. In like manner, the realm of the Father and Son is
not complete without the synthesis achieved by the Holy Ghost;
a synthesis accounted for by no less than a quaternity, and the
restoration of the dual original Yahweh. "Our quaternity formula confirms the rightness of their claims; for the Holy Ghost,
as the synthesis of the original One which then became split,
issues from a source that is both light and dark. 'For the powers
of the right and the left unite in the harmony of wisdom' we are
told in the Acts of John."[74] God is a quaternity, and the revelation of the unconscious through the manifestation of the Holy
Ghost reveal the dark aspect, already suppressed by the Church.

Gods are personifications of the contents of the unconscious;
hence, the Holy Ghost is understood as an idea or an abstract
concept endowed with personality, representing the hypostasis
of life. But this is not exempt from difficulties because the Holy
Ghost as breath of life presupposes the revelation of the self
helped by the activity of the archetype of the spirit, none of
which usually have human personality. Many symbols of the self

73. *Ibid.*, XI, 161. Cf. XI, 194, 160; XI, 162: "The Holy Ghost is a process
of human reflection that irrationally creates the united Third."
74. *Ibid.*, XI, 178. Cf. XI, 187.

are not endowed with personality, as for instance spheres, circles, squares, and so forth. Even some of the Christian symbols of the Paraclete lack personality, like, for example, the spirit descended on the disciple in tongues of fire. The Holy Ghost is incommensurable and paradoxical, he has no proper name.[75]

Christ and the Holy Ghost are both related to the archetype of the self, but they are not identical. Psychologically, Christ must be understood as a symbol of the self; the descent of the Holy Ghost, however, as the self-actualization in man. Christ took on man's bodily nature; the Holy Ghost took on man as spiritual force. It is obvious that in Jungian terms the supremacy belongs to the Holy Ghost.

The incarnation of Christ is incomplete, for Christ is not an empirical human being as he is sinless and we all are born in sin. His incarnation, therefore, needs to be complemented by a new incarnation because, according to strict divine justice, the wrong done to Job by God, and through him to mankind, can only be repaired by the incarnation of God in common, ordinary human beings; just as man must suffer from God, so God must suffer from man.[76]

But is that possible? The incarnation appears as a unique historical event, and no repetition of it was to be expected. But the Catholic Church, Jung asserts, is cautious in this regard, believing that with the assistance of the Holy Ghost the dogma can progressively develop and unfold in agreement with Christ's own teaching about the Holy Ghost. Hence there is a possibility of a further continuation of the incarnation. Even more, it seems highly unlikely that the bond between God and man was broken with the death of Christ. On the contrary, this bond is stressed again and again by the sending of the Paraclete.[77]

The new incarnation is realized through the indwelling of the Holy Ghost, which makes the believer a child of God and fellow heir with Christ, because the Paraclete is also God. The deifying effect of the Holy Ghost is naturally assisted by the image of God stamped in the elect. God in the shape of the Holy

75. *Ibid.*, XI, 185–186, 159. Thomas Aquinas, *Summa Theol.*, I, q. 36, a. 1.
76. *Ibid.*, XI, 161, 194.
77. *Ibid.*, XI, 432, 412–413, 414.

Spirit puts up a tent in man, for he obviously wishes to realize himself continually. He descends into the human realm and through reflection acquires new consciousness. On the other hand man finds redemption, individuation, and mounts up to the realm of the divinity: "Everybody who possesses the Holy Ghost will be a new rock, in accordance with 1 Peter 2: 5: 'Be you also living stones built up.' "[78]

Hence, Jung says, the continuous indwelling of the Holy Ghost entails a real danger for the Church, who discourages and ignores the indwelling as much as possible. Why? Because through the indwelling man is included in God's sonship, and the words of Christ, "Ye are gods" (John 10: 34) appear in a significant light. In addition, the Holy Ghost as spirit is not subject to any control and authority, and that will pose a serious problem to the teaching authority of the Church.[79]

The continuous incarnation leads to a quaternity which will take place in many yet to come, none of whom would enjoy the privilege or even the probability of being born without the sting of sin. God fills us with evil as well as with good, and since he wants to become man the uniting of his antinomy must take place in man. The incarnation of Christ is the proto-type which is continuously being transferred to the creature by the Holy Ghost. In other words, the psychological process repre-senting the revelation of the self is endowed with a religious significance and symbolism, for the union of opposites in the self represents the heavenly *hieros-gamos* which unites Yahweh and Sophia, whose fruit is the divine child, a symbol of the self:[80] "The Holy Ghost is a comforter, like the Father, a mute, eternal, unfathomable One in whom God's love and God's terri-bleness come together in wordless union. And through this union the original meaning of the still unconscious Father's world is restored and brought within the original scope of human experience and reflection. Looked at from a quaternity standpoint the Holy Ghost is the reconciliation of opposites

78. *Ibid.,* IX,ii, 88.
79. *Ibid.,* XI, 433.
80. *Ibid.,* XI, 462, 468, 438.

and hence the answer to the suffering of the Godhead which Christ personifies.[81] This is the answer to God's continuous incarnation: his desire to acquire continuously greater consciousness, and to restore the dual unconscious Yahweh into a conscious God in whom the opposites are united.

81. *Ibid.,* XI, 176.

IV

Critique of Jung's Ideas on
Religion and Individuation

Jung's Methodology

Jung has steadily insisted that his views on religion are not theological or metaphysical but simply empirical. He relies on empirical observation rather than on abstract theories which he humbly confesses he is unable to comprehend. However, no modern science is merely a collection of facts, and though Jung says that he finds access to religion only through psychological understanding of inner experience, he also points out that his psychology, like every empirical science, cannot go along without auxiliary concepts, hypotheses and models. His method is descriptive, but he is also aware that nowhere does the observer interfere more drastically with experiment than in psychology. Psychic experience, he says, is very difficult. Likewise, he sees that in dealing with religious factors his feelings are challenged as much as his intellect, and that he cannot write in a coolly objective manner, but must allow his emotional subjectivity to speak.[1]

In *Two Essays on Analytic Psychology* he says that his work is a pioneer work, and often a bitter one—"hence not everything I bring forth is written out of my head, but much of it comes from the heart also, a fact I would beg the gracious reader not to overlook."[2] In *Religion and Psychology* Jung realizes that he is beyond the territory of psychology. Furthermore, he asserts that even a layman in theology like him can, or perhaps must, make a contribution. He also points out that the great mistake

1. *Coll. Works,* XI, 306; XVII, 86; XI, 363.
2. *Ibid.,* VII, 116.

of Freud was to turn his back on philosophy and, finally, he writes; "I fancied I was working along the best scientific lines, establishing facts, observing, classifying, describing causal and functional relations, only to discover in the end that I had involved myself in a net of reflections which extend far beyond natural science and ramify into the fields of philosophy, theology, comparative religion, and the human sciences in general. This transgression, as inevitably as it was to suspect, has caused me no little worry."[3] In other words, the work of Jung is basically empirical, sometimes partially empirical, and, on occasions, theoretical rather than empirical. It is important to bear this distinction in mind in order to give a fair evaluation to Jung's work.

But whether or not the work is empirical, we must be aware of the different approaches to religion of Jung, the theologian, and philosopher. Jung's ideas on religion are rooted in the facts observed in the experience of his patients. With these observations in hand he speculates psychologically in order to discover the auxiliary hypotheses, explanations of the empirical facts. But it is relevant to point out that Jung not only relies on the facts of immediate experience but also on a more or less world religious literature ranging from myth, astrology, alchemy, gnosticism, and oriental mysticism, to Sacred Scripture and the dogmas of Christianity. He uses everything available to support his psychological views. Jung considers doctrines and objects which strictly belong to theology or metaphysics from another point of view: the psychological one. For instance, Christ, for theology, is God; for Jung, Christ is a symbol of the archetype of the self. Psychology and man are the pillars of Jung's approach to religion; all the rest revolves around them and is subordinated to them. He attempts to build a psychology of religion rooted and ending in man, a closed human system. "I must expressly emphasize," he says, "that I am not dabbling in metaphysics or discussing the question of faith, but I am speaking of psychology. Whatever religious experience or metaphysi-

3. C. G. Jung, "The Spirit of Psychology," in *Spirit and Nature* (London, 1955), ed. J. Campbell, p. 426.

cal truth may be in themselves, looked at empirically they are essentially psychic phenomena, that is, they manifest themselves as such and must therefore be submitted to psychological criticism, evaluation, and investigation. Science comes to a stop at its *own* borders."[4]

A close look at the work of Jung also shows a manifest connection between psychology and history. The nature of the psyche is fully evaluated when viewed from the historical point of view because history is contained in each individual, especially in the archetypes of the unconscious. Jung studies history, observing the behavior of the psyche; he studies the psyche analyzing its continuous manifestations through the centuries.

Scientists and philosophers, accustomed to the analytic and detailed empirical approach, find difficulty in reading his works and even more difficulty in understanding them. Moreover, clarity is not Jung's special gift. As Ira Progoff remarks, Jung often gives up the reductive study of man in terms of efficient causes to adopt a teleological point of view. The emphasis is placed on the evolution of the purpose of life within the human being. Jung also stresses the social approach in psychology. "Whereas the psyche had previously been biological, it now becomes inherently social, and for Jung, it meant that the psyche now had to be understood in historical terms. Jung took this step and asked the question: What are the historical roots from which the contents of the psyche are derived?"[5]

Furthermore, different points of view on God usually pose serious semantic problems. The same words may entail different significations. This is the case here, and Jung himself is aware of the semantic implication as the source of bitter misunderstanding between his views and those of theology and metaphysics. "One of the main difficulties lies in the fact that both appear to speak the same language, but this language calls upon their mind two different fields of association. . . . Take, for instance, the word 'God.' The theologian will naturally assume that the metaphysical *Ens Absolutum* is meant. The empiricist,

4. *Coll. Works.*, XVI, 192 fn.
5. Ira Progoff, *Jung's Psychology and its Social Meaning* (New York, 1953), p. 267.

on the contrary does not dream of making such a far-reaching assumption. . . . He just as naturally means the word 'God' as a mere statement, or at most as an archetypal motif which prefigures such statement."[6] For the theologian trained in traditional ways and for the layman the semantic problem encountered in the reading of Jung is almost insurmountable.

Is Jung's method with regard to religion totally justified? Although Jung's initial attitude claims to be neutral, it is not; it is philosophical and as old as philosophy itself. The initial rejection of a transcendent God, of the possibility of metaphysics, and of a relativistic morality is common in the history of thought. Jung's initial attitude, although essentially Kantian, is at times more radical than that of Kant himself. Both Kant and Jung deny the possibility of the science of metaphysics. But the German philosopher compensates for this denial by means of the postulates of the practical reason. The existence of God and the spirituality of the soul are the starting points of Kant's ethics. Not for Jung, who on occasions seems to maintain a relativistic idea of morality without reference to anything absolute. God and man are intimately related; but not for him who, seeing religion only from the psychological point of view, fails to transcend the limits of human experience. "An absolute God," Jung says, "does not concern us in the least, whereas a 'psychological' God would be *real*."[7] There lies the incompleteness of Jung's conception. The science of psychology is incomplete without the science of metaphysics to which it corresponds to prove the connection between the psychology of religion and the object upon which religious activity falls, namely, God.

Sources and Interpretation of Sources

Christian revelation is founded on an unusual manifestation of a transcendent God who reveals himself to man by means of the prophets, apostles, and Christ himself. After the death of the apostles, private revelations are limited to the doctrine

6. *Coll. Works,* XI, 303.
7. *Ibid.,* VII, 233 fn.

already known or to the direction of human activity. Christian revelation presupposes a special intellectual illumination called "inspiration," which is a special intellectual light superior to the natural light of reason.[8] Jung's ideas on revelation are legitimate, according to his viewpoint: revelation is a manifestation of the collective unconscious which reveals itself in the experience of the numinous. The starting point of his psychology is therefore empirical, namely, the numinous experience of his patients. But to support his ideas on revelation and religious functions he uses sources which for centuries have been considered not necessarily as projections of the unconscious but rather as conscious manifestations of man—and even as objects existing independently of human consideration. Furthermore, these sources from myth to Sacred Scripture are of such a variety of origin and nature that the first and most urgent need is the empirical critical evaluation of them, as well as of their applicability to the psychological problems which religion poses. The selection of the material that Jung uses is not always based on the intrinsic values of these manifold sources, but some-

8. Thomas Acquinas, *Summa Theol.*, II–II, q. 174, a. 6: ". . . In the time of grace the entire faith of the Church is founded on the revelation vouchsafed to the apostles, concerning the faith in One God and three Persons, according to Matt. 16: 18, *On this rock,* i.e. of thy confession, *I will build My Church.*" *Ibid.,* ad 3: "At all times there have not been lacking persons having the spirit of prophecy, not indeed for the declaration of any new doctrine of faith, but for the direction of human acts. . . ." *Ibid.,* II–II, q. 171, a. 1 ad 4: "It is requisite to prophecy that the intention of the mind be raised to the perception of Divine things: wherefore it is written (Ezech. 2: 1): *Son of man, stand upon thy feet, and I will speak to thee.* This raising of the intention is brought about by the motion of the Holy Ghost, wherefore the text goes on to say: *And the Spirit entered into me . . . and He set me upon my feet.* After the mind's intention has been raised to heavenly things, it perceives the things of God; hence the text continues: *And I heard Him speaking to me.* Accordingly inspiration is requisite for prophecy, as regards the raising of the mind, according to Job 32: 8, *The inspiration of the Almighty giveth understanding:* while revelation is necessary, as regards the very perception of Divine things, whereby prophecy is completed; by its means the veil of darkness and ignorance is removed, according to Job 12: 22, *He discovered great things out of darkness.*" *Ibid.,* a. 2: "Since prophecy pertains to a knowledge that surpasses natural reason, it follows that prophecy requires an intellectual light surpassing the light of natural reason. . . ."

times on their usefulness for supporting his ideas on religion and man. Furthermore, as Eliade says, the significance of symbols regarding religion cannot be solved by depth psychology alone, "for the symbolisms which decipher the latter are for the most part made up of scattered fragments and of the manifestations of a psyche in crises, if not in a state of pathological regression. To grasp the authentic structures and functions of symbols, one must turn to the inexhaustible indices of the history of religions; and yet even here, one must know how to choose."[9] This makes the problem involved and difficult.

Moreover, Jung's interpretation of these sources, although psychological, is not without difficulties. For instance, he considers Yahweh as a symbol expressing the motion of the libido of the objective psyche, according to his psychological point of view. But the theologian cannot help having misgivings concerning the plausibility of his approach because: (1) Jung's conception of how some of the books of Sacred Scripture were written, e.g., St. John's Apocalypse, differs from the Christian interpretation. (2) Jung's interpretation of the contents of these books, although claiming to be psychological, is sometimes opposed to the interpretation of theologians. Consequently, he has been accused of holding heretical doctrines. Jung, sensitive to criticism, was infuriated by the imputation and reassured the reader by saying that he asserted nothing positive or negative about the existence and nature of a transcendent God. On the contrary, he adds, "Psychology thus does the opposite of which it is accused. . . . It opens people's eyes to the real meaning of dogmas, and far from destroying them, it throws open an empty house to new inhabitants."[10] His answer is partially true but not totally convincing, for although in theory his views and those of theologians belong to different realms, in practice it is not always easy to keep them independent, or to harmonize them. For instance, theologians consider God as a Trinity; Jung's psychological approach demands a quaternity.

9. Mircea Eliade, *Images and Symbols,* p. 37.
10. *Coll. Works,* XII, 15.

Jung's Positive Philosophical Attitude

Jung calls himself an empiricist, but he also says that it is impossible to write psychology without models, auxiliary concepts, and hypotheses. Hypotheses, concepts, and models are tentative principles set up by the scientist to explain facts and laws. With them scientists try to explain their respective fields; with them Jung tries to explain man. His hypotheses are dialectical principles established to make the complex facts of human behavior understandable. Jung holds for a structure of personality based on the theory of opposites; a dynamic of personality based on the concepts of psychic energy, the law of conservation of energy, and psychic entropy. He also professes a philosophy of individuation. Jung's initial attitude, as explained before, is not neutral but philosophical. His views on the unconscious of man, on the four functions and two attitudes, are philosophical. His ideas on duality and opposition, on morality and evil, on evolution, etc., are philosophical ideas that influence every one of Jung's voluminous writings.

And we do not blame him, because there is no possibility of being a psychologist without being a philosopher: "Insofar as it was purely a question of method," Baynes says, "Freud and Jung found themselves in harmony, but the study of psychological processes can never remain a mere question of method; sooner or later it must challenge the investigator to produce a philosophical standpoint. And there a basic psychological difference began to make itself felt . . . a psychology that excludes the most vital problems of life from its sphere of responsibility requires no further criticism. It is already moribund."[11] Psychology challenges the investigator and poses the perennial and most important problems of philosophy, like morality, religion, immortality, death, suffering, passions, knowledge, and love. There is something more. As Jung honestly professes, he writes with his heart as much as with his mind. Every single page of his works manifests not only facts but also the unequivocal imprint of the man, of Jung. His erudition is phenomenal,

11. H. G. Baynes, in *Coll. Works,* VI, iii–iv, and ix.

perhaps without a par in Western tradition. But this erudition sometimes betrays him because then, leaving aside any material which may possibly jeopardize him, he selects other material which enhances his views. The work of Jung is a mixture of facts, marvelous intuitions, philosophical concepts, amazing erudition, and the continual projection of his unusual and extraordinary personality.

Religious Functions

Is it possible to investigate the religious function of man? Yes, there exists a psychology of religion simply because the phenomenon of religion is a human manifestation which psychology cannot overlook. Jung studies the religious psychological manifestation characterized by the numinous. The amount of empirical material he has gathered as a psychotherapist is so important that it is simply impossible to evaluate; perhaps it is unique in modern research in this field. He describes the properties of the numinous; the contribution of the rational and irrational factors in religious experience; the relation between the numinous and the collective unconscious; the connection between dreams and religious factors; the meaning of myth and its religious implications; the manifestation of religion according to different cultures in the Western world, in primitive and Oriental peoples; the connection between types and their religious characterizations; the relation between ministers, priests, and the needs of the faithful; the meaning of the symbols appearing in contemplation, in addition to many other things.[12]

12. Jung blames theologians, philosophers, and especially scientists for ignoring the irrational element of religion: *Coll. Works,* XI, 291–292: ". . . in order to survive, Christianity had to defend itself not only against its enemies but also against the excessive pretensions of some of its adherents. . . . Increasingly it had to rationalize its doctrines in order to stem the food of irrationality. This led, over the centuries, to that strange marriage of the originally irrational Christian message with human reason, which is so characteristic of the Western mentality. But to the degree that reason gradually gained the upper hand, the intellect asserted itself and demanded autonomy. And just as the intellect subjugated the psyche, so also it sub-

Jung is indeed a pioneer in the field of religious phenomenology, but his research on the therapeutical value of religion is itself unique. Jung knows the weaknesses, passions, sufferings, and problems of modern man perhaps better than any psychologist of the present century, and as a psychiatrist he was especially interested in the connection between mental health and religion, as shall be explained later. Through the practical knowledge of thousands of patients he saw the absolute necessity of religion as a factor in the integration of man. He also investigated the relationship between neurosis and religion, the function of religion in the development of human personality, and the abnormal manifestations of religion.

Scientists should very carefully consider Jung's priceless contribution to the phenomenology of religion, his best empirical work in a field which until recent years has been almost untouched. Neither scientists nor those engaged in pastoral theology and religious psychology can afford to ignore the material and the observations gathered by him in sixty-five years of pioneer work.

Man's Ideas of God

The psychology of religion, Jung points out, is not a question of God at all, but of man's ideas of God. There are people who do have such ideas and who form such conceptions, and these things are the proper study of psychology.[13] However, we must be cautious in respect to this assertion. Man's ideas of God are one thing, and Jung's ideas of God are another. The interpretation he gives to the contents of man's ideas of God is sometimes

---

jugated Nature and begat on her an age of scientific technology that left less and less room for the natural and irrational man. Thus the foundations were laid for an inner opposition which today threatens the world with chaos. . . . By a strange *enantiodromia,* the Christian spirit of the West has become the defender of the irrational, since, in spite of having fathered rationalism and intellectualism, it has not succumbed to them so far as to give up its belief in the rights of man, and especially the freedom of the individual. But this freedom guarantees a recognition of the irrational principle, despite the lurking danger of chaotic individualism."
13. *Coll. Works,* XI, 163 fn.

strange to those who had such ideas. Jung, the philosopher-psychologist, interprets man's ideas of God within the framework of his own ideas of God. In this area of research his position, although very valuable, is open to doubt and requires further investigation. This occurs mainly in Jung's psychological interpretation of the content of Christian dogmas, namely, God, the Trinity, Christ, and the Holy Ghost.

Dogmas

The formulation of Christian dogmas does not entail the unveiling of the depths of our unconscious. They are expressions concerning an infinite and transcendent God, and not the archetype of our psyche.[14] But it is also true that our ideas of God usually bear anthropomorphic traits of both a rational and an irrational character. The common man, even the educated one, knows a little about a spiritual God, much about a picture of him framed somewhat by his mind but more so by his senses, as well as by the irrational needs of our appetite. Jung sees only the human projection which is not necessarily nor exclusively unconscious, and he investigates the psychological characteristic of its contents in the light of the religious literature over the centuries.

It is the relationship between dogmas and the needs of the human psyche discovered empirically which makes Jung's ideas of dogmas valuable. There is in man a religious instinct endowed with energy which finds its natural object in dogmas, especially Christian dogmas. In other words, aside from the truths about God that dogmas contain, dogmas fulfill a collective and individual psychological function related to the unconscious needs of our psyche. There is a true psychological affinity between the needs of the unconscious and the Gods formulated

14. Thomas Aquinas, *Summa Theol.,* II–II, q. 1, a. 1: "If we consider, in faith, the formal aspect of the object, it is nothing else than the First Truth. For the faith of which we are speaking, does not assent to anything, except because it is revealed by God. . . ." *Ibid.,* a. 6: "The object of faith is something unseen in connection with God. Consequently any matter that, for a special reason, is unseen, is a special article. . . ."

in dogmas. In Jung's own words: "The solution is normal and satisfying in that the dogmatically formulated truths of the Christian Church express, almost perfectly, the nature of psychic experience. They are the repositories of the secrets of the soul, and this matchless knowledge is set forth in grand symbolic images. The unconscious thus possesses a natural affinity with the spiritual values of the Church, particularly in their dogmatic form, which owes its special character to centuries of theological controversy—absurd as this seemed in the eyes of later generations—and to the efforts of many great men."[15]

Moreover, dogmas absorb the perilous energy of the unconscious; they are like dams or walls storing and keeping its energy under control. Without the protecting walls of dogmas the energy released by the unconscious erupts into consciousness overpowering the ego of man and thus disposing the individual for neurosis and even psychosis. The nations without the protecting shields of dogmas are easy prey to collective destructive ideas which in modern times have appeared exemplified as *ism,* communism, Hitlerism, fascism, etc. Repression of religion presupposes mass murder on an unparalleled scale.[16]

Dogmas are the objects of faith, but the pure and exclusive intellectual surrender to an object which transcends the possibility of our understanding—as are by definition all Christian dogmas—finds no room in Jung's approach unless it goes together with experience. St. Paul defines faith as "the substance of things to be hoped for, the evidence of things that appear not" (Heb. 11: 1). Faith inclines man to assent to truths which are not apparent to the mind: the Trinity is the object of Christian faith. Thus there is always an obscurity in the act of faith which needs the impulse of the will in order to give assent because its object lacks evidence. The reason for being an obscure habit is that it makes us to believe truths revealed by God Himself, which transcend all the natural light and exceed all human understanding. For this reason St. John of the Cross says: "Faith is a dark night for the soul, and it is in this way that it gives light; and the more it is darkened, the greater light

15. *Coll. Works,* XVI, 193.
16. *Ibid.,* VII, 104.

comes to it. For it is by blinding that it gives light."[17] For Jung, the object of faith lies not in the existence of an infinite God outside man, but rather in the contents of the collective unconscious as they reveal themselves in consciousness as the symbol of an incomprehensible content.

> Legitimate faith must always rest on experience. There is, however, another kind of faith which rests exclusively on the authority of tradition. This kind of faith could also be called "legitimate," since the power of tradition embodies an experience whose importance for the continuity of culture is beyond question. But with this kind of faith there is always the danger of mere habit supervening. . . . The much-vaunted "childlikeness" of faith only makes sense when the feeling behind the experience is still alive. . . . Since faith revolves round those central and perennially important "dominant ideas" which alone give life a meaning, the prime task of the psychotherapist must be to understand the symbols anew, and thus to understand the unconscious compensatory striving of his patient for an attitude that reflects the totality of the psyche.[18]

Thus Jung stresses experience, as against Christianity which stresses the intellectual surrender even against our own feelings, as happens in periods of aridity and especially in the mystic purification of faith—the dark night of the soul. But, although faith in itself depends essentially on the intellect and will—the two spiritual powers—it is also true that it is man who believes, the whole man, and feelings and human experiences undoubt-

---

17. St. John of the Cross, *The Complete Works of St. John of the Cross*, ed. Allison Peers (Westminster, Maryland, 1949), *Ascent of Mount Carmel*, Bk. II, ch. 3, n. 4. *Ibid.*, n. 1: "Faith . . . the reason for being an obscure habit is that it makes us to believe truths revealed by God Himself, which transcend all the natural light, and exceed all human understanding, beyond all proportion."

18. *Coll. Works*, V, 232–233. Cf. XII, 17: "The religious point of view, understandably enough, puts the accent on the imprinter, whereas scientific psychology emphasizes the *typos*, the imprint—the only thing it can understand. The religious point of view understands the imprint as the working of an imprinter; the scientific point of view understands it as the symbol of an unknown and incomprehensible content."

edly help the assent of the act of faith, especially in the first stages of Christian life. As Tolstoy put it, faith is the sense of life, that sense by virtue of which man does not destroy himself but continues to live on; it is the force whereby we live.

God

The God of Jung's religious experience is not transcendent, since "psychologically the God-concept includes every idea of the ultimate, of the first, or last, of the highest or lowest."[19] Hence God seems to be reduced to a human factor, very important indeed, but human; when Jung speaks on God, he usually means the God-image, not the Godhead.

The unconscious is the only available source of religious experience, the medium from which religious experience seems to flow, though "this is certainly not to say that what we call the unconscious is identical with God or is set up in his place."[20] Jung defends himself against the critics who accuse him of deifying man. "I have been accused of 'deifying the soul.' Not I but God himself has deified it! I did not attribute a religious function to the soul. I merely produce the facts which prove the soul is *naturaliter religiosa,* i.e., possesses a religious function."[21] We are in sympathy with him; he is not deifying the soul but perhaps humanizing God, because religious experience, religious factors, and Gods themselves do not transcend the human domain. They are considered as human psychological factors, leaving unsolved their ultimate relationship to a personal God. It is more difficult to follow Jung, however, when he invests God with the properties of omniscience, eternity, and other attributes of this kind, unless we strip these words of their traditional meaning. These attributes belong exclusively to a transcendent and infinite God.

The pscyhe is evolving. Consequently, God, the expression of its contents, is also evolving. Yahweh is an unconscious God of dual nature, evil and good, just and unjust, light and dark. The

19. *Coll. Works,* XI, 455 fn.
20. *Ibid.,* X, 293. Cf. *Jung and the Problem of Evil,* p. 15.
21. *Ibid.,* XII, 13.

starting point of the redemption is not sin but the confrontation of an unjust God, Yahweh, with a just man, Job. Man is
more just and conscious than God, therefore God must incarnate both in order to attain a greater consciousness and redress
the wrong done to Job.

Are these ideas then a symbolic expression of the process of
individuation? For Jung, yes; but is this conception the conception of the author of the Book of Job? Certainly not; the Book
of Job confronts a just man with the mysteries of the Providence of God, mysteries which are beyond human understanding. Jung prefers his own to the traditional interpretation.
But it is not sufficient to resort to psychology in order to justify
his views because that would imply that this book symbolizes
the motions of the collective unconscious of the writer, a principle impossible to prove empirically. Jung himself is aware of
the implications of his views. He says: "The idea of a God has
become burningly topical. It is no longer a problem of experts
in theological seminaries, but a universal religious nightmare
. . . to the solution of which even a layman in theology like
myself . . . must make a contribution."[22]

Interpreting the Book of Revelation, Jung asserts that the
psychotherapist has more to say on these matters (the visions of
St. John) than does the theologian. Consequently, the irritation
of theologians who accuse Jung of intruding into their field is
understandable, although their interpretation of Jung's ideas
is usually wrong. Reading Jung's *Answer to Job,* we do not
know much about Yahweh or Job but we certainly know a great
deal about Jung's ideas and personality. What Jung actually
attempts is to pose and solve the thorny problem of evil. He
chooses the Book of Job simply because it affords him the
opportunity to expand his ideas. His interpretation is unique,
astonishing to the neutral reader unaware of the problem of
the unconscious.

Jung's attitude is human, understandable; he sees and touches
evil; he witnesses wars, poverty, injustice, murder, tragedy, suffering, neurosis, and death. No wonder, if driven by his feel-

22. *Ibid.,* XI, 453.

ings, he rejects St. Augustine's formula of evil as *privatio boni*. His approach is not metaphysical and abstract, but psychological and concrete; he speaks from his heart, even from his passions. The Augustinian solution teaches him nothing.

Jung's belief in the existence of evil is natural, even logical. But, as will be explained later, less natural and logical is the solution he proposes through duality and opposition. Evil is a positive factor and as essential for man as is good; without evil there is no opposition or tension and consequently no psychic energy. Therefore we have to assimilate evil as we assimilate good. Here Jung lacks the power of abstraction so important in philosophical thought.

Trinity

The dogma of the Trinity, psychologically speaking, is a symbol representing the process of the collective unconscious towards consciousness. The projection of the Trinity presupposes a developed consciousness which is nonexistent in archaic man whose unconscious projections are myths depicting God as One. The Trinity is the outcome of the natural evolution stemming from myth in the same way as modern man is the natural evolution of archaic man.

But insofar as dogmas go, Christians look with indifference at the idea that the mystery of the Trinity symbolizes the process of assimilation of the unconscious by the ego. It is true that Jung is always coming up against the misunderstanding that "a psychological treatment reduces God to 'nothing but' psychology."[23] But is it possible to harmonize the two viewpoints, namely, the psychological and the theological? The theologian considers the Trinity as existent outside man and the universe and only known by external revelation, by the revelation of God Himself. Jung considers the Trinity, however, as the projection of a psychological unconscious process and known by internal revelation—as if a little Trinity were hidden in the inner recesses of our psyche. Jung's treatment is essen-

23. *Ibid.*, XI, 163 fn.

tially—especially concerning the Holy Ghost—an unconscious process, as against St. Augustine's psychological interpretation which finds in knowledge and love the analogy for the Trinitarian formula: "For, we are, and we know that we are, and we love to be and to know that we are. And in this trinity of being, knowledge, and love there is not a shadow of illusion to disturb us."[24] And even clearer in Aquinas: "In the knowledge by which our mind knows itself there is a representation of the uncreated Trinity according to analogy. It lies in this, that the mind, knowing itself in this way, begets a word expressing itself, and love proceeds from both of these, just as the Father, uttering Himself, has begotten the Word from eternity, and the Holy Spirit proceeds from both."[25] Are both points of veiw compatible? Perhaps, if we remember that Jung sees in the Trinity not a dogmatic formula expressing the nature of God, but a psychological symbol which expresses the development of the Christian psyche. The words used are the same but their signification calls for two different kinds of concepts. The semantic problem, however, will produce much misunderstanding; moreover, Jung himself seems on occasion to oppose his views to traditional Christian views, as was noted before.

But the theologian rejects as false the idea of a psychological quaternity which Jung claims to be the voice of nature. The Trinity should be a quaternity, he says, because Satan (the dark part of God) or Mary (the feminine partner) is missing. The proof that Jung provides, in spite of the amount of material ranging from literature to alchemy and gnosticism, bears no conviction. Why? First, because Jung rejects as irrelevant a much more important wealth of material supporting the Trinity, namely, all the writings of the Fathers and almost twenty centuries of Christian theology. Jung, on the other hand, adduces gnosticism and alchemy plus his own personal interpretation to prove his assertion. "This was the time when the Greeks started criticizing the world," Jung says, "the time of 'gnosis' in the widest sense, which ultimately gave birth to Chris-

24. St. Augustine, *The City of God,* Bk. 11. ch. 26. Cf. *De Trin.* XI, 2: XI, 7.
25. Thomas Aquinas, *De Verit.,* q. 10, a. 7.

tianity."[26] But modern scholars in the field deny the importance and influence of gnosticism on Christianity: "The trend of Biblical and typological studies during the last quarter of a century shows a reaction against the tendency to explain Christianity by means of the mysteries and of syncretic Gnosticism, and also a reaction against the 'confusionism' of certain comparativist schools. Christian liturgy and symbolism are connected directly with Judaism. Christianity is a historical religion, deeply rooted in another historical religion, that of the Jews. Consequently, in order to explain or better to understand certain sacraments or symbols, one has to look for their 'prefiguratives' in the Old Testament."[27] Christianity is not rooted in gnosticism but mainly in Judaism.

Furthermore, the different methodologies of theology and psychology explain the deep cleavage between the Christian dogmatic truth on the Trinity and Jung's psychological approach to the mystery as a quaternity. "Trinity and quaternity symbols," Jung says, "occur fairly frequently in dreams, and from this I have learnt that the idea of the Trinity is based on something that can be experienced and must, therefore, have a meaning. This insight was not won by a study of the traditional sources. If I have succeeded in forming an intelligible conception of the Trinity that is in a way based on empirical reality, I have been helped by dreams, folklore, and the myths in which these number of motifs occur."[28] Dreams and symbols express psychic needs, not necessarily the nature of God. Dreams, folklore, and myth are not the source of doctrine of the Trinity, but the words of Christ in the gospel: "Go, therefore, and

26. *Coll. Works*, XI, 134. *Memories, Dreams, Reflections*, pp. 200–201: "The psychologist must depend therefore in the highest degree upon historical and literary parallels if he wishes to exclude at least the crudest errors in judgment. Between 1918 and 1926 I had seriously studied the Gnostic writers, for they too had been confronted with the primal world of the unconscious and had dealt with its contents, with images that were obviously contaminated with the world of instinct."
27. Mircea Eliade, *Images and Symbols*, p. 157. E. J. Homyard and H. E. Stapleton, the former a specialist in alchemy, the latter in magic circles, deny the importance of the number four. See H. L. Philp, *op. cit.*, pp. 74–75.
28. *Coll. Works*, XI, 189.

make disciples of all nations, baptizing them in the name of the Father, and of the Son, and of the Holy Spirit" (Matt. 28:19).

Even more, the operations of the unconscious do not prove the inadequacy of the Trinity. The visions of the mystics were always Trinitarian, and the presence of the Trinity in the soul of Christians not only is a dogmatic truth but also a mystery experienced by a multitude of souls. "By some mysterious manifestation of the truth," Teresa of Avila says, "the three Persons of the most Blessed Trinity reveal themselves, preceded by an illumination which shines on the spirit like a most dazzling cloud of light. The three Persons are distinct from one another; a sublime knowledge is infused into the soul, imbuing it with a certainty of the truth that the Three are of one substance, power, and knowledge and are one God. Thus that which we hold as a doctrine of faith, the soul now, so to speak, understands by sight."[29]

Christ

The historical Christ is irrelevant for Jung. But Christ as a symbol of the archetype of the self is the living myth of our culture. His properties and miraculous life express faithfully the needs and motions of the collective psyche. Consequently, the life of Christ is collective, embodying myth as constituting the quintessence of the Gospels.

What can be said about this conception of Christ? Reading *Psychology and Religion,* and especially *Aion,* one cannot help admiring Jung's psychological penetration and tremendous erudition. But his style is so obscure and the materials he chooses so diverse that the reader ends up quite perplexed. A psychological conclusion is however very important; namely, the life of Christ is in perfect harmony with the needs of the uncon

29. St. Teresa of Avila, *The Interior Castle,* Seventh Mansion, ch. 1, n. 9; *The Relations,* Rel. IX, 12: "I understood, and, as it were, saw,—I cannot tell how, unless it was by an intellectual vision which passed rapidly away, —how the Three Persons of the most Holy Trinity, whom I have always imprinted in my soul, are One. This was revealed in a representation so strange, and in a light so clear, that the impression made upon me was very different from that which I have by faith. . . ."

scious: "Had there not been an affinity—magnet!—between the
figure of the Redeemer and certain contents of the unconscious, the human mind would never have been able to perceive
the light shining in Christ and seize upon it so passionately. The
connecting link here is the archetype of the God-man, which on
the one hand became historical reality in Christ, and on the
other, being eternally present, reigns over the soul in the form
of a supraordinate totality, the self."[30] In *Aion,* the self is not
a symbol of Christ, but Christ a symbol of the self, which is
equivalent to saying that in our collective unconscious there
exists an archetype of the Redeemer which is perfectly realized
by Christ. "Christianity as a whole," Jung says, "is less concerned with the historical man Jesus . . . than with the mythological Anthropos or God-Son figure. . . . Moreover it is not
the Jewish rabbi and reformer Jesus, but the archetypal Christ,
who touches upon the archetype of the Redeemer in everybody
and carries conviction."[31] These words are similar to Caruso's,
who says: "Neurosis searches for a redeemer. The 'Christ archetype' is the central factor in all psychotherapy."[32] Depth psychology, therefore, has found a psychological archetype in perfect affinity with the message of Christ. This conclusion is of
capital importance for the psychology of religion.

But on the other hand, to identify, for instance, the mythical
death of the hero with Christ's death is, in Jungian terms,
equivalent to saying that Christ's death symbolizes the regres-

---

30. *Coll. Works,* IX,ii, 181–182.
31. C. G. Jung, in H. L. Philp, *Jung and the Problem of Evil,* pp. 253–254.
32. Igor Caruso, *Existential Psychology,* p. 84. The fact that Jung's research
on religion starts not with faith but psychology makes this conclusion
especially valuable. He says: "As Christ never meant more to me than I
could understand of Him, and inasmuch as this understanding coincides
with my empirical knowledge of the self, I have to admit that I mean the
self dealing with the idea of Christ. As a matter of fact I have no other
access to Christ but the self" (*Jung and the Problem of Evil,* p. 247). Jung
writes again: "This amounts to saying that in unconscious humanity there
is a latent seed that corresponds to the prototype Jesus . . . accord with
psychology" (*Coll. Works,* IX,ii, 67). "The fish symbol is thus the bridge
between the historical Christ and the psychic nature of man, where the
archetype of the Redeemer dwells. In this way Christ became an inner
experience, the 'Christ within' " (*Coll. Works,* IX,ii, 182–183).

sion of the libido into the unconscious. His resurrection, likewise, is a symbol of the coming into consciousness of the contents of the collective unconscious, which, if relevant to psychology, is of little bearing to the believer, and needs to be complemented with conscious factors. Not only is the figure of
Christ an embodiment of the collective needs of the unconscious, it is also the reflective and conscious consideration of the
life of Christ which attracts Christians to the Redeemer—his
doctrines, his wisdom, his evangelic life, his miracles, his compassion and love, his mercy, his poverty, his self-denial, and the
panorama of the beatitudes. The message of Christ appeals
indeed to the unconscious, but primarily to the ego as a symbol
of everything good and worthy in life.

Christians are surprised by Jung's ideas on the incarnation.
The purpose of the coming of Christ is not the redemption of
mankind from sin. Rather, he comes to beg the help of man in
order to acquire a greater consciousness and to redress the injustice done to Job by an unconscious God. Where is the root of
the psychological interpretation to be found here? In individuation, because the unconscious (which represents the divinity of Christ) and the ego (which represents his humanity) have
to endure struggles and sufferings in order to acquire wholeness.
The sufferings of Christ symbolize these sufferings; his humanity (the ego) is suffering the tension and the opposition of his
divinity (the unconscious).

But Jung's own words seem sometimes to be a direct denial
of the traditional interpretation, as, for instance, in this passage taken from *Psychology and Alchemy*: "Whereas Catholicism
emphasizes the effectual presence of Christ, alchemy is interested in the fate and manifest redemption of substances, for
in them the divine soul lies captive and awaits the redemption
that is granted to it at the moment of release. The captive soul
then appears in the form of the 'Son of God.' For the alche-
mist, the one primarily in need of redemption, is not man, but
the deity who is sleeping in matter. . . . His attention is not
directed to his own salvation through God's grace, but to the
liberation of God from the darkness of matter."[33]

33. *Coll. Works,* XII, 299.

Moreover, since in the practical realm the process of individuation entails the necessity of withdrawing the projection
from the figure of the Redeemer, Jungians and Christians in
the end follow different roads leading them to their goals. For
Christians, Christ is the way, the truth, and life; hence his imitation is their goal. Jungians treat dogmas as projections of the
contents of the objective psyche; their goals cannot be the imitation of Christ. "The demand made by the *imitatio Christi*—
that we should follow the ideal and seek to become like it—
ought logically to have the result of developing and exalting
the inner man. In actual fact, however, the ideal has been
turned by superficial and formalistically-minded believers into
the external object of worship, and it is precisely this venera-
tion for the object that prevents it from reaching down into
the depths of the soul and transforming it into a wholeness in
keeping with the ideal . . . of realizing the ideal on one's own
account."[34] This is, naturally, an easy oversimplification, for
Christian life presupposes a profound internal transformation
without which there is no holiness nor wholeness. The imitation
of Christ is not possible without a transformation equivalent
to the death of the carnal man and the birth of a spiritual one,
clearly explained by St. Paul's words: "For we were buried with
him by means of Baptism into death, in order that, just as
Christ has arisen from the dead through the glory of the Father,
so we also may walk in newness of life. . . . For we know that
our self has been crucified with him, in order that the body of
sin may be destroyed, that we may no longer be slaves to sin"
(Rom. 6: 4–8). A worship of the historical Christ should not
prevent the reaching of Christ in the depth of our soul where
the Trinity dwells.[35]

---

34. *Ibid.,* XII, 7; XIII, 53. To some Jungians the process of individuation
is like a substitution for religion. See, Cary F. Baynes, in C. G. Jung, *Modern Man in Search of a Soul* (New York, 1933), p. viii.
35. The absolute dependence of Christians upon Christ is summarized in
the cannon of the Mass in these words. "Through Him, and with Him, and
in Him, is to thee, God the Father almighty, in union of the Holy Ghost,
all honor and glory."

The Holy Ghost

Taking into account Jung's ideas on God, man, evil, opposition, and duality, his approach to the doctrine of the Holy Ghost not only is logical but pregnant with meaning. He finds in it the reconciliation of opposites in the deity, the religious significance of the self in Christian man, and, finally, the explanation of how the unconscious God is continuously acquiring a greater consciousness with the help of man.

Naturally, in theology the breathing of the Holy Ghost by the Father and the Son is not interpreted as a projection and hypostatization of the process of a human reflection that irrationally creates the united Third. The breathing of the Holy Ghost or the spiration is simply a word to designate a procession, that is to say, an immanent divine action. "It can be said that the Father spirates the Holy Ghost through the Son, or that the Holy Ghost proceeds from the Father through the Son, which has the same meaning. . . . The same spiritive power belongs to the Father and to the Son; and therefore the Holy Ghost proceeds actually from both."[36]

Although Jung does not explicitly deny this procession, he nevertheless seems to ascribe to projection and to the activity of the archetype of the spirit manifestations that Christians usually ascribe to the activity of the Holy Ghost.[37] Furthermore, the Holy Ghost is not something begotten, but spirit precisely because it is a divine Person which proceeds not from the immanent action of the intellect, as the Son does, but from the immanent action of the will. The well-known psychological Augustinian analogy recourses to the appetite, not as Jung does

36. Thomas Aquinas, *Summa Theol.*, I, q. 37, a. 3 and ad 2.
37. For example, Jung writes about Joachin of Flora, a Benedictine monk who lived in the eleventh century: "Consciously, Joachin thought he was beginning the status of the Holy Ghost into reality. But unconsciously—and this is psychologically what probably happened . . . Joachin was seized by the archetype of the spirit, which is characterized by numinous experience. He understood the spirit in the dogmatic sense of the Third Person of the Godhead, and not in the sense of the empirical archetype" (*Coll. Works*, IX,ii, 86).

to the revelation of the archetype of the self, although the activity of the latter may perhaps contain a remote similarity to the activity of the former. "The procession of the Word (the Son)," Aquinas says, following Augustine, "is by way of an intelligible operation. The operation of the will within ourselves involves another procession, that of love, whereby the object loved is in the lover, as by the conception of the word, the object spoken of our understanding is in the intellect. Hence, besides the procession of the Word in God, there exists in Him other procession called the procession of love."[38] This action of the will is not called generation because "the will is made actual not by any similitude of the object willed within it, but by its having a certain inclination to the thing willed. Thus the procession of the intellect is by way of similitude, and is called generation, because every generator begets its own like; whereas the procession of the will is not by way of similitude, but is rather by way of impulse and movement towards an object so what proceeds in God by way of love, does not proceed as begotten, or as son, but proceeds rather as spirit; which name expresses a certain vital movement or impulse accordingly as anyone is described as moved by or impelled by love to perform an action."[39]

Jung's activity of the archetype of the spirit may have a certain similarity to the procession corresponding to love for both are unconscious, but the similarity is very obscure. And since the actions of the will which correspond to the procession of love are always much less known than the actions of the intellect, the Holy Spirit has no proper name: "We can name only from creatures. As in creatures generation is the only principle of communication of nature, procession in God has no proper or special name, except that of generation. Hence, the procession which is not generation has remained without a special name; but it can be called 'spiration' as it is the procession of the Spirit."[40]

38. Thomas Aquinas, *Summa Theol.*, I, q. 27, a. 3.
39. *Ibid.*, I, q. 27, a. 4.
40. *Ibid.*, I, q. 27, a. 4 ad 3. Cf. Also, *Ibid.*, I, q. 28, a. 4: "The procession of the Word is called generation in the proper sense of the term, whereby it is applied to living things. Now the relation of the principle of generation in perfect living beings is called paternity; and the relation of the

Although the three Persons of the Trinity are spiritual and hence incapable of being depicted or imagined, it is also true that by analogy with human images our fantasy finds it easier to imagine and symbolize the Persons of Father and Son than the Person of the Holy Ghost in whom the convenient analogy is difficult to find. Even Augustine himself humbly acknowledges the difficulties to figure out the nature of the procession of the Holy Ghost. "This I know," he says, "that I know not how to distinguish between this generation and this procession; I am not able, I am inadequate to do so."[41] Man depends on his cognitive powers so much that he finds no concepts and images to describe the obscure activity of his will, only indirectly known by consciousness. That is why the Holy Ghost has no proper name.

A further continuation of the incarnation of God is possible by the sending of the Paraclete, Jung asserts: God, in the shape of the Holy Ghost, puts up a tent in man, for he obviously wishes to realize himself continuously through the unconscious reflection of ordinary man. At the same time, the indwelling of the Holy Ghost makes the believer a child of God, a new rock, and the words of John "you are gods" appear in a new light, which entails danger for the Church which discourages the indwelling as much as possible.

Naturally, a new incarnation of God—as against Jung's contention that the Church is cautious in this regard and does not rule out its possibility—is absolutely impossible, because although the presence of the Trinity in the soul of Christians

---

one proceeding from the principle is called filiation. But the procession of Love has no proper name of its own; and neither have the ensuing relations a proper name of their own. The relation of the principle of this procession is called spiration. . . ."

41. St. Augustine, *II Against Max.*, ch. 14, n. 11, M.L. 42, 770. Augustine, as Jung, is puzzled by the procession of the Holy Ghost: "Because, then, if he is born, not only of the Son, but of both, he is indeed born; he is truly called the son of both. But since he is in no sense the son of them both, it is needless to say that he is born of them. Because he is placed between being born and proceeding, who can explain in words this most excellent nature? Not everything that proceeds is born, although everything that is born indeed proceeds, just as not every two-legged animal is a man, though every man is a two-legged animal. This I know: that I know not how to distinguish between this generation and this procession: I am not able, I am inadequate to do so."

is real, the presence does not make man divine. Christians are adoptive children of God not natural sons of God, which is exclusive to Christ. Pius XII, in his encyclical *Mystici Corporis,* advises to "reject every kind of mystic union by which the faithful of Christ should in any way pass the sphere of creatures and wrongly enter the divine."[42] The Church, however, does not discourage the indwelling; on the contrary, she emphasizes its importance and encourages Christians to gaze inward where the Trinity dwells. Leo XIII says in his encyclical *Divinum Illud*: "Moreover God by grace resides in the just soul as in a temple, in a most intimate and peculiar manner. From this proceeds that union of affection by which the soul adheres most closely to God, more so than the friend is united to this most loving and beloved friend, and enjoys God in all fullness and sweetness. Now this wonderful union, which is properly called 'indwelling,' although it is certainly produced by the presence of the whole Blessed Trinity, nevertheless is attributed in a peculiar manner to the Holy Ghost. . . . The fullness of divine gifts is in many ways a consequence of the indwelling of the Holy Ghost in the souls of the just."[43]

Furthermore, the mystery of the indwelling is the root of infused contemplation, and it has been experienced continuously by innumerable number of souls. St. Teresa, in her *Way of Perfection*, remarks that God is not only in heaven but in the inmost center of the soul, and we must know how to recollect ourselves to seek and find Him there. She also says in her *Relations*: "I am in peace within; and my liking and disliking have so little power to take from me the presence of the Three Persons, of which, while it continues, it is impossible to doubt, that I seem clearly to know by experience what is recorded by St. John, that God will make His dwelling in the soul."[44] With-

42. Pius XII, *The Mystical Body of Christ,* n. 78.
43. Leo XIII, *The Holy Spirit.*
44. St. Teresa of Avila, *The Relations,* XI, 8. Sister Elizabeth of the Trinity: "My only practice is to enter 'within,' and to lose myself in Those Who are there." *The Spiritual Doctrine of Sister Elizabeth of the Trinity,* by M. M. Philipon, O.P. (Westminster, 1947), p. 46. The indwelling of the Trinity is the root of contemplation. See Santiago Ramirez, O.P., *De Hominis Beatitudine* (Madrid, 1947), III, pp. 335–336. "The contemplative souls have intuition of God without any discourse through certain direct experience which is the result of the indwelling of God in the soul."

out the Trinity the soul is deserted. It is inhabited when by baptism the infant has become, in St. Paul's words, "the temple of the Holy Ghost" (1 Cor. 6: 19). "Do you know," the apostle says again, "that you are the temple of God and that the Spirit of God dwells in you? If anyone destroys the temple of God, him will God destroy: for holy is the temple of God, this temple you are" (1 Cor. 3: 16–17). The indwelling of the Trinity is indeed one of the prominent mysteries of Christian spirituality. But the Holy Ghost is neither the reconciliation of opposites in the deity nor the cause of a continuous incarnation of God in empirical man.

Finally, let us say that though Christ is spotless and without sin, He assumed a human body as our own, descending from Adam. "God was able to assume human nature elsewhere than from the stock of Adam, who by his sin had fettered the whole human race," Augustine says, "yet God judged it better to assume human nature from the vanquished race, and thus to vanquish the enemy of the human race."[45] Christ assumed a body subject to human infirmities, as death, hunger, thirst, suffering, and the like, because a human nature without these defects would not have made him a true man. However, there was no sin in Christ, for the truth of his human nature is not proved by sin, since sin does not belong to human nature as such (the cause of which is God) but rather sin is against its nature, as John Damascene says.[46] Because Christ is spotless he set up the long-awaited bridge between heaven and earth and redemption was possible; a new incarnation of the Holy Ghost in ordinary man makes no sense at all.

The Self and Religion

The starting point for the existence of the self is psychological observation. Jung discovered in his patients, empirically, the existence of a totality supraordinate to consciousness. This totality which ontologically considered is indescribable reveals itself to consciousness as something numinous in dreams, visions,

45. St. Augustine, *De Trinit.*, xiii, 18.
46. St. John Damscene, *De Fide Orthod.*, iii, 20; Thomas Aquinas, *Summa Theol.*, III, qq. 14–15.

active imagination, and spontaneous drawings. There exists in man an archetype of wholeness which manifests itself spontaneously in symbols, like trinities, quaternities, circles, mandalas, etc. This archetype relates other archetypes to its center, and the totality contains the union of opposites because if the opposites were not contained in the symbol it would not be a symbol of totality.

But how does Jung establish the connection between the self and man's religious factors? Through the identity of symbols; the self produces a symbolism that is identical to the symbolism produced by human religious activity. For example, the image of God in man reveals itself to consciousness in the form of trinities, quaternities, mandalas, union of opposites, and other symbols that are also symbols of the self. In physics, Jung says, we can do without a God-image, but not in psychology; psychology does have to reckon with the existence of a God-image. Consequently, it seems probable that the archetype of wholeness occupies a central position which approximates it to the God-image, for it produces a symbolism which has always characterized and expressed the deity.[47] The symbols of the self that, on one side, appear as a psychological experience signifying psychic wholeness, express, on the other, the idea of God. It should be pointed out, however, that although the original experimental source of the self rests on the observation of his patients, Jung seeks the full explanation of its symbolism by recourse to history by comparing the new symbols to similar symbols that have continuously appeared over the centuries.

If the fantasies are expressed in drawings, Jung says, symbols appear which are chiefly of the so-called mandala type. This is in agreement with Caruso, who asserts that analytic drawing will indeed produce the mandalas almost with absolute certainty. Jung's historical mandalas found in the East, as well as the Christian mandalas, are instruments of contemplation, and they have usually a deity in the center—as, for instance, the rose stained-glass of Christian medieval cathedrals, with the meaning of totality. For Eliade, "the mandalas can be used in

47. *Coll. Works*, XIII, 22.

support, either at the same time or successively, of a concrete ritual or an act of spiritual concentration or, again, of a technique of mystical physiology. This multivalence . . . is a characteristic of the symbolism of the Center on general. This is easily understandable, since every human being tends, even unconsciously, towards the Center, and towards his own center, where he can find integral reality—sacredness. . . ."[48] Therefore Eliade interprets mandalas in the light of myth in connection with the myth of the Center. In man, mandalas are expressions of the deep conscious or unconscious desire to attain sacrality, to find himself at the very heart of the real, in the center, where gods dwell.

But to Jung's astonishment, modern mandalas lack the deity in the center. He remarks: "Prejudiced by historical analogies, we could expect a deity to occupy the center of mandalas. The center is however empty. The seat of deity is unoccupied . . . we find no deity in the mandala, but on the contrary a mechanism (a peculiar mental condition). . . . The center, as a rule, is emphasized. But what we find there is a symbol with a very different meaning. It is a star, a sun, a flower . . . but never a God. There is no deity in the mandala, nor is there any submission or reconciliation to a deity. The place of the deity seems to be taken by the totality of man."[49]

---

48. Mircea Eliade, *Images and Symbols*, p. 54. Cf. *Ibid.*, pp. 51–52: "We have seen that it was not only temples that were thought to be situated at the 'Centre of the World,' but that every holy place, every place that bore witness to an incursion of the sacred into profane space, was also regarded as a 'centre.' These sacred spaces could also be constructed; but their construction was, in its way, a cosmogony—a creation of the world—which is only natural since, as we have seen, the world was created in the beginning from an embryo, from a 'centre.' . . . The mandala thus represents an *imago mundi* and at the same time a symbolic pantheon." In *Patterns in Comparative Religion* (New York, 1958), Eliade says: "The assimilation of the temple with the mandala is obvious in the case of Borobudur and the Indo-Tibetan temples built under the influence of Tantric doctrine. All these sacred constructions represent the whole universe in symbol: their various floors are identified with the heavens or levels of the cosmos. In one sense, every one of them reproduces the cosmic mountain, is, in other words, held to be built at the centre of the world" (p. 373).
49. *Coll. Works*, XI, 80–82.

How is it possible to explain these facts? According to Jung, the experience formulated in modern mandalas is typical of people who cannot project the divine image any longer and are in danger of inflation and dissociation of personality. The mandala denotes and assists exclusive concentration on the center, the self, a much needed self-control for the purpose of avoiding inflation and dissociation. This is similar to what in Greek is called *temenos,* which signifies the precincts of a temple or sacred place. The circle in this case protects an inner content that should not get mixed up with things outside. The inhabitant of the *temenos* was a god, but the prisoner in the mandala does not seem to be a god, since the symbols used—star, crosses, globes—do not signify a god but an important part of human personality. Man himself, or his innermost soul, is the prisoner of the mandalas. And since modern mandalas are close parallels to the ancient magical circles which usually have a deity in the center, it is clear that in modern mandalas man, the self, is not a substitute but a symbol for the deity.

Thus when the idea of God is no longer projected as an autonomous entity, the unconscious produces the idea of a deified or divine man who is imprisoned, protected, usually depersonalized and represented by an abstract symbol. The symbols contain allusions to medieval conceptions, especially alchemy, but in the last analysis the historical roots of these symbols extend beyond the Middle Ages and are to be found in Gnosticism.[50] Therefore, "In the light of these historical parallels," Jung says, "the mandala symbolizes either the divine being hitherto hidden and dormant on the body and now extracted and revivified, or else the vessel or the room in which the transformation of man into a divine being takes place."[51] This conclusion reminds us of Jung's theory of the Holy Ghost, the continuous incarnation of God, and the indwelling of the Paraclete in man.

But it seems to us that—using his own words, "prejudice by historical mandalas"—Jung forces himself to find in Gnosticism

50. *Ibid.,* XI, 95–104.
51. *Ibid.,* XI, 104.

and Alchemy the explanation for the lack of the divine image in the center of mandalas. However, the historical mandalas of Christianity (like, for instance, the rose stained-glass of medieval cathedrals with Christ in the center) as well as the historical parallel explained by Eliade are conscious symbols of contemplation, not unconscious. They are genuine expressions of a religious attitude, but conscious because the symbols are known to their authors and to their worshippers. They are not identical to the spontaneous and unconscious content of modern mandalas that reveal and express an unconscious attitude unknown even to the patients themselves. Therefore the interpretations of modern mandalas seems more likely to follow rather pure natural lines: they simply express the improvement of the mental conditions of patients, as an indication that their conditions are now better. "Perhaps Jung," Caruso says, "has unintentionally exaggerated its significance, inasmuch as his writings give the impression that the production of the mandalas is the culmination of the analytic process by the discovery and release of the 'self.' But it seems more likely that the production of the mandala is no more than a sign of progress; it shows the patient's ability to grope his way towards his own Self. The mandala may be taken as sign that the analysand might now be ready to correct his own problems, do without the 'scapegoat,' withdraw his projection and admit that the most important problem is that set by the self in need of salvation. . . . The mandala, then, stands for a need for salvation and not, as one might think, for the completed integration."[52]

In other words, the modern mandalas appear to be no more than symbolic expressions of the patient's improvement. The dissociation characteristic of neurosis is disappearing, and the patient is on the road towards unity and wholeness—a partial unity and wholeness, not a total one. The total unity including God has not been achieved yet; if there are spontaneous mandalas symbolizing the total unity, they will probably be more like the religious historical mandalas described by Jung himself and Eliade, with a deity in the center. The mandalas drawn

52. Igor Caruso, *op. cit.*, pp. 199–200.

by neurotics are just the beginning of a much needed unity, which, naturally, will foster a further unity; they are the first step of a long process. Full individuation, Jung always insists, is possible only after a long and painful process, and it is achieved by only a few.

Furthermore, much new research is required to determine the exact meaning of some of the symbols of the mandala. Trinities and quaternities, Jung says, occur fairly frequently in dreams; but he considers trinities as a vehicle of the synthesis in which the individual process culminates in the putting together of the four. But Jung has been influenced by Buddhism and Gnosticism, and psychological experience alone can verify the plausibility of his views. "The quadruple mandala," Caruso writes, "includes the 'shadow.' As yet a state of tension, a 'crucifixion' obtains. We do not really know whether the rarer combination of the mandala with a triangle stands for successful integration, and whether it should not, accordingly, be regarded as an advance over the quadruple mandala. Jung holds the opposite opinion. . . . He maintains that the triangle could stand for the repression of the shadow . . . yet much difficult research remains to be done. We know of cases where the triangular mandala in fact represented the peak of the process of integration, but whether this is general rule cannot as yet be said with certainty."[53] Symbols, besides, are polyvalent; the exact meaning of a symbol is hard to know; its message is hidden, difficult to decipher and see, dealing with God and the unconscious even much more.

Coincidence and Opposites

The archetype of the self unites all the opposites in a transcendent synthesis. Hence its totality is perfectly symbolized by

53. *Ibid.,* p. 200. Jung says: "When I began to understand alchemy I realized that it represented the historical link with Gnosticism. . . . Grounded in the natural philosophy of the Middle Ages, alchemy formed the bridge on the one hand into the past, to Gnosticism, and on the other into the future, to modern psychology of the unconscious" (*Memories, Dreams, Reflections,* p. 201). This continuity is hardly substantiated by facts. The historical connection between gnosticism and alchemy would be difficult to prove. But in Jung both gnosticism and alchemy play an important role.

the union of opposites, which is common in myth, and appears often as an expression of the divinity. "These myths, rites, and theories involving the *coincidentia oppositorum* teach men that the best way of apprehending God or the ultimate reality is to cease, if only for a few seconds, considering and imagining divinity in terms of immediate experience; such an experience could only perceive fragments and tensions."[54] Hence, this formula reminds man that the sacred, the divine, defies all possibilities of rational comprehension and transcends the limitation of the fragmentary human existence. For Nicholas of Cusa, for example, the coincidence of opposites was the best definition of God.

But more significant than the formula as expression of the divinity is the psychological need it reveals; namely, man's deep dissatisfaction with the human condition. "Man feels himself torn and separated. . . . Ultimately, it is the wish to recover this lost unity that has caused man to think of the opposites as complementary aspects of a single reality. It is the result of such existential experiences, caused by the need to transcend the opposites, that the first theological and philosophical speculations were elaborated . . . the mystery of totality forms an integral part of the human drama."[55] Hence, the importance of the symbol does not rest on the explanation it gives to the divinity, but rather on the psychological craving it entails; namely, the human dissatisfaction with its fragmentary existence and his yearning for a perfect state where all the opposites are transcended in a mode of perfect being.

Moreover, not all the expressions of the coincidence of opposites are equivalent. "By transcending the opposites," Eliade says, "one does not always attain the same mode of being. There is every possibe difference, for instance, between spiritual androgynization and the 'confusion of the sexes' attained by orgy. . . . The element common to all the rites, myths, and symbols lies in this, that all seek to come out of a particular situation in order to abolish a given system of conditions and reach a mode of 'total' being."[56] This is of great importance; natu-

54. Mircea Eliade, *The Two and the One*, p. 82.
55. *Ibid.*, pp. 122–123.
56. *Ibid.*, p. 123 fn.

rally, the gods have to transcend time and space, good and evil, death and life, and all pairs of opposites. And man attaining sacredness seeks to share this state by transcending himself all the antinomies and riddles of life. But as noted above, "the union of opposites" formula is endowed with a great variety of meanings and degrees of unity, ranging from the material to the spiritual from the purely "material orgy" which abolishes the sexes, to a theological formula for the divinity. To which of them does the symbol appearing in myth, dreams, and drawing correspond? It will probably depend on the state of psychological integration of those in whom these symbols appear, as was explained before regarding mandalas. The formula corresponding to the archetype of the self, however, requires the integration of man and God, for as Jung says, there is no totality without God. In these latter cases is probably true Jung's contention that it is impossible to distinguish empirically the self from the image of God in man. Here faith and philosophy alone can decide, he adds. Philosophy and theology, in consequence, must clarify and complement the empiricist's work.

The Image of God in Man

The conception we have of the God-image in man will depend, naturally, on our conceptions of the nature of God and man. Jung approaches this problem from the empirical viewpoint. There exists in man an image of God that has revealed its presence continuously over the centuries in the form of symbols and concepts. Jung uses the word *image* simply in the sense of a representation. A psychic entity can be a conscious content only if it has the quality of an image; all conscious contents are called images or are related to images. Hence God-images are simply the conceptions we have of the divinity. "God is always man-made," Jung says, "and the definition he gives is therefore finite and imperfect. The definition is an image, but this image does not raise the unknown fact it designates into the realm of intelligibility. The master we choose is not identical with the image we project of him in time and space."[57] Accordingly, an image of God is a representation of God in time and space; hence when Jung is speaking of God he usually means a psychological image, not God as such.

For Christians, the image of God is a philosophical-theological concept partly rooted in revelation. "Man's excellence," Augustine says, "consists in the fact that God made him to His image by giving him an intellectual soul, which raises him above the beast of the field."[58] And Aquinas, going beyond this general idea, writes: "Since man is said to be to the image of God by reason of his intellectual nature, he is the most perfectly like God according to that in which he can best imitate God in his intellectual nature. Now the intellectual nature imitates God chiefly in this, that God understands and loves Himself."[59] Hence the image of God in man is found primarily in the mind when the mind understands and loves the Deity. Consequently, the image of God exists in man through the mind which is the superior part of our nature. This is an important mark of man's anthropology, and does not correspond to him on account of his psychosomatic nature but only because of his intellectual and spiritual nature. Since through knowledge and love we possess in a certain way the object we know and love, by knowing and loving God we are assimilated to Him in a special way which is the image of God in man.

We are in consequence facing a semantic problem. The image of God as revealed in myths, dreams, and other religious manifestations explained by Jung, emphasizes *typos,* the imprint, the symbol of an incomprehensible content; not the imprinter, nor the activity of the mind knowing and loving God, although the latter may be the root of the former. Myth, symbols, images, and ritual are essential factors of religious manifestations, and the image of God in the Jungian sense appears in these mani-

57. *Coll. Works,* XI, p. 87.
58. St. Augustine, *Super Gen., ad litt.,* ch. 12; M.L. 34, 348.
59. Thomas Aquinas, *Summa Theol.,* I, q. 93, a. 4. Cf. *De Verit.,* 10, 7: "In the cognition by which the mind knows God the mind itself becomes conformed to God, just as every knower, as such, is assimilated to that which is known. . . . Therefore, properly speaking, the image of the Trinity is in the mind primarily and mainly, insofar as the mind knows God, and it is there in a certain manner. . . ."

festations in a genuine variety of forms. But myth, symbols, and
ritual are not directly concerned with the scientific analysis of
God's nature which properly belongs to metaphysics and theology. Let us suppose, for example, that the quaternity is the
symbol of the self. What does this mean? Does it perhaps prove
that God is not a Trinity but a quaternity? Not at all; it only
proves the connection between the symbol and its unconscious
psychological need. The definition of God as pure act cannot
be expressed by the union of opposites, not any other symbolic
expression emerging spontaneously from the unconscious. The
revelation of the unconscious does not teach us theology; it
merely manifests the basic craving of our nature, sometimes
unknown even to ourselves.

Immanence

Jung has been repeatedly accused of making the unconscious,
and especially the self, a substitute for God; as if everything
concerning religion could be explained by recourse to pure
human factors. Disturbed by the accusation, Jung blames his
critics of gross ignorance of his ideas and writings. "It is a
misunderstanding to accuse me of having made out of this an
'immanent God' or substitute God' . . . the self never at any
time takes the place of God, though it may perhaps be a vessel
for diving grace."[60]
For Jung the important factor is the image of God, and when
he speaks he speaks of a psychological image, for psychology
must deal with these images only insofar as they come under
our experience. But this, he insists, has nothing to do with God
as such. "How could any sane man suppose he could displace
God, or do anything whatever to him? I am not so mad that I
should be suspected of intending to create a substitute for
God. How could any man replace God? . . . The best I can do
is to have a divine *image,* and I am not the idiot to say that the
image I behold in the mirror is my real, living self."[61] It is
therefore the fault of the contamination of the object and image

60. *Coll. Works,* X, 463.
61. C. G. Jung, in Victor White, *God and the Unconscious,* p. 267 fn.

that people can make no conceptual distinction between "God" and "God-image," and therefore he says, think that when one speaks of the God-image one is speaking of God and offering theological explanations. Psychology cannot demand the hypostatization of the God-image, but it does have to reckon with the existence of a God-image in the same way it reckons with instinct. What God is in himself remains a question outside the competence of all psychology.[62]

On the other hand, however, he seems to contradict himself when he asserts that the God-image in man is *homoousia*, namely, of the same nature as God, and not *homoisia*, which is of similar nature. He even says: "It is impossible for psychology to establish the difference between the image of God (or the self) and God himself (i.e., in reality) not merely conceptually. For even the concept of the self indicates something transcendental; an empirical science is incapable of making positive statements about it."[63]

In the limitation of the purely empirical method lies the apparent contradiction of some of Jung's statements, for as he himself points out, it is beyond the realm of empirical psychology to discover the meaning of what the image of God is in itself, let alone the existence and nature of God. So in truth he can perhaps say that "we cannot tell whether God and the unconscious are two different entities. Both are border line concepts for transcendental contents." And on the other hand, he can say that "there is no doubt in my mind that there is an original behind our images, but it is inaccessible."[64] Therefore, although Jung is steadily insisting on the distinction of God and God-image, in the last analysis he leaves the problem open, for, being a Kantian, the Godhead is totally beyond the sphere of his knowledge; and even for a Thomist beyond the sphere of empirical psychology. This belongs to metaphysics.

On empirical grounds, however, Jung proves the affinity of Christ as an embodiment of the archetype of the self; and Caruso insists on saying that depth psychology has discovered

62. *Coll. Works*, VIII, 278.
63. C. G. Jung, in Victor White, *God and the Unconscious*, p. 265 fn.
64. *Coll. Works*, XI, 468. Cf. *Jung and the Problem of Evil*, p. 15.

the archetype that "brings salvation" as essential for therapy. In addition, he notes the danger of making man an absolute, for then there is no redemption in the immanence. Man cannot redeem himself alone. Naturally, the convenience of the existence of a factor is not sufficient proof for its existence, and nobody should try to prove the existence of a transcendent Redeemer within the scope of depth psychology. But depth psychology stresses the capacity of the human soul for transcendence: redemption, beatitude, incarnation, etc., are in correspondence to deep psychic needs. In the anthropology of man there seems to exist room for a Redeemer.

Furthermore, religious experience without the existence of a transcendent God would manifest the absurdity of the most important human instinct, and accordingly, the absurdity of man as such, baffled and frustrated in the deepest layer of his personality. This is not a valid argument for the existence of God—it is explicitly rejected by Aquinas—it would only prove the absurdity of nature failing in its superior creature, man.

But whether or not a transcendent God exists, the psychology of religion cannot afford to ignore the belief of religious man in transcendence; the psychological structure of faith is founded on that belief. The religious experience resulting from the belief in a transcendent God is, psychologically speaking, totally different from any other religious experience lacking this belief. "We would urge that the fact that men make these affirmations of God's transcendence is a psychological fact of immense importance and influence, which the empirical therapist can ignore only at his peril," Victor White says.[65] For example, as Eliade explains, the religious attitude of the Judeo-Christian people, rooted in transcendence, differs diametrically from other

---

65. Victor White, O.P., *God and the Unconscious*, p. 94. Rudolf Otto, *Mystique d'Orient and Mystique d'Occident* (Paris, 1951), p. 145. "Not only is the relation to the divine different . . . but also the object of that relation, namely, the Absolute, inasmuch as this object is considered as immanent or as transcendent. In order to establish a diversity of relations to the divine the important factor is not the man, but the object of the relation; this distinction of the relation rests in the diversity of the term, that is to say, an immanent or a transcendent deity."

religions because a new concept of faith was introduced into their worship, giving their religious manifestation a unique mark irreducible to any archaic form of worship.[66]

The Self and Mysticism

What is the relation between individuation and mysticism? Is the Jungian individuation, especially the union of opposites, characteristic of the revelation of the archetype of the self, equivalent to Christian holiness?

Rudolf Otto, from whom Jung borrows several ideas on the holy, defines mysticism as "the stressing to a very high degree, indeed the overstressing, of the non-rational or supra-rational elements of religion." Or again, "while sharing the nature of religion, it shows a preponderance of its non-rational elements and an over-stressing of them in respect to the 'over-abounding' aspect of the *numen*. . . . Christianity since St. Paul and St. John is not mysticism, but religion with a mystical coloring."[67] These definitions seem to over emphasize the *numen*, and supra-rational elements of religion, that which is extraordinary and endowed with awe. However, mysticism in Christian theology is not an extraordinary grace, like prophecy, visions, locutions, gifts of tongues, and so forth, which constitute epiphenomena of Christian life. Mysticism is the full development of the grace

66. Mircea Eliade, *Cosmos and History*, p. 109 fn.: "It may be of some service to point out that what is called 'faith' in the Judeo-Christian sense differs, regarded structurally, from other archaic religious experiences. The authenticity and religious validity of these latter must not be doubted, because they are based upon a universally verified dialectic of the sacred. But the experience of faith is due to a new theophany, a new revelation, which, for the respective elites, annuls the validity of other hierophanies." *Ibid.*, p. 108–110: "In this respect, the classic example of Abraham's sacrifice admirably illustrates the difference between the traditional conception of the repetition of an archetype gesture and the new dimension, faith, acquired through religious experience. . . . Isaac was given them through their faith. . . . By this act, which is apparently absurd, Abraham initiates a new religious experience, faith . . . God reveals himself as personal, as a 'totally distinct' existence that ordains, bestows, demands, without any rational justification, and for which all is possible. This new religious dimension renders 'faith' possible in the Judeo-Christian sense."
67. Rudolf Otto, *The Holy*, pp. 22 and 85 fn.

received in Baptism, and its essential trait is the actuation of the gifts of the Holy Ghost in a suprahuman manner which ordinarily produces a passive experience of God in the soul. The activity of the gifts reaches and touches the inner recesses of our personality and affects profoundly the psychology of mystics, especially in contemplation which consists in a high and special infused knowledge of God.

The data of contemplation are vague and obscure because the experimental knowledge proper to it is neither the scientific abstract knowledge of metaphysics when it considers God as the First cause of being, nor the knowledge of theology which speculates on the divine based on the data of revelation. The knowledge corresponding to contemplation is intuitive, rooted in love and reduced to created categories only with difficulties. The mystic experiences the supernatural, but he is incapable of conceptualizing this experience for it is totally unique and irreducible to any previous experience and hence incommunicable. "Henceforth," St. Teresa says, "they begin to be supernatural and it will be most difficult to speak clearly about them. . . . So subtle are the things seen and heard in them, that the mind cannot give a lucid idea of them to those inexperienced in the matter."[68]

This experience is ineffable, absolutely and invariably beyond our understanding. Or, in Teresa's words: "I know of no other words whereby to describe it or to explain it; neither does the soul then know what to do—for it knows not whether to speak or to be silent, whether it should laugh or weep. It is a glorious folly, a heavenly madness, wherein true wisdom is acquired; and to the soul a kind of fruition most full of delight."[69]

The infused knowledge of contemplation, however, is not usually revealed to the soul through dreams, active imagination, visions, or any other psychological methods used in psychotherapy. These graces are simply granted by God through prayer to souls far advanced in the road of Christian perfection.

68. St. Teresa of Avila, *The Interior Castle,* Fourth Mansion, ch. 1, nn. 1–2.
69. St. Teresa of Avila, *Life,* ch. 16, n. 1. Cf. Rudolf Otto, *The Holy,* pp. 28 and 31.

Here there is no need of mandalas with or without deities in the center; a simple gaze inside, where God dwells, is often sufficient to start the infused contemplative activity which, naturally, assumes a diversity of forms depending on the disposition of the individual soul and of the will of God whose spirit is granted to souls according to the inscrutable design of his will.

In order to attain the state of infused contemplation, the soul ordinarily has to pass through a double purification called nights and described by John of the Cross in the following way: "This night, which is contemplation, produces in spiritual persons two kind of darkness or purgation, corresponding to the two parts of man's nature—namely, the sensual and the spiritual. And thus the one night of purgation will be sensual, wherein the soul is purged and stripped according to sense, which is subdued to the spirit; and the other is a night or purgation which is spiritual; wherein the soul is purged and stripped according to the spirit, and subdued and made ready for the union of love with God."[70] These purifications produce a double unity and totality; in the purgative the desires, affections and passions of the soul are put to sleep, mortified, and quenched; all the powers of man are united under the control of the intellect and will. The night of the spirit unites man, already a partial whole by the first night, with God with whom total wholeness is achieved.

The road is painful; so many and so great are the afflictions of these nights, John of the Cross says, that strength fails to write of them. The first purgation is terrible and bitter to sense. The second, however, bears no comparison with it for it is horrible and awful in the spirit. The psychological explanation of these nights is simple. In order to receive the pure and high light of contemplation it is required to purify the appetite and cognitive powers that are going to receive it. The high light on contemplation is pure, but the soul which it assails is in the beginning dark and impure; it follows that the soul suffers a great pain when it receives the light. "For the nearer the soul

70. John of the Cross, *Dark Night of the Soul*, Bk. I, ch. 8, n. 1.

approaches God, the blacker is the darkness which it feels and the deeper the obscurity which comes through its weakness. So immense is the spiritual light of God, and so greatly does it transcend our natural understanding, that the nearer we approach it, the more it blinds us and darkens us."[71] No mention of these purifications can be found at all in Jung, although perhaps the "terrible aspect of God" emphasized by Otto and Jung bears a certain similarity with these purifications.

Comparison of Jung's Self and the Christian's Self

The full development of mysticism leads to a complete and permanent union of the soul with God who is, as it were, the very center of the soul; this is the self in the Christian sense of the word. God lives and works in the center and transforms the soul of man. This is "the lover transformed in the Beloved," of John of the Cross.

St. Teresa describes the peace and joy of this state in this way: "This 'center of the soul' or 'spirit' is so hard to describe or even to believe in, that my inability to explain my meaning saves your being tempted to disbelieve me; it is difficult to understand how there can be crosses and sufferings and yet peace in the soul. . . . Although the mind regrets these troubles, they do not disturb it nor rob it of its peace, for the passions are too subdued to dare to enter here where they would only suffer still further defeat."[72] This peace is so deep that it produces a bliss which is like an anticipation of the bliss of eternal life. "That which the soul knows and feels in this awakening concerning the excellence of God," John of the Cross writes, "is wholly indescribable, for, since there is a communication of the excellence of God in the substance of the soul . . . there is heard in the soul an immense power of the voice of the multitude of excellences, of thousands upon thousands of virtues which can never be numbered."[73]

71. *Ibid.,* Bk. II, ch. 16, n. 11.
72. St. Teresa of Avila, *The Interior Castle,* Seventh Mansion, ch. 2, nn. 14–15.
73. St. John of the Cross, *Living Flame,* Stanza IV, n. 10. St. Teresa of Avila, *The Interior Castle,* Seventh Mansion, ch. 2, n. 3. "So mysterious is the secret and so sublime the favor that God thus bestows instantaneously

When the soul reaches that stage the intellectual vision of the Three Persons seems ever present, and to this state may perhaps correspond some of Jung's descriptions of the self, as when he says: "Consequently, it does not seem improbable that the archetype of wholeness occupies as such a central position which approximates it to the God image. . . .The religious need longs for wholeness, and therefore lays hold of the images of wholeness offered by the unconscious which, independently of the conscious mind, rises up from the depths of our psychic nature."[74] But the wholeness is not a quaternity but a Trinity without any shadow, and the unconscious is the center of the soul vivified by sanctifying grace. John of the Cross describes the picture better: "The center of the soul is God, and when the soul has attained to Him according to the whole capacity of its being, and according to the whole force of its operation, it will have reached the last and the deep center of the soul, which will be when with all its power it loves and understands and enjoys God, Who is its center."[75]

The psychological attitude which follows the experimental awareness and knowledge of this "Christian center" is totally different from the religious attitude expressed by the mandalas drawn by Jung's patients. Furthermore, the Christian center has little to do with the mandalas found in Asia and even less with the union of opposites representing dualities, evil gods, or Antichrists. In the summit of contemplation there are no quaternities but Trinities, no evil but only good, no fear of God but only love. For as the Apostle says: "There is no fear in love; but perfect love casts out fear, because fear brings punishment. And he who fears is not perfected in love. Let us therefore love, because God first loved us" (1 John 4:18).

Otto's and Jung's approach to religion stresses too much the primitive and archaic conception of religious man, and fear rather than love. In that kind of mysticism fear is as essential

---

on the soul, that it feels a supreme delight, only to be described by saying that our Lord vouchsafes for the moment to reveal to it His own heavenly glory in a far more subtle way than by any vision or spiritual delight . . . the spirit of the soul is made one with God Who is Himself a spirit."
74. *Coll. Works*, XI, 469.
75. St. John of the Cross, *Living Flame*, Stanza I, n. 12.

a manifestation of religious experience as is love. If God is a duality, fear has to be a factor as important as love. In consequence Jung chooses Nicholas of Claus, Eckhart, and especially Jacob Bohme as authentic exemplars of Christian mysticism, ignoring Teresa of Jesus and John of the Cross. As Otto puts it: "In our Western mysticism the writer in whom the non-rationally 'dreadful' and 'demonic' phase of the numinous remains a most living element is Jacob Bohme . . . supra-rational identification of good and evil and therewith the possibility of the dual nature of deity itself."[76]

In Jung the picture of Christian mysticism is incomplete and often erroneous, for neither is the doctrine of these mystics a genuine source of Christian contemplation, nor have gnosticism and alchemy any bearing on authentic Christian spirituality. We identify the self with wholeness and holiness, but also with perfection, a total perfection which cannot include evil, but only good. Jung's capital mistake is to ascribe duality to the Godhead; then, accordingly, the human self as a faithful image of God requires duality, too.

76. Rudolf Otto, *The Holy*, p. 106. Cf. Jung, *Memories, Dreams, Reflections;* "The visionary genious of Jacob Boehme recognized the paradoxical nature of the God-image and thus contributed to the further development of the myth. The mandala symbol sketched by Boehme is a representation of the split of God, for the inner circle is divided into two semicircles standing back to back" (p. 333–334). Jacob Boehme's mandala is reproduced in *Coll. Works*, IX,i, 297.

V

Jung's Ideas on Evil

One of the thorniest riddles concerning philosophical and theological inquiries is the determination of the nature of evil. The problem is even more difficult for minds who, although brilliant in other fields, are not trained in the complex art of philosophical and theological thinking. The principles of any relevant philosophical or theological system cannot be grasped without profound meditation and a considerable amount of painstaking training. This is perhaps the case regarding Jung's ideas on evil; hence we should not be surprised if the writings of the most outstanding thinkers of Christianity are in disagreement with what he contends to be empirical observation.

His approach to the problem, he asserts, is neither theological nor philosophical, but empirical. How does then the conflict arise? Because metaphysics encroaches on experience and interprets it in a way that is not justified empirically. It is therefore the interpretation of empirical observation which poses the collision between his psychological views and the views of speculative thinkers, especially St. Augustine's idea of evil as *privatio boni*. It is then when theologians and philosophers have a certain right to fear the intrusion on the part of the empiricist who criticizes the idea of *privatio boni* as disagreeing with his psychological findings. Psychological experience shows that whatever we call "good," Jung says, is balanced by an equally substantial "evil" which contradicts abstract speculations not grounded on reality. In consequence, "psychology must insist on the reality of evil, and must reject any definition that regards it as insignificant or actually non-existent. Psychology is an empirical science and deals with realities."[1]

1. *Coll. Works,* IX,ii, 53. Cf. XI, 357; IX,ii, 54.

Hence, it is primarily the empirical evidence of the existence of evil which makes Jung reject the idea of *privatio boni*. But there is something else, the disastrous moral consequences that follow from this principle, as clearly illustrated by the case of a patient,

> a scholarly man with an academic training, who had got involved in all manner of dubious and morally reprehensible practices. He turned out to be a fervent adherent of the *privatio boni,* because it fitted in admirably with his scheme; evil in itself is nothing, a mere shadow, a trifling and fleeting diminution of good, like a cloud passing over the sun. This man professed to be a believing Protestant and would therefore have had no reason to appeal to a *sententia communis* of the Catholic Church had it not proved a welcome sedative to his uneasy conscience. It was this case that originally induced me to come to grips with the *privatio boni* in its psychological aspect.[2]

Furthermore, there exists a final implication of this principle, which Jung again thinks to be unacceptable: "If evil is non-existent then whatever there is must needs be good. Dogmatically, neither good nor evil can be derived from man since the 'Evil one' existed before man as one of the 'Sons of God.' "[3] In other words, the existence and nature of evil depend on God, from whom they are derived as divine effects; and God is a duality containing two opposites, good and evil, Christ and Satan. Hence evil and good are as real and positive as are Christ and Satan.

Augustine's principle paves the way to another theoretical conclusion which runs against empirical psychology: "I also criticize the dictum derived from the *privatio boni,* namely, *'omne bonum a Deo, omne malum ab homine';* for then, on the one hand, man is deprived of the possibility of doing anything good, and on the other he is giving a seductive power of doing evil. The only dignity left him is that of the fallen angel."[4]

2. *Ibid.,* XI, 304.
3. *Ibid.,* XI, 357. Cf. IX,ii, 41.
4. *Ibid.,* XI, 305.

This idea together with the common belief in the doctrine of original sin formed the foundation of a moral consciousness which was a novel development in human history: "One-half of the polarity (Satan), until then essentially metaphysical, was reduced to a psychic factor (original sin), which meant that the devil had lost the game if he could not pick on some moral weakness of man."⁵ Thus, both the impossibility of doing good and the doctrine of original sin deprive man of any constructive value; God has been robbed of his dark side which is now attributed to man, who, as a consequence, suffers damage in his psychology and in his education. "Cases are not unknown where rigorous exercises and proselytizings of the Catholics, and a certain type of Protestant education that is always sniffing out sin, have brought about psychic damage that leads not to the Kingdom of Heaven, but to the consulting room of the doctor."⁶

How is it possible to compensate this psychological blunder? The exclusive attribution of evil to man leaves him psychologically one-sided; so in order to restore the necessary equilibrium, the Church protects his views under the varnish of "moral probabilism" which is a disguise for the real pair of opposites existing in man, namely, good and evil.⁷

Nature of Evil

If St. Augustine's definition of evil is erroneous, who can explain its elusive nature? Jung does not hide the difficulties encountered in the investigation, and humbly confesses his inability to give a definition of good and evil that could be considered universally valid. We do not know what good and evil are in themselves; we know it only abstractly. To see through a concrete situation to the bottom is God's affair alone, he adds. But this leaves him unmoved, for "as I am definitely

5. *Ibid.*, XIV, 79.
6. *Ibid.*, XII, 20–21.
7. *Ibid.*, XII, 21: "Although sin is the gravest and most pernicious thing there is, it is still not so serious that it cannot be disposed of with probabilistic arguments."

not a philosopher," he says, "I am shy of general definitions which are only good for philosophical talk, but of little or no use to the empiricist."[8] He nevertheless writes: "I mean by 'sin' the offense against our moral code; by 'evil' the black fiend ever working in man's nature."[9] But this depends on many factors, and there is nothing which at times cannot be called evil, since the judgment depends on subjective views supported by a more or less general consent.

In spite of the obscurity inherent in the concept of evil, one of its traits is clear: evil is not a negative entity, a shadow, as Augustine says: "I am indeed convinced that evil is as positive a factor as good. Quite apart from everyday experience it would be extremely illogical to assume that one can state a quality without its opposite. If something is good, then there must needs be something that is evil or bad. The statement that something is good would not be possible if one could not discriminate it from something else."[10] Furthermore, "the identification of good with *ousia* (entity) is a fallacy, because a man who is thoroughly evil does not disappear at all when he has lost his last good. . . . According to this theory even the devil, the incarnate evil, must be good, because he exists, but inasmuch as he is thoroughly bad, he does not exist."[11] This seems an obvious contradiction to Jung, if we accept St. Augustine's idea of evil as *privatio boni.*

Therefore, although good and evil are not derived from one another, they are always together. Evil, like good, belongs to the category of human values and represents one extreme of a polarity, well pictured by Ruth Strauss in the following personal recollection: "He was looking at me seriously with a twinkle in his eyes. 'Being good,' he said, must happen to you in the same way as it happens to you being bad. If you set out

8. C. G. Jung, in H. L. Philp, *Jung and Problem of Evil*, p. 209. Cf. *Coll. Works*, X, 457.
9. C. G. Jung, in H. L. Philp, *Jung and the Problem of Evil*, p. 211. Cf. *Ibid.*, p. 212.
10. *Ibid.*, p. 18. Cf. *Coll. Works*, IX,ii, 41, 53.
11. C. G. Jung, in H. L. Philp, *Jung and the Problem of Evil*, p. 19.

to be good it almost gives me the creeps. It makes me see the devil rising up behind your chair."[12]

Relativity of Evil

Jane Wheelright says that Jung's biggest intellectual contribution was his concern about morality, his paradoxical ideas on good and evil: "No one saw better than he how often there is something good in what is bad; how also sometimes, in a subtle way, bad *is* good."[13]

Does Jung really believe in the relativity of evil? At times it seems he does, in a relativity depending on the contingency of concrete circumstances and on the uncertainty of moral judgment. "Although sin is the gravest and most pernicious thing there is, it is still not so serious that it cannot be disposed of with 'probabilist' arguments."[14] Again he writes these words: "Evil is a relative thing, partly avoidable, partly fate—just as virtue is, and often one does not know which is worse. . . . Good and evil are simply the moral aspects of this natural polarity . . . good and evil are feeling values of human provenance, and we cannot extend them beyond the human realm."[15]

At times, however, he himself seems to deny explicitly the relativity of evil. "But because I take an empirical attitude, it does not mean that I relativize good and evil as such. I see very clearly: this is evil; but the paradox is just that for that particular person, in this particular situation, at this particular stage of development, it may be good. Contrariwise, good at the wrong moment in the wrong place may be the worst thing possible."[16] This appears to refer not to what is usually con-

---

12. Ruth Straus, "A Personal Recollection," in *Contact with Jung*, p. 74. Cf. *Coll. Works*, IX,ii, 47.
13. Jane Wheelwright, "A Personal Experience," in *Contact with Jung*, p. 228.
14. *Coll. Works*, XII, 21.
15. *Ibid.*, XI, 197.
16. *Ibid.*, X, 459. Cf. *Memories, Dreams, Reflections*, p. 329: "In practical terms, this means that good and evil are no longer self evident. We have to realize that each represents a *judgment*. In view of the fallibility of all human judgment, we cannot believe that we will always judge right. . . .

sidered as "moral evil" or "sin," but rather to what is thera-
peutically convenient—although this distinction does not seem
to be relevant to Jung, as will be explained later.

Evaluation of Jung's Ideas on Evil

Jung himself recognizes the difficulties of a dialogue with
philosophers and theologians regarding the riddle of evil. "I
have the impression," he says, "that they are not talking about
the thing itself, but only about words, about the concepts
which denote and refer to it."[17] The reason, however, explaining the difficulties encountered in the dialogue does not lie
primarily in words or concepts, but in the complexity and
obscurity of the problem as such, which is far from being
purely empirical. On the contrary, although initially empirical,
the solution of the riddles of evil requires a whole system of
philosophical principles ranging from ethics, psychology, metaphysics, and theodicy, to revelation and theology, which is what
makes the dialogue so difficult. Jung's own interpretation of
empirical facts is highly philosophical; philosophical is his
criticism of Augustine and Aquinas, and philosophical are the
principles and ideas with which he approaches and attempts to
solve the difficulties that evil poses. In addition, the customary
semantic problems underlying the discussions hamper and blur
the mutual understanding. We are not sure that concepts such

The relativity of 'good' and 'evil' by no means signifies its characteristic
psychological consequences. I have pointed out many times that as in the
past, so in the future the wrong we have done, thought or intended will
wreak its vengeance on our souls. Only the contents of judgment are subject to the different conditions of time and place and, therefore, take cor-
respondingly different forms. . . . But once we know how uncertain the
foundation is, ethical decision becomes a subjective, creative act . . . harsh
as it may sound, we must have the freedom in some circumstances to avoid
the known moral good and to do what is considered to be evil, if our
ethical decision so requires. . . . Naturally, it is difficult to know sometimes
the moral qualification of particular events. But this does not signify that
morality is relative and subjective. It only emphasizes that often the
knowledge of what is good and bad is far from simple. When a conclusion
is far from the principles is difficult to know; but our ignorance does not
destroy the principle of morality."
17. *Ibid.*, X, 456.

as good, evil, sin, ethics, morality, etc., bear the same meaning when they are used by Jung as when they are used, for example, by Augustine. Let us try, nevertheless, to interpret and evaluate some of his ideas and criticisms.

Existence of Evil—Jung's interpretation of the definition of evil as *privatio boni* is incorrect. Neither St. Augustine nor St. Thomas can deny the existence of so manifest a fact of experience. Evil is very real in the universe; and in man, evil exists: "On the assumption that evil does not exist," Aquinas says, "all prohibitions and penalties would be meaningless, for they exist only to hold back evil. . . . Hence it is clear that evil is found in things, as corruption also is found: for corruption is itself an evil."[18]

Evil therefore exists; it is real, very real. And we will heartily agree with Jung in stressing its existence and importance. Therefore Augustine's definition of evil cannot be an excuse for denying its existence—and even less for justifying morally reprehensible practices, or any other consequences that follow as a result of erroneous interpretations of that definition. There are wars, poverty, injustices, sufferings, sins, oppressions, death, nakedness, cruelty, ignorance, and countless other evils. The existence of evil is as manifest as the existence of death or the feeling of pain: nobody can deny them and both are evils.

Nature of Evil—Jung blames theologians for contradictions but he himself falls on them. On the one hand, he violently rejects any definition that regards evil as insignificant, actually nonexistent, or a mere shadow, as totally unacceptable and psychologically wrong. On the other, however, he accuses Christianity for sniffing out evil, for ascribing all evil to man, and for leaving him only with the dignity of a fallen angel. If St. Augustine denies the existence of evil man cannot be a sinner nor a fallen angel, but a sinless creature, a true angel, a saint. If evil does not exist, then the dogma of original sin cannot exist either, and consequently it is not logical to sniff out evil, as Jung says the Church does.[19]

18. Thomas Aquinas, *Summa Theol.*, I, q. 48, a. 2.
19. *Coll. Works*, IX,ii, 54: "If Christian metaphysics clings to the *privatio boni*, it is giving expression to the tendency always to increase the good and diminish the bad."

A full philosophical analysis is needed to explain the nature of evil as *privatio boni*. Evil exists, but with what kind of existence? Here lies the riddle that baffles so many. Evil exists always in the good, it exists in the good when the good is deficient, when the good does not attain the totality of perfection corresponding to its nature. Hence, it is an evil to be blind or ignorant; evil certainly exists in the man deprived of sight or knowledge, but these evils are privations, lack of perfections which correspond to an integral man. Thus evil is the privation of the good which is due; and since privation necessarily requires the subject which is deprived, paradoxically evil exists only in the good. Blindness as such is not an entity, but the privation in the man who is good as man but suffers from evil because he is deprived of sight. Thus the expression *privatio boni* should be understood in this way. Although pains, sufferings, tragedies, and sins are all privations, they are also real because there are men really afflicted by them.

Does evil need a cause? And if it is needed, what kind of cause does produce evil? Naturally, the kind of cause that produces evil will depend on the kind of cause a privation requires. That something fails from its natural disposition can come only from some agent drawing it out of its proper disposition. Thus the agent which produces the effect produces also accidentally the evil joined to it; as productive of the effect the agent is efficient; as responsible for the lack of perfection the same agent is deficient. Saint Augustine says:

> The more the things have a being, the more their causes are efficient; but insofar as they fail or are defective and, in that sense, "do evil"—if a defect can be done—then their causes are deficient. . . . There is no essential cause of evil; what makes evil is, in reality, an "unmaking." The very defection is deficient in the sense of having no cause. Trying to discover causes of such deficiency is like trying to see darkness, or hear silence. True, we have some knowledge of both darkness and silence; of the former only by the eyes, of the latter only by

the ears. Nevertheless, we have no sensation but only the privation of sensation.[20]

For example, a child born blind is blind by the same agent that causes him to be a child. The blindness belongs to the child as a privation produced by the deficient action of the parents. But blindess as such is not intended by them, nor is it essential to their action which is only the new child; for this reason the deficiency is accidental, or, using Augustine's own words, not essential.

Consequently, Aquinas cannot deny even God's causality in certain evils, although never in sins. Hence the old aphorism, *ome bonum a Deo, omne malum ab homine,* taken literally is only half true and needs explanation, for the universality of divine promotion goes as far as evil inasmuch as God, as First Agent, causes the perfection to which privations join. But even in these cases God never seeks evil for evil's sake but for the sake of good. As Augustine says, "God would never have created a single angel—not even a single man—whose future wickedness He foresaw, unless, at the same time, He knew of the good which could come of this evil."[21] Evil neither belongs to the perfection of the universe nor is essentially part of its order except accidentally (that is to say, by reason of some good joined to it). "To Thee," Augustine says, "there is no evil at all; not merely to Thee, but to the totality of Thy creatures. For, beyond it, there is no thing which might break in and break up the order which Thou hast placed upon it."[22]

And yet, God cannot be the cause of sin, for although God

20. St. Augustine, *The City of God,* Bk. XII, ch. 7–9. Cf. Thomas Aquinas, *Summa Theol.,* I, q. 49, a. 1.
21. St. Augustine, *The City of God,* Bk. XI, ch. 18. Cf. Thomas Aquinas, *Summa Theol.,* I, q. 49, a. 2. "The evil which consists in defect of action, or which is caused by defect of the agent, is not reduced to God as to its cause. But the evil which consists in the corruption of some things is reduced to God as a cause. . . . The order of justice belongs to the order of the universe, and this requires that penalty should be dealt out to sinners. And so God is the author of the evil which is penalty, but not of the evil which is fault, by reason of what is said above."
22. St. Augustine, *Confessions,* Bk. 7, ch. 13, 19.

is the cause of every action, He is not the cause of the defect of the action, which is sin. The defect is from a created cause, namely, the free will as falling away from the order of the First Agent—God: "Consequently this defect is not reduced to God as its cause, but to the free will: even as the defect of limping is reduced to a crooked leg as its cause, but not to the motive power, which nevertheless causes whatever there is of movement in the limping. Accordingly God is the cause of the action of sin; and yet He is not the cause of sin, because He does not cause the act to have a defect."[23]

Order, totality, and subordination are therefore essential elements to delve into this problem if we wish to get a glimpse of its nature, however scanty it may be. The judgment of the goodness of anything does not depend upon its order to any particular thing; but rather upon what it is in itself, and on its order to the whole universe, wherein every part has its own perfectly ordered place. Our partial and imperfect vision of the universe as a whole prevents us from seeing the good hidden behind particular evils. Synthesis and order are the work of wisdom; analysis and fragmentary vision merely of science.

Good and evil are opposites, but of what kind is the opposition corresponding to them? In the opposites known as "relative" the mere existence of one extreme of the relation necessarily presupposes the existence of the other. The concept of father, for example, presupposes necessarily the concept of son and vice versa. This is perhaps what makes Jung think that it is "extremely illogical to assure that one can state a quality without its opposite."[24] But this is not the case regarding good and evil. Good and evil pertain to the opposition known as "privative." The concept of God as supreme good not only does not imply any evil at all, but on the contrary, evil is positively excluded as incompatible with the divine nature. Even more, the concept of created good as such does not necessarily presuppose connection to evil, although de facto evil exists in nature. Evil, however, implies a connection to the good, inas-

23. Thomas Aquinas, *Summa Theol.*, I–II, q. 79, a. 2.
24. C. G. Jung, in H. L. Philp, *Jung and the Problem of Evil*, p. 18.

much as the privation needs the subject which is deprived of something pertaining to its integral nature. The concept of man does not presuppose blindness, but blindness necessarily presupposes the man inflicted by this privation.[25]

The above-mentioned remarks belong to the ontological order. In the cognitive order, the good leads to the knowledge of evil, as its privation. Nonentities, like negations and privations, are known by their connection to entities: negation by the thing negated, privation by the relation to possession. Thus one opposite is known through the other, and what evil is must be known from good. Augustine says:

> True, we have some knowledge of both darkness and silence; of the former only by the eyes, of the latter only by the ears. Nevertheless, we have no sensation but only the privation of sensation. So there is no point in anyone trying to learn from what I know I do not know—unless, perhaps, he wants to know how not to know what, as he ought to know, no one can know. For, things we know, not by sensation, but by the absence of sensation are known—if the word says or means anything—by the same kind of "unknowing," so that they are both known and not known at the same time. For example, when the vision of the eyes passes from sensation to sensation, it sees darkness only when it begins not to see. So, too, no other sense but the ear can perceive silence, yet silence can only be heard by not being heard. So, too . . . when the realities are no longer intelligible, the mind, too, knows by "unknowing," for who can understand sins?[26]

25. St. Augustine, *Ench.*, ch. 4, 14. "Yet, although there is no doubt that good and evil are contraries, not only can they exist together, but evil without good and in anything that is not good cannot exist at all; good, however, can exist without evil. For whereas a man or an angel can be other than wicked, it is only a man or an angel that can be wicked: good because he is a man or because he is an angel, evil because he is wicked. And the co-existence of these two contraries is so conditioned that, were there no good in which it could reside, evil simply could not exist, because corruption would neither have place of existence nor a source from which to spring, if there were nothing which could be corrupted; since corruption is nothing other than the destruction of good."
26. St. Augustine, *The City of God*, Bk. XII, ch. 7.

Positive Aspect of Evil

Evil is as positive a factor as is good, Jung asserts. Here we witness the transformation of a psychological observation into a philosophical principle; from the fact that something is really existing, to the speculative principle saying that everything that exists exists as a "positive" factor. Since evil exists, it exists as a positive factor, and as a positive factor it is also convenient, a "good evil." Are we perhaps confused by semantics? By words that although written in the same way signify different concepts? To know what Jung means by evil is far from simple, for it is a manifest fact of experience that we are always seeking for happiness, for what is convenient and pleasant, and not for evil—as vision is always looking for color and not for darkness, and the intellect seeks truth and not error. In other words, the object of the will is the good, and whenever we are intending something we are intending its goodness, and whenever we are rejecting something we are rejecting its evil as opposite to what is good and suitable to our nature.[27]

These considerations are not conclusions; they are first principles discovered by simple introspective analysis of our actions. And as first principles they cannot be demonstrated, but merely apprehended by observing our behavior. It is against the operative formality of our appetite to intend evil. Even when we believe we operate for the sake of evil it is not evil as such we are pursuing, but the good which comes with it: "Someone has killed a man. Why did he do it? He coveted the victim's wife or his goods, or he desired to commit robbery so as to make a living, or he was afraid of this man causing him to lose something, or he had been injured and burned for revenge. Would he have killed a man without a motive, just out of love of homicide itself? Who would believe this? . . . Therefore not

27. Thomas Aquinas, *Summa Theol.*, I, q. 48, a. 1 ad 4. "Everything which is desired as an end, is a perfection. And therefore, as Dionysius says: Evil does not act nor is it desired, except by virtue of some good joined to it: while of itself it is nothing definite, and beside the scope of our will and intention."

even Catiline himself loved his own crimes, but something else, for the sake of which he committed them."[28]

All these considerations prove how perplexing are Jung's ideas on evil as a positive factor. A convenient evil is for us a good; for Jung, perhaps, an evil. And vice versa, a nonconvenient good is an evil even if it is a partial good—a baffling paradox summarized by Augustine in this sentence: "Anyone who loves perversely the good of any nature whatsoever, and even, perhaps, acquires this good makes himself bad by gaining something good and sad by losing something better."[29]

We are dealing with principles, and there is little possibility of changing them. We only try to clarify the semantics involved in these concepts, and to examine initial viewpoints in order to find, if possible, a common ground.

With these ideas in mind, nobody should be surprised by the objections raised against Jung's ideas on integration of evil, as well as the polarity of the self. Evil is indeed the unfailing companion of human existence, and some evils, as sufferings and pain, can be integrated; for suffering and pain have never been regarded without significance. Eliade says that the superiority of Christianity is what gives value to suffering, transforming pain from a negative condition to an experience with positive content. But even so, he adds, no religion has ever considered suffering as blind and without meaning. Jung shares his views and ascribes to suffering an important psychological value: "All creativeness in the realm of the spirit as well as every psychic advance of man," he says, "arises from the suffering of the soul, and the cause of the suffering is spiritual stagnation, or psychic sterility."[30] But suffering and pains in these cases are the evil we undergo or suffer, not the evil we do, our evil actions, our sins. To be punished is not an evil; but it is an evil to be made worthy of punishment. Sins are always

---

28. St. Augustine, *Confessions,* Bk. II, ch. 5, 2.
29. St. Augustine, *The City of God,* Bk. XII, c. 8.
30. *Coll. Works,* XI, 331. Cf. Victor White, O.P., *Soul and Psyche,* pp. 164–165; Mircea Eliade, *Cosmos and History,* p. 96: Thomas Aquinas, *Summa Theol.,* I, q. 48, a. 6.

against our nature and therefore can never be integrated.[31] Thus evil actions can never be a necessary factor with which we have to reckon for individuation. On the contrary, they make individuation impossible to achieve. "Woe unto them that call evil good and good evil: they put darkness for light, and light for darkness: they put bitter for sweet, and sweet for bitter" (Isa. 5:20).

And yet, paradoxically, there is no evil that cannot produce good, and good that cannot produce evil. For, as Augustine says: "Not even the Almighty God . . . would permit any evil in his works, were not His power and goodness such that even out of evil He can do good."[32] Why? Because evil is always mixed with good; communism as such is evil but indirectly causes good as long as it fosters a greater awareness of the necessity of social justice. On the other hand, good may accidentally be occasion of scandal for the weak, as Christ himself was for the Pharisees. But evil as such cannot produce good as such or vice versa—only in the sense explained.

A careful analysis of Jung's speculations shows that his ideas on evil revolve around two main considerations: the need of his patients, and the concept of God as a duality. First, the necessity of his patients, for so many factors are involved to know what is good and bad for them that we are often ignorant of what is convenient for their needs. "Perhaps he knows something is really bad, and does it anyway, and then gets a bad conscience. From the therapeutic, that is to say, the empirical, point of view, this may be very good indeed for him."[33] Therefore, the doctor from this standpoint must weigh whether a thing is for or against health. "On paper the moral code looks clear and neat enough; but the same document written on the

31. St. Augustine, *The City of God*, Bk. XIV, ch. 7; Victor White, O.P., *Soul and Psyche*, p. 164: "Such evils are, of their very nature, contrary to our will, our comfort, our pleasure. Here we are bidden to take our crosses, to accept them willingly, even lovingly, though with full awareness that they are evils, contrary to what our nature and inclinations quite rightly desire and hold to be good. These . . . are indispensable to our growth, health, wholeness, and holiness."
32. St. Augustine, *Ench.*, ch. 3, 11.
33. *Coll. Works*, X, 459–460.

'living tables of the heart' is often a sorry tatter, particularly in the mouths of those who talk the loudest."[34] So Jung seems to measure goodness by the pure therapeutical necessity of his patients. His own words seem to endow this principle with supreme moral validity, rejecting the possibility that a good therapeutical resolution may perhaps be evil from the ethical viewpoint, that is, sinful; what appears as a rejection of objective morality. "The Church distinguishes between physical ills and moral ills," Jung says. "The former may be willed by divine Providence (e.g., for man's improvement), the latter not, because sin cannot be willed by God even as a means to an end. It would be difficult to verify the Church's view in concrete instances, for physical and somatic disorders are 'ills,' and as illnesses, they are moral as well as physical."[35] Thus Jung is unwilling to distinguish between the fault we freely do, and the pain we undergo. The psychic or physical need of the individual is his only moral criterion, and morality is purely pragmatic, subordinated to "human health."

The final key for understanding Jung's speculations on evil rests in his erroneous concept of God. Jung solves the riddle of evil in simple fashion, ascribing duality to God. Yahweh had two sons, Christ and Satan, the former spotless and good, the latter totally evil. And since creation is, according to his own

34. *Ibid.*, XII, 30; Victor White, O.P., *Soul and Psyche.* "It is increasingly recognized in the course of therapy that there had been good and bad on both sides; and if this is what Jung means by the 'relativation' of good and evil, it is thoroughly acceptable, and expresses known psychological facts" (p. 160).

The concrete judgment of morality is often difficult to attain. Ethical science and prudence are distinguished as the universal from the particular. Ethics considers the problem in universal, like any other science. Prudence and conscience, however, deal with concrete cases, and fall under the realm of the singular and contingent, which is always difficult to judge and to know. Hence, the difficulty of knowing the right moral decision in particular instances, for the singular as such is only known through experience and the senses. For example, to know in universal when the war is justified belongs to ethics. But to know, now, in concrete, if the Viet Nam war is justified or not is much more difficult, because it entails the knowledge of all individual circumstances surrounding the conflict, which no man can master.

35. *Coll. Works,* XI, 169 fn.

words, "God himself in every part," it has to mirror necessarily the attributes of the Creator, namely, his duality and polarity. Hence Jung's ideas on God presuppose—although he bitterly resents the accusation—a renewal of the old Manichean idea of God as a duality. "I did not know that evil is but the privation of the good," Augustine says, explaining how he fell into the Manichean error. "How could I have seen this, for my vision was limited with my eyes, to material bodies; with my mind, to phantasm?"[36] Does Jung partake of the same principles that plunged Augustine into error? Perhaps no; one thing is however clear: his errors are not empirical but philosophical. The duality of God is not observable, nor are his ideas on evil and sin. Philosophically speaking our ignorance of the true nature of God paves the way to anthropomorphism and, consequently, to a version of Him depicted from our knowledge of material bodies and of our own; from duality in nature and man to duality in God, a common mortal jump. And what is easier and even worse: from duality in God to duality in nature and man. In spite of his insights and valuable observations, Jung here appears to us as a tentative philosopher, groping in the dark.

36. St. Augustine, *Confessions,* Bk. 3, ch. 7, 12; Thomas Aquinas, *Summa Theol.,* I, q. 49, a. 3, explains the Manichean error in these words. "Because they failed to consider the universal cause of all being, and considered only the particular causes of particular effects . . . because they found two contrary particular causes of two contrary particular effects, they did not know how to reduce these contrary particular causes to the universal common cause; and therefore they extended the contrariety of causes even to the first principles. . . ." See also *Coll. Works,* IX,ii, 61 fn.

VI

Religion and Myth

Among the majority of theologians and philosophers myth enjoys a poor reputation. For them, myth means a kind of knowledge opposite to reality and synonymous with story, tale, or fiction. This is however an easy simplification; for although this may perhaps be true regarding the object upon which the mythological thinking falls (usually the image of the sacred), it is false regarding the psychological and religious significance revealed by mythical thinking. If we take myth as "a narrative resurrection of a primeval reality, told in satisfaction of deep religious wants, a vital ingredient of human civilization . . . a pragmatic charter of primitive faith and moral wisdom,"[1] then myth should be considered primarily not as a tale or fiction but as a psychological expression of man's deepest needs. Myth reveals and manifests the marks of primitive man and, in a sense, also of modern man, because paradoxically myth is yet an important factor determining our behavior and dreams.

Character of Myth

For primitives, everything lacking exemplary models is meaningless and without reality, for reality is acquired solely through repetition of models. Objects and actions become real insofar as they imitate or repeat archetypes; and since only the first manifestation of a thing is significant and valid, objects and actions acquire values and are real if they reproduce the mythical acts of primordial beings. For this reason the cosmogonic myth is ordinarily the exemplary model for every kind

1. B. Malinowski, *Magic, Science and Religion*, p. 101.

of creation and doing. As gods did, so must man too: this is the pattern of the behavior of primitive man. Hence, the enchanted world of gods, heroes, and ancestors is endowed with special meaning because they provide the paradigmatical personages for archaic society. Therefore, the myth, teaching the first story of everything that is meaningful to primitive life, supplies models for human behavior. "The return to the origins and to primordiality is a basic feature of every mythology," Kerenyi says. "The philosopher tries to pierce through the world of appearance in order to say what 'really is,' but the teller of myths steps back into primordiality in order to tell us what 'originally was.' "[2] Good and evil, life and death, gods and demons and rest of human puzzles find solution and explanation in these archetypal histories which shape the life of primitive man, whose life is meaningful and real only as he imitates extra-human models depicting the deeds of extraordinary exemplars.

The repetition of the mythical cosmogony is equivalent to a re-creation of the cosmos, and accordingly it projects the primitive man into mythical time. Primitive man transports himself to the time in which the creation took place to live there in a continuous present partaking thus the mysterious world of gods.[3] And when primitives fly from time and space to be submerged in mythical time and space, they also fly from history, from the irreversibility that history entails, and from the meaninglessness of the historical present. For primitives history is not connected with the mysterious and elusive "now" which continuously passes away, but with primordial time and the primordial event that occurred in the beginnings. Primitive people abolish continuous history and give meaning to it only in connection with archetypal events, usually the happening of the gods and their deeds.[4]

2. Carl Kerenyi, *Essays on a Science of Mythology* (New York, 1949), p. 10. See a full explanation of these ideas in Mircea Eliade, *Cosmos and History* and *Myth and Reality*.
3. Mircea Eliade, *Images and Symbols*, p. 71.
4. This idea is fully developed and explained by Mircea Eliade in *Cosmos and History*.

Philosophical and Theological Implications of Myth

Myth reveals the theology and psychology of primitive man; therefore, theological and psychological elements are underlying the continuous appearance of myth over the centuries. Lévy Bruhl pointed out the identification of primitives with the tribe and with the cosmos, identification that he called "mystique." Accordingly, myth and ritual are cosmic in the sense that the history of myth and elements of ritual are always rich in cosmic objects and cosmic rhythms. And since the myth is holy, nature in this way becomes sacred. "By imitating the gods man remains in the sacred, hence in reality; by the continuous reactualization of paradigmatic divine gestures, the world is sanctified. Man's religious behavior contributes to maintaining the sanctity of the world."[5]

The spiritual attitude of primitives is not scientific. It is rather an attitude known as existential, a consequence of its peculiar situation in the universe. The myth is the answer to the riddle and mystery of his existence, a mystery which belongs to the awareness of sexuality, the consciousness of death, the puzzle of nature, the existence of good and evil, and above all the experience of the sacred. Hence, myth poses and solves the same problems as philosophy, but not by analysis and intellectual penetration of reality, proper to scientific speculation, but by drama, action, experience, and intuition. The myth gives meaning to life in the sequence of events making up the sacred history, answering thus how, by whom, and why things were made. Myth is like a primitive philosophy for it explains to the bewildered archaic man the perennial enigmas of life.

For Lévy Bruhl, myths are the holy histories of primitive society; the myth shows not dialectically, but by acting, the spiritual attitude of primitive man, actions that are genuine manifestation of man. As Aquinas says: "Just as human reason and will, in practical matters, may be made manifest by speech, so may they be known by deeds: since seemingly a man chooses

5. Mircea Eliade, *The Sacred and the Profane*, p. 99.

as good that which he carries into execution."[6] And this spiritual attitude is highly significant, for although myths, rituals, and symbols change, there always remains the common denominator underlying all them: "However their differences may be," the French anthropologist says, "the source remains the same; the mystical power of the supernatural."[7]

The myth reveals man's profound desire to go beyond the human condition, for religious experience leads towards transcendence. Man is not satisfied with what he attains here, with purely human models, and he longs for extraterrestrial paradises and suprahuman models: "The religious figure," Jung says, "cannot be mere man, for it has to represent what it actually is, namely, the totality of all the primordial images which express the 'extraordinary potent,' always and everywhere. What we seek in visible human form is not a man, but a superman, the hero or God, the *quasi-human* being who symbolizes the ideas, forms and faces which grip and mould the soul."[8]

The myth does not delve into the secrets hidden in God's nature; the myth proceeds differently, for it describes the divinity as a wish fulfillment of man, revealing in this fashion the deep ontological religious craving of primitive man. The yearning for transcendence is the source from which springs the image of the mysterious gods. Hence, God has to be a hero, a superman, a being all powerful whose deeds and actions transcend the facts that make the human condition miserable, like duality, contingency, corruption, evil, fragmentary existence, and death. "Man desires to be always, effortlessly, at the very heart of the world of reality, of the sacred, and, briefly, to transcend, by natural means, the human condition and regain a divine state of affairs; what a Christian would call the state

6. Thomas Aquinas, *Summa Theol.*, I–II, q. 97, a. 3. Jung, referring to the Indians, writes: "Their religious conceptions are not theories for them . . . but facts, as important and moving as the corresponding external realities" (*Memories, Dreams, Reflections*, p. 250).
7. Lévy Bruhl, *Les Carnets de Lucien Lévy Bruhl*, p. 189. Cf. Jung, *Memories, Dreams, Reflections*, p. 340: "For it is not that God is a myth, but that myth is the revelation of a divine life in man."
8. *Coll. Works*, V, 177–178.

of man before the Fall."[9] The primitive longs for ideal space, ideal time,. ideal conditions, ideal unity, ideal forms, absolute values, and absolute realities. Through the magical power of ritual man escapes from terrestial limitations in order to attain the realm of the ideal state, which is patrimony of the gods. And if transcendence is attained, so is unity, as its natural sequel, for there will always exist an unquenchable thirst to abolish fragmentary existences and disunity. In the divinity the opposites are symbolically unified, and by imitating the gods, "man no longer feels himself to be an 'air tight' fragment, but a living cosmos open to the other living cosmoses by which he is surrounded."[10]

Transformation and Corruption of Myths

History teaches that myths are sometimes corrupted, sometimes desacralized, and sometimes they simply disappear. Naturally, if we remember the distinction between the image of the sacred, and the psychological function of myth, then it is easy to understand the continuous transformation and metamorphosis of sacred images, rites, and symbols throughout the ages on the one hand, and the continuity of mythical thinking over the centuries on the other.

Since the image of the sacred in myth is colored by the strong affectivity of the sacred and by the primitive's need to identify himself with the cosmos and cosmos rhythms, these images are imbued with anthropomorphic marks and cosmic traits, both in need of purification. The metamorphosis of the gods is therefore a necessity and a logical consequence of the nature of myth itself. Little by little the gods are pictured less passionate, less carnal, and less cosmic, and their images more spiritual. Sometimes, strong personalities are the cause of profound religious revolutions, as history teaches for example with the prophets of Judaism, and in modern age with the secular Aryan myth of national socialism in Hitler's time. The majority of the

9. Mircea Eliade, *Patterns in Comparative Religion*, p. 383. Cf. *Ibid.*, *p.* 184.
10. *Ibid.*, p. 455. Cf. *Ibid.*, p. 385; *Myth and Reality*, pp. 139–140.

people always follow the impact made by strong and magnetic personalities, either for good or bad, as in the example of Hitler or Lenin.[11]

Philosophical thought also purifies the image of the gods and the sacred, as happened for example in Greece at the time of Plato and Aristotle. A good philosophical speculation gradually strips the gods of crude anthropomorphic ideas, alien to the nature of the divinity. And since philosophy is founded on first principles, the ritualistic going back in search of paradigms, characteristic of myth, is replaced by an intellectual going back in search of intelligibility and evidence rooted in principles, characteristic of philosophy.

Finally, myth is sometimes corrupted by science, because science (like philosophy) gradually strips the gods of the cosmological elements ascribed to them by primitive man that science continuously purifies down to our time.

Mythological Thinking

However, although the metamorphosis of the gods goes on and should go on continuously for good, the mythical way of thinking as such does not disappear, for it is the expression of a profound psychological need. Men like Plato and Aristotle accepted the existence and importance of myth, although their speculations stripped the gods of erroneous traits, like passions and immorality. As Eric Veogelin writes: "Plato knows that one myth can and must supersede the other, but he also knows that no other human function, for instance 'reason' or 'science,' can supersede the myth itself. The myth remains the legitimate expression of the fundamental movement of the soul."[12]

11. Mircea Eliade, *Cosmos and History*, p. 108 fn: "Without religious elites, and more especially without the prophets, Judaism would not have become very different from the religion of the jewist colony of Elephantine, which preserved the popular Palestinian religious viewpoint down to the fifth century B.C."
12. Eric Voegelin, *Ordo and History* (Lousiana, 1957), Vol. III, p. 186. Cf. *Ibid.*, p. 191. "He rejects the old myth because it has become historically untrue; but he defends it, nevertheless, against the enlightened materialists who, from the historical untrue, will draw the conclusion that myth has no truth."

Therefore, if myth responds to a deep psychological need, its suppression is tantamount to the suppression of a vital human function which cannot be done without impunity. Plato warns of the serious consequence that the stability both of personality and society will endure from the postulate of a freedom from myth, because "the myth has a fundamental function in human existence and myths will be created no matter what anybody thinks about them. We cannot overcome the myth, we can only misunderstand it . . . the real danger to the soul does not come from the ancients; it comes from the enlightened moderns who not only misuse the old myth but also in their illusionary inflation through science have lost the truth of myth altogether."[13] Thus the acceptance of myth seems to be the condition for a realistic understanding of the soul.

In other words, it is the spiritual psychological fact which is of paramount significance; and accordingly: "It matters little if the formula and images through which the primitive expresses 'reality' seem childish and even absurd to us. It is the profound meaning of primitive behavior that is revelatory; this behavior is governed by belief in an absolute reality opposed to the profane world of "unrealities' . . . this behavior corresponds to a desperate effort not to lose contact with being."[14] Myth reveals the religious instinct of archaic societies.

When myth is desacralized and stripped of its religious connotation, life and cosmos lose part of their mystery to be replaced by purely intellectual explanations—more accurate and objective indeed, but less attractive and poetic—which usually leave cold the human heart. For it is mystery, and not the purely rational explanation that pleases man and fills his appetite. In science these explanations are to be expected, but man does not live out of science alone. Poetry, music, art, morality, religion and the unconscious world of drives shape the pattern of our personality as well. The loss of sacrality disposes man for a pessimistic vision of the cosmos and himself.

We find it difficult to understand the psychological attitude underlying mythical thinking. Why? Because myth cannot be

13. *Ibid.,* pp. 187–190.
14. Mircea Eliade, *Cosmos and History,* p. 92.

accounted for exclusively by pure rational elements, but primarily by recourse to the unconscious. For Neitzsche, myth is a style of thinking according to the manner of the unconscious, and according to Zimmer the power of myth is derived from its position in the historical depths of the psyche: "There is no explicit commentary on the meaning of the mythological action. The tale goes straight to the listener through an appeal to his intuition, to his creative imagination. It stirs and feeds the unconscious. By an eloquence rather of incident than word, the mythology serves its function as a popular vehicle of the esoteric wisdom of yoga experience and of orthodox religion."[15] For Plato, the world of myth can only be understood assuming the existence of the unconscious and its relation to consciousness. Accustomed as we are to sheer rational explanations and demonstrative thinking appealing exclusively to the intellect, the strange, intuitive, and affective charged world of myth appears foreign to the psychology of contemporary man, reluctant as he is to accept any explanation not in line with our ordinary process of scientific speculation. But there lies the crux of the matter; for primitives, the approach to reality is neither exclusively nor primarily rational, but emotional, intuitive, even irrational. It is the reaction of the "whole man" who, by appeal to cognitive and appetitive powers, to rational and irrational elements, to conscious and unconscious factors, solves thus the enigma of his existence, of nature, and of the gods.

Myth and Contemporary Man

Although gradually disappearing in the secular city, myth is, nevertheless, much more alive than it may appear at first glance. Myth indeed exists, perhaps not in its archaic and original sacred form, but in a more profane fashion, desacralized. "In every word of consciousness," Jung says, "such things hardly exist; that is to say, until 1933 only lunatics have been found in possession of living fragments of mythology. After this date, the world of heroes, of monsters, spread like a devastating force

15. Heinrich Zimmer, *Myths and Symbols in Indian Art and Civilization* (New York, 1946), p. 40; Nietzsche, *Human All Too-Human*, p. 25.

over whole nations, proving that the strange world of myth had suffered no loss of vitality during the centuries of reason and enlightenment."[16] Not only is the racist utopian of Aryanism mythical, as is Hitler's Germany; communism is also mythical which presupposes eschatological and millennialistic structure, as well as the archetypal slogan of liberation, freedom, peace elimination of social conflict, abolition of classes, perfect justice, and final and utopical terrestrial bliss.[17]

The comic strips, like the batman, the phantom, the superman, etc., pivot around the exemplary struggle of good and evil, hero and criminal, light and darkness. The same occurs with stories, novels, and movies depicting fantastic adventures, ideal planets, missions impossible, world organizations, strange beings and animals, superior men, etc., and the final victory of the good cause. They satisfy the secret longing of contemporary man for heroic and suprahuman achievements.

Mythical is the obsession for success, wealth, efficiency, fulfillment, and wishful thinking characteristic of contemporary man. "The old perfectly realizable Puritan imperative for the moment, 'work, save, deny the flesh,'" Margaret Mead says, "has shifted to a set of unrealizable imperatives, 'be happy, be fulfilled, be the ideal.'"[18] To this is to be added the desire for novelties, for the exotic, for occultism, for astrology, for narcotics and drugs and for anything esoteric and mysterious, all of which will transport man to the realm of the unknown and mystical, of paradisaical experiences far beyond the dull experience of everyday.

16. *Coll. Works*, IX,ii, 35.
17. For a complete account of modern myths see, Mircea Eliade, *Myth and Reality*, pp. 181–193.
18. Margaret Mead, *Male and Female*, p. 193. Jung, *Memories, Dreams, Reflections*, p. 236. "But it is precisely the loss of connection with the past, our uprootedness, which has given rise to the 'discontents' of civilization and to such a flurry and haste that we live more in the future and its chimerical promises of a golden age than in the present, with which our whole evolutionary background has not yet caught up. We rush impetuously into novelty, driven by a mounting sense of insufficiency, dissatisfaction, and restlessness. We no longer live on what we have, but on promises, no longer in the light of the present day, but in the darkness of the future, which we expect will at last bring the proper sunrise."

Mythical is the sanctification of the cult of absolute freedom, of boundless liberty, of perfect peace, of mystical brotherhood among nations and mankind; of nudism and absolute sexual freedom in which everybody belongs to everybody else, like in a new Paradise where everything is communal, where guilt is absent, and conflict between individuals and society, between flesh and conscience does not arise. Mythical too is the boundless faith in psychoanalysis as the new magical ritual which frees man of the hindrances of the past and paves the way to the future. Mythical is the sacralization of science as the new god and scientists as the modern priesthood, which lead man and society towards a utopic future of infinite possibilities, for science possesses the key unlocking all mysteries and solving all difficulties. Mythical is Walt Disney's magical and fairy world which has enchanted millions of children and grownups; paradigmatical is his magic world of dwarfs, animals playing human roles, witches, angels, fairies of good and evil, of enchanted forests, and the aforesaid triumph of the good cause and punishment of evil.

The imitation of archetypes—of paradigms—which is also a characteristic mark of mythical thinking is also a common modern phenomenon. Naturally, modern man does not imitate the deeds of divine gods; he imitates the deeds, appearances, and even little details of human gods, of extraordinary exemplars that, because they symbolize the fulfillment of their dreams, give meaning to their lives, and the impression of achieving, even in a modest way, what the exemplar is famous for. Identification, projection, and imitation, are, as Freud put it so well, the characteristic feature of man's wish fulfillment. And so, archetypal are the images of millionaires, adventurers, kings, aristocrats, men in power, all America's beauty queens, heroes, play boys, beatles, fashions and looks. All these figures and images are paradigmatical for they give man a feeling of identification with the model, thus achieving reality. What the gods did we do—this is the pattern of behavior of primitive man achieving thus reality. What the modern gods did we do —this is the slogan of contemporary man who achieves a certain reality in this way. The power of our wishes will always transport us beyond the realm of our limited existence, to the magic and enchanted world of dreams. Wishful thinking and imitation are human traits, but in forms that often assume mythical proportion and archetypal images.

Perhaps the best known manifestation of modern myth are the hippies: their desire to return to the primitive and simple, to the origin of things; their reactions against the norms set up by an artificial society; their revolt against authority and parents, against moral barriers and restrictions; their long hair, showy dresses, bare feet, the beat of drum and folk music; their sexual liberty and primordial brotherhood; their amulets which recall the power of magic; their use of drugs which projects them to an unknown world of fantastic dreams and mystical dimensions, etc. All these manifestations bear the mark of the paradise archetype on earth; of a mythical loneliness for a state of perfect happiness in freedom and love; of a going beyond the human condition, which in them is perhaps more acute because of the force of their desires, the emptiness of their family life, and the frustration of life itself.

All these are mythical manifestations, desacralized or simply hidden under profane dress, and even deprived of cosmic natural elements, which in an era of science are replaced by gadgets and all kinds of artificial tools. They presuppose a deep and inmost desire to escape from reality and to be submerged in a time and space that is fantastic, away from the time that crushes and kills. Never before in history has the desire to escape from reality been so manifest and common; it is the mark of contemporary humanity, showing that although we despise mythologies and theologies, this does not prevent us from recourse to paradigmatical images and symbols. As Eliade says, "Man whatever else he may be free of, is forever the prisone of these archetypal intuitions; the extirpation of myth is illusory."[19] Man's view of the theme changes but the mythical theme does not, as happens, for example, to the exemplary

19. Mircea Eliade, *Images and Symbols*, p. 19. Cf. *Patterns in Comparative Religion*, p. 433. Jung, *Memories, Dreams, Reflections*, p. 282. "Some ten years before, I had discovered that in many places in England the myth of the Grail was still a living thing. . . . Myths which day has forgotten con-

fight of good and evil which has undergone countless alterations over the centuries, although the theme and final victory of good cause always remain the same.[20]

Not everybody shares this viewpoint: "If theology is to survive and to make any sense to the contemporary world," Harvey Cox says, "it must neither cling to a metaphysical world view, nor to collapse into the mythical mode. It must push on into a living lexicon of the urban-secular man."[21] But a theology without metaphysics would rapidly lead to a variety of urban myths, beginning with the myth of a paradisaical city only existing in the minds of thinkers who transpose the paradise of Marx's utopian classless society to the new paradise of the secular city where the gods have fled. The problem is not so simple; Lewis Mumford, who knows too well the goods and evils of the modern city, writes: "If we continue in science and technology along the lines we are now following, without changing our direction. . . towards more valid human goals, the end is already in sight. Cybernetics, medical psychology, artificial insemination, surgery and chemotherapy have given the rulers of men the power to create obedient automatons, under remote control, with just enough mind to replace the machine when its cost would be prohibitive. The polite name of this creature is 'man in space' but the correct phrase is 'man out of his mind.' "[22]

Hence, myth will survive in more or less sacred form because contemporary man did not lose yet the power of imitation of archetypal paradigms; nor the desire of transcendence and

---

tinue to be told by night, and powerful figures which consciousness has reduced to banality and ridiculous trivialities are recognized again by poets and prophetically revived; therefore they can also be recognized 'in changed form' by the thoughtful person. The great ones of the past have not died, as we think; they have merely changed their names."

20. Mircea Eliade, *Patterns in Comparative Religion,* p. 433. "The function of the paradisaical land in perfect freedom remain unchanged; it is just that man's view of it has undergone a great displacement—from Paradise in the Biblical sense, to the exotic paradise of our contemporary dreams . . . at all levels of human experience, however ordinary, archetypes continue to give meaning of life and create cultural values. . . ."

21. Harvey Cox, *The Secular City* (New York, 1966), p. 251.

22. Lewis Mumford, *The City in History* (New York, 1961), p. 176.

suprahuman models; nor the longing for unity, for paradise,
for salvation; nor the riddles of life, sexuality, evil, suffering,
religion, and death; nor his desire for integration with the
cosmos; nor the horror of history, nor the craving of being
beyond time and space; nor the desire for eternity and eternal
happiness; nor his attraction for heroes, monsters, fairies, angels,
demons and gods. In other words, as long as man remains
human, wishing and dreaming in a human way, myth will
certainly appear, probably more rational and reflective and less
intuitive and unconscious. Myth seems to spring still now from
the inner recesses of man, at least partly from the unconscious,
as explained by Jung, who ascribes to mythical thinking the
archaic manifestation of the objective psyche, hidden though it
may be to our conscious ego. But it is real and alive, and since
it is alive, no human prophet is capable of foreseeing its reaction were we to try to abolish it. Reason is not enough; an
exclusively rational world would appeal merely to a few individuals of unusual personality. The irrational is also part of our
wholeness, as history continuously teaches over the centuries.

These reflections should be taken into consideration to
understand what Jung wants to say in these words: "Theologians would do better to take account of these psychological
facts than to go on 'demythologizing' them with rationalistic
explanations that are a hundred years behind the times."[23]
Although this idea cannot be accepted without reservations and
severe qualifications, it expresses the demands of the irrational
nature of man, often ignored by philosophers, theologians, and
even psychologists.

The Christian Myth

With Judaism myth assumes new dimensions; the believer is
indeed aware of the past, but in the first place he is looking to

23. *Coll. Works*, IX,i, 105. Cf. *Memories, Dreams, Reflections*, p. 300–301.
"Unfortunately, the mythic side of man is given short shrift nowadays. . . .
As a result, a great deal escapes him. . . . Mythic man, to be sure, demands
a 'going beyond all that,' but scientific man cannot permit this. To the
intellect, all my mythologizing is futile speculation. To the emotions, however, it is healing and valid activity; it gives existence a glamour which we
would not like to do without. Nor is there any reason why we should."

the future. Time ceases to be the mythical time of our ancestors, and reality is not realized by the imitation of the primordial deeds of the gods. For the first time history is endowed
with a value itself, because every irreversible event appears as
a manifestation of God's Providence, who reveals his will
through the continuous flow of happenings.

With Christianity, God himself incarnates in history, and
time is reckoned as before and after the birth of Christ, who
gives history a meaning in connection with the unique historical event of his incarnation. Hence, Christianity and Judaism
abolish the eternal return of things, the regeneration of time,
and the going back of primitives in search of primordial paradigms. But Christianity is, as it were, mythical, because Christ
is now the archetypal God whose deeds we have to imitate. He
is the answer to everything in life, for he is the life, the truth,
the way; he gives meaning to the cosmos, sanctified as it is by
his terrestrial presence; even the eternal cycle of death and resurrection is fulfilled in him, because by his death and resurrection
he conquered death itself to give us life. Furthermore, he is the
embodiment of the self and the living myth of our culture
because his person possesses the qualities of man and God. The
Christian liturgy, on the other hand, pivots around the drama
of his death and brings to us as present the sacrifice of the cross
enacted as it is daily in the Mass. Moreover, Christ himself
is ever living among us by his mysterious presence in the
Blessed Sacrament. The Christian liturgical year is a continuous
remembrance of the life of the Master, who is presented to
the believer as the unique exemplar to imitate: annunciation,
nativity, hidden life, preaching, miracles, passion, death, resurrection and ascension—that is to say, the whole life of Christ
on earth is reenacted and remembered yearly through the power
of ritual. This enables the Christian to share the fruits of the
Redemption by his continuous incorporation into the mysteries
of the life of Christ.[24]

24. See Mircea Eliade, *Images and Symbols,* pp. 169–172; *Cosmos and History,* p. 140; *Myth and Reality,* p. 65. "The end of the World will occur
only once, just as the cosmogony occurred only once. The Cosmos that will
reappear after the catastrophe will be the same Cosmos that God created

Therefore, with Christianity the ritual of myth is invested with double dimension: it is eschatological inasmuch as the present is projected into the future, into eternity, into the heavenly kingdom that faith promises to the believer. And it is also paradigmatical and looks at the past inasmuch as the ritual reenacts the time sanctified by the presence of Christ upon the earth. Hence, in a certain sense, Christianity and Christ embody the fulfillment of every myth—because it is eschatological and paradigmatical; because it is an imitation of God who Christ is; because it presupposes the restoration of the paradise in heaven; and because it incorporates into myth the supreme reality of an unique event which entails the fulfillment of every wish and the restoration of the heavenly Jerusalem. Not only does Christianity represent the fulfillment of Judaism, it also represents the fulfillment of every myth.

Philosophical Considerations on Myth

"Nature," Aquinas says, "has implanted in man an appetite for his last end in general so that he naturally desires to be completed in goodness. But, in just what that completeness consists . . . has not been determined for him by nature."[25] In other words, man is endowed with an unquenchable thirst for being, for happiness, for completion, for totality, for unity. But since happiness may assume a great variety of forms, it is far from easy to know the object that really fulfills man's need; the determination of that object is the consequence of an intellec-

---

at the beginning of Time, but purified, regenerated, restored to its original glory. This Earthly Paradise will not be destroyed again, will have no end. Time is no longer the circular Time of Eternal Return; it has become a linear and irreversible Time. Nor is this all: the escatology also represents the triumph of a Sacred History. For the End of the World will reveal the religious value of human acts, and men will be judged by their acts."
25. Thomas Aquinas, *De Verit.*, 22, 7. Cf. Mircea Eliade, *The Sacred and the Profane,* p. 64. "Religious man can live only in a sacred world, because it is in such a world that he participates in being that has real existence. Thus religious need expresses an unquenchable ontological thirst. Religious man thirsts for being. His terror of the chaos that surrounds his inhabited world corresponds to his terror of nothingness."

tual inquiry followed by a free choice. Hence, a deep ontological desire for happiness is underlying every myth of primitives
who have already made their choice: the sacred. For them,
ontology is identified with sacrality, with the sacred revealed to
them by the history of myth. This idea is like a re-echo of
Plato's concept of participation for, according to Platonic
thought, all created beings are beings by participation because
they receive their entities from the First being who is God. In
Aquinas' terms: "Every being has the act of existing in the
proportion in which it approaches God by likeness. But according as it is found to be unlike Him, it approximates non-
existence. And the same must be said of all the attributes which
are found both in God and in creatures."[26]

Therefore, although the natural appetite for happiness is
being, in the last analysis the only object capable of filling
man's capacity for being is the First being, Who is the end of
everything existing and in a special way of man. The imitation of God is the end of everything created because God
created the universe as an artist. And in the same way as the
work of art has to imitate as perfectly as possible the idea
existing in the mind of the artist, so every being has to reproduce the idea existing in the divine intellect. Hence, we must
say that in the divine intellect are the types of all things which
are called ideas, or exemplary forms existing in the divine
mind. "Now, different things," Aquinas says, "imitate the
divine essence in different ways, each one according to its own
proper manner, since each has its own act of existence, distinct
from that of another."[27]

In this manner, therefore, God is the First exemplar of all
things. In man, however, the imitation of God is most perfect
and assumes an especial modality which is precisely the image
of God in man. As explained before, the image of God consists
primarily in the actual exercise of knowledge and love having
God as the object; hence, inasmuch as man knows and loves

26. Thomas Aquinas, *De Verit.*, 23, 7.
27. *Ibid.*, 3, 2. Cf. *Summa Theol.*, I, q. 44, aa. 3–4; *De Verit.*, 22, 7.

God he imitates God.[28] Accordingly, the mythical imitation of
the gods by primitives has ontological and theological foundation, however archaic and imperfect the form of this knowledge
and love may be. The knowledge of primitives is affected by
strong emotions, emotions that have their roots in the vivid
awareness of the supernatural. Naturally, archaic man is totally
foreign to the idea of God as pure spirit, or any other abstract
formulation of the divinity. He conceives God as a being who
reveals himself with power and majesty, sometimes as a dreadful
being, the God of terror, which profoundly affects the psychology of primitives. It is Rudolf Otto's *mysterium tremendum* which grips them with a feeling of hopelessness and awe.
But although this Knowledge of God is imperfect and archaic,
it nevertheless shapes their whole lives, no matter how subordinated and dependent these lives are upon the emotional
awareness of the supernatural.[29]

In man, the imitation of the gods is also a consequence of
love, because through love man can attain God even more
intimately than by knowledge. "The perfection of knowledge,"
Aquinas says, "requires that man should know distinctly all
that is in a thing, such as its parts, powers, and properties. On
the other hand, love is in the appetitive power, which regards
a thing as it is in itself: wherefore it suffices, for the perfection
of love, that a thing be loved according as it is known; since
it can be loved perfectly, even without being perfectly known
in itself. Hence it is, therefore, that a thing is loved more than
it is known; since it can be loved perfectly, even without being

28. Thomas Aquinas, *De Verit.*, 28, 3: "The human soul in some sense
touches God by knowing Him and loving Him." *Contra Gentes*, III, ch. 25,
2: "A thing is more closely united with God by the very fact that it attains
to His very substance in some manner, and this is accomplished when one
knows something of the divine substance." *De Verit.*, 10, 7: "In that cognition by which the mind knows God the mind itself becomes conformed to
God, just as every knower as such is assimilated to that which is known."
29. Lévy Bruhl, *op. cit.*, p. 68. "The cognitive point of view is totally accidental, subordinated and hidden by the emotions which are inseparable
from the presence and action of supernatural forces. What occupies the
conscience of primitives at the moment is the emotional category of the
supernatural."

perfectly known. . . . The same applies to the love of God."[30] Accordingly, although the knowledge of primitive man is vague and erroneous, it is nevertheless sufficient for the purpose of fostering love, which produces a certain imitation of the gods; for what is loved is in the lover by way of inclination.[31] Moreover, since God is the First exemplar of everything created, when primitives imitate the primordial actions of the gods they are attempting to identify themselves with them, because every imitation is for the sake of attaining similarity with the exemplar which is imitated. This imitation, however naive and imperfect the form it may assume in itself, is revelatory of the religious instinct of archaic societies, whose activity springs from the belief that everything existing and real depends in the first place upon the presence and activity of all powerful gods. As explained above this idea has profound theological and metaphysical roots.

There are indications, Jung says, that at least a part of the psyche is not subject to the laws of space and time; there are experiments proving that the psyche at times functions outside of spatiotemporal law of causality. This is true indeed, for the human soul, by reason of its perfection, is not a form entirely embraced by matter: "The soul is capable of an operation which is accomplished without any bodily organ at all, for understanding is not affected through any bodily organ. That is why the intellective soul by which man understands and which transcends the condition of corporeal matter, must not be wholly encompassed by or imbedded in matter, as material forms are. This is proved by its intellectual operation, wherein corporeal matter has no part."[32]

---

30. Thomas Aquinas, *Summa Theol.*, I–II, q. 27, a. 2 ad 2.
31. Thomas Aquinas, *Contra Gentes*, IV, ch. 19, 4: "What is loved is not only in the intellect of the lover, but in his will as well. It is in the intellect by reason of the likeness of its species; it is in the will of the lover, however, as the term of a movement is in its proportioned motive principle by reason of the suitability and proportion which the term has for that principle. . . ."
32. *Ibid.*, II, ch. 68. Cf. *Summa Theol.*, I, q. 76, a. 1 ad 4: "The human soul, by reason of its perfection, is not a form merged in matter, or entirely embraced by matter. Therefore there is nothing to prevent some power

From the independence of the higher powers of the soul from matter follows an important property concerning myth: man in the sphere of the "spirit" possesses a kind of immobility, for immobility is the hallmark of spiritual substances, as against material ones, the trait of which is mobility. And since time depends on motion, a being independent of motion is also independent of time, which is the case of spiritual substances. Man, therefore, as composed of spirit and matter is "on the border line between eternity and time,"[33] as Aquinas put it. Hence, a vision exclusively irreversible of history, as unfolding continuously in time, cannot fully satisfy the higher powers of our being. Man as "spirit" craves for something absolute, immutable, and permanent in the turmoil of the particular, contingent, and corruptible, which is the world as revealed to us by the senses. The continuous resistance to irreversible history is a consequence of the immobility of man's mind. Even history considered as the Epiphany of God, essential mark of the Judeo-Christian tradition, points to something absolute and immutable. Why? Because, although God reveals Himself in time through concrete historical events, in the last analysis He does this for the sake of eternity; in eternity everything and everybody will be restored to eschatological dimension. Even irreversible history is salvation history; and salvation, Eliade notes, is equivalent to deliverance from cosmic time. Augustine poetically writes at the end of his *City of God*: "This 'seventh day' will be our Sabbath and it will end in no evening, but only in the Lord's day—that eighth and eternal day which dawned when Christ's resurrection heralded an eternal rest

---

thereof not being the act of the body, although the soul is essentially the form of the body." Jung expresses a similar idea: "There are indications that at least a part of the psyche is not subject to the laws of space and time. Scientific proof of that has been provided by the well-known J. B. Rhine experiments. Along with numerous cases of spontaneous foreknowledge, nonspatial perceptions, and so on. . . . These experiments prove that the psyche at times functions outside of the spatio-temporal law of causality" (*Memories, Dreams, Reflections,* p. 304). See J. B. Rhine, *Extra-sensory Perception* (Boston, 1934), *The Reach of the Mind* (New York, 1947).
33. Thomas Aquinas, *Contra Gentes,* III, ch. 61.

both for the spirit and for the body. On that day we shall rest and see, see and love, love and praise—for this is to be the end without end of all our living, that Kingdom without end, the real goal of our present life."[34]

This explains the resistance of primitives to history, their continuous flight to mythical time, and their tendency to seek refuge in the gods. Primitives are utterly ignorant but profoundly religious—a religiosity that because it is spontaneous possesses the fresh and simple value of revealing the significance of their religious instinct, however childish and absurd their images and ideas on the sacred may appear to people now.

Modern Man, Religion, and the Unconscious

The sacred realities of myth and its religious implication are lacking in the conscious life of the majority of contemporary Western man. His religious instinct, however, has not yet disappeared; it is now sometimes repressed, sometimes underdeveloped, for the majority is simply in the unconscious. Jung has proved that the contents and structure of the collective unconscious exhibit astonishing similarities with primitive images and symbols. And Eliade says that the only real contact with cosmic sacrality is realized by the unconscious; religion and mythology are now veiled in darkness.

The instinct is there, yes, but in desperate need of nourishment lest it dies of pure anemia. Although the desire of happiness is natural to everybody, the choice of the sacred is not; it is the result of a free election on the part of man's will. Religion demands a choice followed by strong determination and the continuous exercise of religious activity. It can die of stagnation, of pure indifference, or by positive repression. But even in those who have repressed God or have never thought in religious terms, the problem is far from being solved. Since anyone possesses an unconscious desire for God, when the sacred is ignored or repressed, dreams, tales, stories, fables, terrestrial paradises, supermen and all sorts of human gods replace the

34. St. Augustine, *The City of God*, Bk. XXII, ch. 30. Cf. Mircea Eliade, *Images and Symbols*, p. 73.

sacred. The sacred in all these instances will never attain its due stature; but neither does nonreligious man remain purely secular, for his human manifestations assume then a "hybrid" status that displays its nature in the variety of secular modern myths described before.

Are myth and religion identical? This question cannot be brushed aside because the relation of myth and other religious manifestations is crucial to clarify the meaning of religion as such. The same religious instinct seems to rest at the root of both. But their respective manifestations, although perhaps interwoven and even connected, are reducible to each other only with difficulty. Myth is more primitive, less reflective, more emotional and intuitive. It is the natural sequel of a psychology and human attitude which is the hallmark of primitive mentality. On the other hand, religion as we understand it now is more rational, more reflective, more analytic, less intuitive, less symbolic, less sentimental, and much less affected by Lévy Bruhl's mystique of the supernatural. This is why modern religion is less anthropomorphic, more dogmatic, less cosmic, and more accurate and scientific. Myth always distorts the sacred images, for emotions and irrational elements bear an important part in its formation. Dogma is much more perfect than myth; it will always describe the nature of God better.

But in practice it will always be hazardous to draw a radical separation between the manifestation of both; mythical elements appear sometimes interwoven even with Christian religious images and symbols. The purification of Christianity from pagan elements has not yet been totally successful. "In the folklore and religious practices of the rural population at the end of the nineteenth century there still survived figures, myths, and rituals from earliest antiquity, or even from proto-history," Eliade says. And then he adds: "For the peasants of Eastern Europe this in no sense implied a 'paganization' of Christianity, but, on the contrary, a 'Christianization' of the religion of their ancestor."[35] Furthermore, if the conclusions of Jung are valid, traits of the mythical way of thinking will

35. Mircea Eliade, *Myth and Reality*, pp. 171–172.

appear in contemporary man in fashion more or less unfore-
seeable and unpredictable, though not always in their original
sacred form. The shadow, the anima, the old wise man, and the
self will always reveal themselves into consciousness in a manner not necessarily in conformity with a purely rational way
of thinking. There are factors in the unconscious not easily
detected by reason, and even less easily controlled by the ego.
The magic and spontaneity of religious symbolism have not yet
been lost.

VII

Jung's Ideas on Neurosis

Neurosis is primarily a suffering of the soul; and since the soul affects man in his totality, neurosis affects the whole of man. So neurosis cannot be an isolated, defined phenomenon; it is the reaction of the whole human being. There is not such a thing as a neurosis but rather a man who has a neurosis. "One cannot treat the psyche," Jung says, "without touching on man and life as a whole, including the ultimate and deepest issues, any more than one can treat the sick body without regard to the totality of its functions—or rather, as a few representatives of modern medicine maintain, the totality of the sick man himself. The more 'psychological' a condition is, the greater its complexity and the more it relates to the whole of life."[1] Accordingly, regarding mental health the problem of the unity within the multiplicity of human factors is crucial because all these factors influence the totality and unity of man. And since neurosis affects the whole man, "the significance of human neurosis cannot, admittedly, be purely metaphysical, since man is not spirit; but neither can it be purely biological. Human neurosis has a significance which permeates the biological, the psycho-physical, and the spiritual levels, and which must be acknowledged on all these levels."[2]

For Jung, therefore, the essential factor of neurosis is not the existence of a highly charged emotion but dissociation. He sees in conflict and dissociation of personality the real basis for neurosis; this dissociation arises from the conscious attitude and the trend of the unconscious, which are sometimes opposites.

1. *Coll. Works,* XVI, 76–77. Cf. XI, 300, 328–331.
2. Igor Caruso, *Existential Psychology,* p. 68.

Neurosis is an inner cleavage, the state of being at war with oneself, a splitting of personality, hence disunity.[3]

There exists a double unity in living beings: (1) Static, for the good of each thing consists in a certain unity. Every being has, united to itself, the elements of which its perfection consists. Hence, everything naturally desires unity. (2) Dynamic, which consists in the operative subordination of the different parts which, working as a whole, attain the goals corresponding to their natures. This presupposes growth, for the aims of living beings cannot be attained without continual motion and continual development. So unity demands both a static harmony and continuous growth.

In man this unity is constituted by: (a) the substantial union of body and soul; (b) the dynamical subordination of the different elements and powers making up the human organism which, for being the most perfect, it is also the most complex and hierarchical. The more perfect the soul, the more it needs to exercise a variety of operations; and in order to exercise all the necessary operations that characterize its nature, it requires a diversity of organs and bodily instruments. Thus since the soul is one and the powers are many, there must be some hierarchical subordination among them in order to attain the required unity. The vegetative and sensitive powers are for the sake of the intellect; finally, the intellect and the whole man has to be united to God. And since the unity is the condition of health, the essential conditions upon which human health depends are order, subordination, and growth. Thus disunity does not exclusively mean lack of harmony among the parts; disunity also means the privations of integral factors we have to acquire for the full development and growth of the human personality.

But how is to be explained the general disorder or disunity which seems to be inherent in human nature? By recourse to the doctrine of original sin. All the parts of man before the fall were reduced to perfect unity; the reason was submissive to God, the lower powers to the reason, and the body to the

3. *Coll. Works*, XVI, 131, 20; IV, 129; XI, 340.

soul. This harmony and ideal state, commonly known as "original justice," was lost as the consequence of original sin, and now man's unity is not as perfect as it was before the fall. The order of original justice chiefly depended upon the intellect and will, for it belonged to them to move all the other powers towards man's final end. Once the will turned away from God, then the disorder in all the other powers of the soul followed as a natural sequel. This disorder is commonly designated by the term "concupiscence" or "fomes," that infects the different parts of the soul insofar as they are parts of one whole. Its common manifestation is the disorderly attraction for the goods that pass away.[4]

Causes of Neurosis

The essential mark of neurosis is dissociation, and so all the factors enhancing disorder and disunity can be reckoned upon as sources of mental disorders. The variety of these factors is as great as the complexity of conditions shaping the individual existence, as family, environment, society, morality, religion, sexuality, shock, guilt, fear, sadness, and so forth. Moreover the specific constitution of the individual plays a part that is practically decisive. As men are differently disposed to physical illnesses, so they are differently disposed to mental diseases—depending on their psychic constitutions and psychological mental unity.

Neurosis is a mental disease embracing the psychological mechanism in its totality; hence it is apparent that neurosis can never be "exclusively" caused by sexuality, power drives, or any restricting theory regarding the pattern of our behavior. "Neurosis—let there be no doubt about this—may be a number of things, but never a 'nothing but.' It is the agony of a human soul in all its vast complexity—so vast, indeed, that every theory of neurosis is little better than a worthless sketch. . . . Freud undervalued the neurosis and therefore won the applause of patients and doctors alike, who want nothing better

4. Thomas Aquinas, *Summa Theol.*, I–II, q. 82, a. 3; *Ibid.*, I–II, q. 82, a. 2 ad 3; I, q. 95, a. 1.

than to hear that neurosis is 'nothing but. . . .' "[5] Neurosis is as complex as the complexity of human nature in regard to its psychological unity.

Some neuroses begin with traumatic experience; but even Freud says that neurotic symptoms are not always related directly to actual events but to the phantasies embodying wishes. Jung agrees with him, asserting that some neuroses begin in childhood with this kind of experience. He cautiously adds however, that it remains equally true that hysteria, for example, is only too ready to manufacture traumatic experiences where such are lacking. This point is crucial in evaluating the significance of infantile sexuality as the root of neurosis. Jung insists in saying that the deviation into sex is used—not always, but very frequently—as a means of escaping the real problem which is selfishness, not sexuality. Consequently, an exclusively sexual view is destructive, for it not only offends ideals, it also misinterprets the natural facts of the psyche.[6] Sex is indeed an important factor for the breeding of neurosis, but it is not the dominant one. Man is not defined as a sexual being but as a rational animal. If sexuality is considered as the most important instinct or the exclusive one the result can be only a "vital heresy," and another kind of disunity perhaps worse will affect the patient, even if he is cured of his faulty sexual drives.

5. *Coll. Works*, X, 168–171. Cf. Igor Caruso, *op. cit.*, p. 3: "The 'nothing but' solution." C. G. Jung, *Memories, Dreams, Reflections*, pp. 150–151: "I can still recall vividly how Freud said to me: My dear Jung, promise me never to adandon the sexual theory. This is the most essential thing of all. You see, we must make a dogma of it, an unshakable bulwark. . . . I was bewildered and embarrassed. One thing was clear: Freud who had always made much of his irreligiosity, had now constructed a dogma; or rather, in the place of a jealous God whom he had lost, he had substituted another compelling image, that of sexuality."
6. *Coll. Works*, XVI, 30; XVII, 111–112; IV, 168; V, 155; In X, 171 Jung writes: "The true reason of a neurosis always lies in the present, since the neurosis exists in the present. It is not a hangover from the past, a *caput mortuum*: it is fed as if were new made every day. . . . And because neurosis contains a part of one's own personality, an excursus into a thousand and one possibilities of obscene fantasies and unfulfillable infantile wishes is just a pretext for avoiding the essential question."

Morality and Neurosis

Every spiritual human value influences the mental life of man and, in consequence, cannot be indifferent to neurosis; the moral attitude of patients is an important factor in the appearance of neuroses: "The condition we call neurosis," Caruso says,

> occurs only where guilt has not been accepted—where it has been suppressed, and gives rise only to a diffuse, or even misplaced guilt feeling. . . . Not every guilt leads to neurosis but that only which is admitted and yet feared. Often the neurotic will accuse himself of unimportant matters and refuse to recognize guilt. That is the guilt of pride, of superbia, and this consists in the neurotic's identification with his real image. He will not accept responsibility for the repressed impulses. The desire for perfection and moral purity may also be connected with this superbia. This desire may be outwardly transcendental, but relies for satisfaction upon inadequate means. This shows that theologians may also overlook the connection between guilt and neurosis. . . .[7]

Thus Caruso's theory presupposes that at the root of neurosis there is always a wrong ethical attitude, although often hidden under the varnish of virtue and purity.

On occasions, Jung seems to express similar ideas, stressing the significance of selfishness and egoism in the breeding of neuroses: "The modern man does not want to know in what way he can imitate Christ, but in what way he can live his own individual life, however meager and uninteresting it may be. . . . He may not know it, but he behaves as if his own individual life were God's special will which must be fulfilled at all costs. This is the source of his egoism, which is one of the most tangible evils of the neurotic state . . . one of his most

---

7. Igor Caruso, *op. cit.,* pp. 33–34. Caruso says: "The neurotic locates his guilt falsely from a lack of humility. Pride will not admit any guilt, but will find it more convenient even to invent a false guilt. The neurotic punishes himself for a guilt which he has carefully repressed into his unconscious, and in order to be able to explain his guilt feelings, he searches for a scapegoat."

common symptoms."[8] He places the main source of neurosis in slackness, carelessness, callousness, greediness, spitefulness, and sundry other selfish acts.[9]

What is therefore the connection between mental diseases and morality? Instinct in animals is the power that enables them to discriminate the good things from the things that may harm their nature. Morality in man is similar to the instinct in animals; but since we are rational and free, the good of man has to be evaluated not only by instinct but by reason and the inclination of our will, wherefore the good of man is to be according to reason. Accordingly anything that diminishes or breaks this order of human unity in man, that is to say, the subjection of the lower powers to reason, is to be considered against the mental health of man. Aquinas says:

> Disease (weakness) may be applied to the soul in similar way as to the body. Accordingly, man's body is said to be sick when it is disabled or hindered in the execution of its proper action, through some disorder in the body's parts. . . . There-fore, disease of the soul is when the soul is hindered from ful-filling its proper actions on account of a disorder in its parts. Now as the parts of the body are said to be out of order when they fail to comply with the order of nature, so too the parts of the soul are said to be inordinate, when they are not sub-ject to the order of reason, for reason is the ruling power of the soul's parts. Accordingly, when the powers are affected by any passion, contrary to the order of reason, the result being that an impediment arises in the aforesaid manner to the due action of man, it is said to be a sin of weakness (a mental disease). Hence the Philosopher (*Eth.* vii, 8) com-

8. *Coll. Works*, XI, 341–342.

9. *Ibid.*, XVII, 111: X, 287: "His training directs his medical interest beyond the conscious personality to the world of unconscious instincts, dominated by sexuality and the power drive (or self assertion) which cor-respond to the twin moral concepts of St. Augustine's *concupiscentia* and *superbia*. The clash between these fundamental instincts (preservation of the species and self-preservation) is the source of numerous conflicts. They are, therefore, the chief object of moral judgment, whose purpose it is to prevent instinctual collisions as far as possible."

pares the incontinent man to an epileptic whose limbs move to a manner it appears contrary to his intentions.[10]

Hence, since morality is for the good of man it appears impossible that subordination to reason could constitute a source of mental disorders. Repression takes place only when feelings, disregarding reason, take the dominant role upsetting the ethical order. Therefore, in general, repression seems to be related to the ethical attitudes of the patient, at least in many instances. But to clarify this thorny and complex question we need to delve into the problem of sin and neurosis, for morality is enhanced by virtue and is hampered by sin.

Neurosis and Sin

We have frequently been told that illnesses and suffering are consequences of the original sin; they are penalties we have to endure as a result of the fall of our first parents. As a result of the fall, the reason has no perfect hold upon the lower powers of the soul, and the body is prey to disease and pain.

This way of explaining disease and pain, however, is a gross oversimplification of Aquinas' theological explanation of original sin. It is of crucial importance to note that original sin is not the "direct" cause of diseases either mental or physical. Original sin is merely an "indirect" cause of penalties, in the sense that, as a consequence of the first sin, human nature was deprived of the protection of "original justice." As explained before, this was the gift which unified all the powers of the soul, and the soul to the body, protecting thus the essential unity of man and the body from diseases. Once this protection was lost, human nature is simply left to itself; and it is not an inherent property of this nature to be without diseases as it is, for example, to be rational or risible. Without rationality man is not any longer a man; but a man afflicted by disease is just as much a man as a healthy one, only more miserable. Health is not an essential mark of the human condition because human

10. Thomas Aquinas, *Summa Theol.*, I–II, q. 77, a. 3.

nature is as other natures—corruptible and prey to diseases. Here are Aquinas' own words:

> Accidentally, one thing is the cause of another if it causes it by removing an obstacle; by displacing a pillar a man moves accidentally the stone resting thereupon. In this way the sin of our first parent is the cause of the defects in human nature, insofar as by the sin of our first parent original justice was taken away whereby not only were the lower powers of the soul held together under control of reason, but also the whole body was held together in subjection to the soul. . . . Wherefore, original justice being forfeited through the sin of our first parent; just as human nature was stricken in the soul by disorder among the powers, so also it became subject to corruption, by reason of disorder in the body. . . .[11]

Thus, Aquinas, speaking of those who endure physical diseases, and who are, nevertheless, without sin, says: "These are the effects of original sin (indirectly) . . . and they remain even after baptism . . . and that they are not equally in all is due to the diversity *of nature, which is left to itself.* . . ."[12] Original sin is not the direct and principal cause of diseases and miseries; these causes have to be found in pure natural agents, essential causes of them.

But if original sin does not produce these effects, what about actual sins? Aquinas again denies the direct influence of actual sins in corporal defects and physical diseases: "Two things may be considered in actual sin, the substance of the act, and the aspect of the fault. As regards the substance of the act, actual sin can cause a bodily defect; thus some sicken and die through eating too much. But as regards the fault, it deprives us of the grace which is given to us that we may regulate the acts of the soul, but not that we may ward off the defects of the body, as original sin did (indirectly). Wherefore, actual sin does not cause those defects."[13] Hence physical diseases are

---

11. *Ibid.*, I–II, q. 85, a. 5; I–II, q. 87, a. 7: ". . . The punishment of original sin is that human nature is left to itself, and deprived of original justice. . . ."
12. *Ibid.*, I–II, q. 87, a. 7 ad 1.
13. *Ibid.*, I–II, q. 85, a. 5 ad 3.

not directly caused either by original sin or by actual sin. They are caused by purely natural agents.

In cases of mental diseases, however, the problem is quite different. The good of man, consisting in the unity of man under the direction of reason, is diminished by actual sin; for, by definition, sin opposes the order of reason and opposes virtue. From the fact that man sins, there results a diminution of the good of nature which is the inclination to virtue. Through sin the reason is obscured especially in ethical matters, the will is hardened to evil, good actions become more difficult, and concupiscence more impetuous.

Hence, there must exist a psychological influence in the habitual sinner as a result of sin. Especially when sin is customary and degrades man, then sin upsets the order of reason, the hierarchical order of values, making the vital heresy a reality and breaking thus the human unity based in order and reason. In these cases guilt is nature's healthy reaction to our evil actions. It warns us of the disunity entailed in them: "If the emotional life acts contrary to reason, there will be a defect in the emotional life. . . . It is more than an intellectual awareness of the wrong that has been done; it is an actual feeling of *incompleteness.* This is the way in which well-balanced, mature individuals spontaneously react and it forms the basis of the feeling of guilt which results from performing acts that are morally wrong. It is an experience of the psychological *incompleteness* of the human act."[14] This incompleteness is the consequence of having chosen a lesser value for a greater one, upsetting the hierarchical unity of our nature. Sins and vices, generally speaking, are elements fostering neuroses, for they are contrary to the order of reason which is the essential condition for mental health.

Hence, we should not be surprised if psychiatrists almost unanimously agree in pointing out the close link between neurosis and the wrong ethical attitude of the patient. Lack of humility, selfishness, pride, indifference for others, egocentrism, the consideration of pleasure as the goal of life, and so

14. A.A.A. Terruwe, *op. cit.,* pp. 28– 29.

forth, hatch neuroses and gleam at the dawn of many of them. "The phenomenology of neurosis provides sufficient evidence that it is his greed for experience that makes the neurotic insensible to ordinary experience and that the pleasure principle actually leads him to dislike life itself."[15] Psychiatrists especially detect pride and self love behind the emergence of many neuroses. Self-love and pride are again behind the majority of our sins. Self-love amounting to contempt of God, builds up the city of Babylon, Augustine says in *The City of God* in agreement with Aquinas, who writes: "Self-love is the root of every sin, inasmuch as every sinful act proceeds from inordinate desire for some temporal good, which is due to the fact that he loves himself inordinately. Whereas pride regards him as turning away from God, to whose commandment man refuses to be subject. For which reason it is called the beginning, because the beginning of evil consists in turning away from God."[16] Therefore let us point out the following parallelism:

---

15. Igor Caruso, *op. cit.*, p. 45. Cf. Caruso reports the following case. "As a child, my impatience was constantly being aroused by my parents, who always started preparing me for weeks beforehand for any event which they supposed would give me pleasure. They would whet my appetite a long time in advance; they encouraged me in anticipation. . . . This made me very impatient, and I kept thinking: if only the time would pass! If only it were Christmas now! I could hardly bear to wait. At such times, the present had no meaning whatsoever, it meant senseless waiting. The same happened before the summer holidays; they were talked about weeks in advance; my impatience was strained. And then, when the moment really came, I was always disappointed, because reality fell short of my feverish expectations. The result was infinite boredom. . . ." (pp. 45–46).

16. Thomas Aquinas, *Summa Theol.*, I–II, q. 77, a. 4. Cf. I–II, q. 84, a. 2. Both the psychological necessity of confession, and the "cosmic dimension" of certain sins, is somberly described by Jung: "A lady came to my office . . . What she had to communicate to me was a confession; some twenty years ago she had committed a murder out of jealousy. She had poisoned her best friend because she wanted to marry the friend's husband. She had thought that if the murder was not discovered, it would not disturb her. She wanted to marry the husband, and the simplest way was to eliminate her friend. Moral considerations were of no importance to her, she thought.

The consequences? She had in fact married the man, but he died soon afterward, relatively young. During the following years a number of strange things happened. The daughter of this marriage endeavored to get away from her as soon as she was grown up. She married young and vanished

pride and self love are the sources of many neuroses; pride is the beginning of evil, and self-love the root of every sin. Morality, sin, and neurosis appear to be interwoven at least in many instances. The nature of this connection will probably assume a diversity as great as the individuals involved in them.

Naturally, this does not mean that all persons afflicted by these moral defects are neurotics. To a large extent neurosis depends upon individual dispositions which are unpredictable and unknown even to the best psychiatrist. Neurosis is like a physical epidemic in which the breeding is in the air—some resist the danger of infection and some become its victim, depending on individual disposition and voluntary reactions.

In the aforementioned cases, neurosis may entail imputability. But on the other hand, there are many other cases in which neurosis is free from any kind of personal responsibility; for instance, in the case of individuals who, although in good faith, have nevertheless erroneous moral principles, or a wrong conscience. The knowledge of what is good and evil comes to us through the judgment of our conscience which binds our actions under moral obligation. And the conscience must be obeyed not only when one is in possession of a good one, but also when in good faith we trust the conclusion of an erroneous moral judgment: "Absolutely speaking," Aquinas says, "every will in variance with reason, whether right or erring, is always

---

from view, drew farther and farther away, and ultimately the mother lost all contact with her. This lady was a passionate horsewoman and owned several riding horses of which she was extremely fond. One day she discovered that the horses were beginning to grow nervous under her. Even her favorite shied and threw her. Finally she had to give up riding. Thereafter she clung to her dogs. She owned an unusually beautiful wolfhound to which she was greatly attached. As chance would have it, this very dog was striken with paralysis. With that, her cup was full; she felt that she was morally done for. She had to confess, and for this reason she came to me. She was a murderess, but on top of that she also murdered herself. For one who commits such a crime destroys his own soul . . . sometimes it seems as if even animals and plants 'know' it. . . . She had seen people and animals turn away from her, and had been so struck by this silent verdict that she could not have endured any further condemnation" (*Memories, Dreams, Reflections*, pp. 122–123).

evil."[17] In these cases the neurosis may perhaps be the mere consequence of wrong ethical principles which prevent integration of spiritual values or upset the order of nature, but without personal responsibility. Patients in good faith, for example, may repress any spiritual factor attempting to emerge from the unconscious because they believe it to be harmful to them. False ideas on psychology and man can also lead to neurosis. In "energy neurosis," neurotics stifle and strangle any passion and emotion in order to attain mistaken goals, namely, the absolute suppression of any emotion and feeling. Disunity here means suppression of vital elements; these individuals are simply ignorant of the value of feelings in the development of human personality.

Neurosis also breaks out as a result of shock and traumatic experiences that leave the victim crippled, without the appropriate defense mechanism against fears, anguish, terrors, and so forth. Furthermore, children too are frequently powerless to resist an unfavorable familiar situation. Parents, Jung advises, should be conscious of the fact that they themselves are the principle cause of neurosis in their children.[18] These children are obliged to do, to feel, and to live not as they want, but as their parents want. Culpability presupposes liberty and knowledge, and in these cases liberty—if not totally abolished—is at least reduced to insignificance.

Caruso himself acknowledges the existence of neuroses in animals, as much as in human beings—even though animals are not morally responsible because they lack freedom. The explanation of their neuroses lies in the unnatural treatment of instincts and passions, usually consequent upon their upbringing.[19] In man although instincts and passion are directed by reason and controlled by the will, the control is not absolute but relative and dependent upon the concrete disposition of

17. Thomas Aquinas, *Summa Theol.,* I–II, q. 19, a. 5.
18. *Coll. Works,* XVII, 42; XVII, 78.
19. Igor Caruso, *op. cit.,* p. 68. "Cruel treatment, impatient training, selfish pampering, constant interference, give rise to neurosis in animals as much as in human beings." For the explanation of neurosis as a result of conflict between passions, see Terruwe, *op. cit.,* pp. 37–42.

individuals. Aquinas himself seems to admit the existence of mental diseases as the result of the defective activity of some passions, especially sorrow: "Sorrow is most harmful to the body. . . . For man's life consists in a certain movement . . . these passions which denote in the appetite a movement of flight or contraction, are repugnant to the vital movement . . . wherefore they are simply harmful: such are fear and despair, and above all sorrow which depresses the soul by reason of a present evil, which makes a stronger impression than future evil. . . . Therefore sorrow too sometimes deprives man of the use of reason: as may be seen in those who through sorrow become a prey of melancholy or madness."[20]

Fear also constitutes a source of neurosis, as occurs in instances of sudden and unexpected dangers, and especially of death which is the worst of all fears. "The things we fear," Aristotle says, "are terrible things and these are, to speak without qualifications, evils; for which reason people even define fear as expectation of evil. . . . Now death is the most terrible of all things; for it is the end, and nothing is thought to be any longer either good or bad for the dead."[21] Thus sorrow and fear may take such a hold on neurotics as to deprive them of initiative, paralyzing their activity and even in instances their freedom. Sorrow and fear thus prevent the attainment of essential human goals, goals that are integral elements of unity; or they foster complexes which operate independently. Individuals prone to neuroses are powerless against these evils; far from being guilty they are on the contrary victims of circumstances and poor psychological individual dispositions.

That many neuroses are free from personal responsibility is also proved if we remember the relation of physical illnesses and sin. Bodily disabilities are produced by a variety of agents totally beyond the control and influence of intellect and will,

---

20. Thomas Aquinas, *Summa Theol.*, I–II, q. 37, a. 4, and ad 3.
21. Aristotle, *Nic. Ethic.*, III, 6, 115a 8–28. Cf. C. G. Jung, *Memories, Dreams, Reflections,* p. 314: "Death is indeed a fearful piece of brutality, there is no sense pretending otherwise. It is brutal not only as a physical event, but far more psychically: a human being is torn away from us, and what remains is the icy stillness of death."

and, consequently, beyond the scope of culpability and beyond the scope of ethics. Yet, although neurosis is primarily a disease of the soul it also depends on the body, for many neuroses presuppose a defective functioning of the passions and internal senses, the psychosomatic activity of which is ascribed formally to the soul but materially to the body. In many neuroses the body has suffered a harm, impeding thus the normal functioning of these powers; and since we are not usually responsible for bodily harms, by the same token we are not responsible for the defective psychosomatic activity which is defective on account of the body. In these instances neurotic reactions are free from the control of the will, insofar as the will has no hold upon the bodily activity of the appetite which has become independent, dissociated.

The mental and bodily correlation characteristic of passions is well analyzed in the following modern words:

> Since the emotion is not exclusively a psychological reaction but possesses a somatic aspect, it follows that its mental inclination must be expressed in the body. This is possible only through a change of bodily conditions in the direction of the sensory good which is sought. St. Thomas already taught this by saying that every appetite is accompanied necessarily by a change in the body. . . . Thus there exists a most intimate relationship between the psychomotor reaction and the emotion. They are united together and constitute the emotion in its entirety. . . . Not only does the psychomotor reaction reflect the mental activity; they are both one and the same, a psychosomatic unit.[22]

The somatic disabilities are not necessarily the result of sin, but of purely natural factors beyond voluntary control, as in the case of bodily illnesses. Therefore, it appears that in many cases responsibility and guilt are not necessarily at the source of neurosis: "Though it cannot be denied that a purely materialistic attitude may in certain circumstances foster neurosis or jeopardize its cure, yet the above thesis (the neurotic is

22. A.A.A. Terruwe, *op. cit.*, pp. 21–22. Cf. Thomas Aquinas, *In Ethic.*, Bk. VII, lect. 3, n. 1351.

always responsible) can hardly apply to all forms of neurosis—indeed not to any specific form. . . . It would be fatal if pastors and psychotherapists always assumed guilt in the patient."[23] A. Snoeck, in *Psychology and Confession,* criticizes Hofner's approach to neurosis, who says that the neurotic is always guilty in one way or another. Caruso himself in later works seems to have softened his previous opinion, and says: "Görres shows clearly as against Frankl and Daim that neurosis has no direct connection with personal culpability. . . . Certainly neurosis is not a sin."[24]

In conclusion, some neuroses entail responsibility and some others are free from any kind of personal culpability. But since neurosis is a mental disease, it is often the result of an habitual false moral attitude leading towards disunity.

Effects of Neurosis

Suffering as such is not a disease but the faithful companion of the human condition and not without meaning, especially in Christianity. Yet, this is not the case of the false suffering characteristic of neurosis, for behind a neurosis there is often concealed all the necessary sufferings that the patient has been unwilling to bear. The self-defense mechanism of the patient has the apparent advantage of clearing the conscious mind of worry and troubles, but it causes an indirect suffering from something unreal, that is, a neurosis. We can see this from the hysterical pains which are relieved in the course of treatment, by the corresponding psychic suffering that the patient sought to avoid. Neurosis is always a substitute for legitimate suffering and a psychoneurosis must be understood, ultimately, as the suffering of a soul which has not discovered its meaning and suffers from the lack of unity.[25] Neurosis produces suffering "from a condition that ought not to be," as Caruso put it. The

23. B. F. Mitzka, *Das neue Buch* (Vienna, 1946), p. 4, quoted by Caruso, *op. cit.,* p. 39.
24. Igor Caruso, *Die Psychologie und das sittliche Werden des Menschen* (Oesterr, Furche, 1957), p. 12.
25. *Coll. Works,* XVI, 78–81; XI, 331–332, 81.

condition represents the failure to adapt to reality, an attempt at healing in which the neurotic is unable to cope with the real conflict to dwell instead in a world of his own, of fantasies and dreams. If we love ourselves we love our unity and we suffer when unity is lost. "For what else is pain," Augustine says, "but a feeling which withstands division? Wherefore it is clear that the soul craves for unity, and yields with the greatest reluctance and resistance to those passions of the body which threaten its unity and integrity."[26] Neurosis produces a non-genuine suffering, a consequence of the lack of unity and wholeness.

The suffering of neurotics may assume as many manifestations as different manifestations may assume man's lack of unity. Neurosis is often the consequence of a transmutation of human vital values, a vital heresy, as Caruso put it. Through the self-defense mechanism, the neurosis apparently solves the human conflict, but since the self-defense mechanism violates the hierarchical unity of man it is also a mechanism of self-deception, for nature and reality cannot be supplanted without impunity. The symbolic wish fulfillment of neurosis does not satisfy the essential needs of the sick, entangled in vital conflicts and craving for essential needs; the solution rests not in dream wishes but in the real fulfillment of our basic necessities. By virtue of this heretic transmutation of values and symbolic wish fulfillment of goals many neurotics lose the essential values of life and are searching in the dark, even for a dim ray of light. The disunity here assumes dramatic manifestations, because neurotics, victims of these manifestations, have lost sight of the final goal of man. It is significant that the majority of neurotics, especially in the second half of their lives, do not have terrors, obsessions, phobias, or any other neurotic manifestations. They rather feel a bottomless emptiness and deep solitude that their bewildered mind is powerless to explain, let alone remove. About a third of the patients who came to see Jung were not suffering from chronically definable neurosis, but from the senselessness and aimlessness of their lives. This is the worst and most terrible neurosis, for it affects the inner-

26. St. Augustine, *De Lib. Arbit.*, Bk. III, ch. 23, 69.

most recesses and deepest layers of our mysterious self. We have come into existence and we do not know for what purpose; we ask ourselves many questions and find no answers: "A psycho-neurosis must be understood, ultimately," Jung says, "as a suffering of a soul which has not discovered its meaning. . . . He is looking for something that will take possession of him and give meaning and form to the confusion of his neurotic soul. . . . The neurotic sees that he has no love, but only sexuality; no faith, because he is afraid to grope in the dark; no hope, because he is disillusioned by the world and by life; and no understanding, because he has failed to read the meaning of his own existence . . . and it is only meaning that liberates."[27] Without love we are separated from our fellow men; without faith we are separated from light, and live in darkness; without understanding of our own mysterious person we are alienated even from ourselves, for we do not know what we are. Neurosis has torn us apart, and we suffer from a condition that "ought not to be," from disunity; but at least the suffering makes us aware of something that is going wrong, for the patient is divided and ill, but this illness is nature's attempt to heal him.[28]

Who Is Neurotic?

Inasmuch as original sin infected nature, everyone is to a certain degree mentally wounded; the stronger the movement of

---

27. *Coll. Works*, XI, 330–331. Victor Frankl, *op. cit.*, p. 153: "*Logos* is a Greek word that denotes 'meaning.' Logo-therapy or, as it has been called by some authors, 'The Third Viennese School of Psychotherapy,' focuses on the meaning of human existence as well as on man's search for such a meaning. According to logotherapy, the striving to find a meaning in one's life is a primary motivation force on man. That is why I speak of a *will of meaning* in contrast to the pleasure principle on which Freudian psychoanalysis is centered. . . ." *Ibid.*, p. 166–167: "What man actually needs is not a tensionless state but rather the striving and struggling for some goal worthy of him. . . . I shall now turn to the detrimental influence of that feeling of which so many patients complain today, namely, the feeling of the total and ultimate meaninglessness of their lives . . . they are haunted by the experience of their inner emptiness, a void within themselves; they are caught in that situation which I have called the 'existential vacuum.'"
28. *Coll. Works.*, XVI, 40–41; XI, 336; X, 170.

the passions and other powers against the order of reason, the greater the mental disease of the soul. Hence the degree of disunity existing among humans follows a continuum; there does not exist a clear demarcation between neurosis and health, for the degree of neurosis will depend upon the degree of dissociation, and complete control of passions and will and perfect unity are not the marks of the psyche after the fall. In psychiatry and in society, however, only the extreme cases are considered diseases, but neither society nor psychiatrists are always in agreement upon the norm that measures the normality or abnormality in individuals. Every society, every age, and to some extent every distinct segment of society defines abnormality for itself; it is relative to the patterns of culture of the different societies and civilizations. Regarding this norm, Jung points out several interesting observations.

> To be normal is the ideal aim for the unsuccessful, for all those who are still below the general level of adaptation. But for people of more than average ability, people who never found it difficult to gain successes and to accomplish their share in the world's work—for them the moral compulsion to be nothing but normal signifies the bed of Procrustes— deadly and unsupportable boredom, a hell of sterility and hopelessness. Consequently, there are just as many people who become neurotic because they are merely normal, as there are people who are neurotic because they cannot become normal. . . . To be a social and adapted person has no charms for one to whom such an aspiration is child's play. . . . The needs and necessities of mankind are manifold. So also with normality and adaptation.[29]

In other words, a purely social adaptation is not the solution for those who aim high, with the possible exception of the average person; and yet, there are many talents and possibilities in our nature which, although real, are nevertheless usually unrealized by the majority. So Jung asserts that there are vast

29. *Ibid.,* XVI, 70. Cf. Erich Fromm, *Psychoanalysis and Religion* (1950), p. 83. "While they are healthy from the standpoint of adjustment, they are more sick than the neurotic person from the standpoint of the realization of their aims as human beings."

masses of the population who, despite their notorious unconsciousness, never get anywhere near to neurosis. "The few who
are smitten by such a fact are really persons of higher type who,
for one reason or another, have remained too long on a primitive level. Their nature does not in the long run tolerate per-
sistence in what is for them an unnatural torpor."[30]

But this does not always seem to be the case, and since neurosis is "anything but" there are neurotics who are far from
being of higher type. There are neurotic specimens who are
persons of low type: "The hysterical neurotics in our psychi-
atric practice usually do not possess a sharp and penetrating
intellect, but a mediocre one,"[31] Terruwe says. Jung knows
this too well, for by claiming neurotics to be of higher type
he is, above all, relating neurosis to the process of individuation. Neurosis then appears as a necessary stage man has to go
through in order to attain a higher goal. Growth and wholeness
require much more than humdrum conformism. Disunity in
this case refers to wholeness achieved by development and
growth, a development and growth which is intimately related
to spiritual values.

Therapy

The essential mark of neurosis is dissociation and, accordingly, the main therapeutical problem is how to integrate this
dissociation; how to unite and make a whole out of the diversity of the conscious and unconscious factors which make up
the totality of human personality and are, however, working
independently or are simply underdeveloped. The analyst has
to establish a relationship with both halves of his patient's

30. *Coll. Works,* VII, 182. Cf. Thomas Aquinas, *Summa Theol.,* I, q. 49, a.
3 ad 5: "The good of man as regards the senses is not the good of man as
man—that is, in regard to reason; and more men seek good in regard to the
senses than good according to reason."
31. A.A.A. Terruwe, *op. cit.,* p. 72. Again she says, "There exists also a
relation between repression and intelligence. . . . It can be stated in general
that the more intelligent the patient, the more deeply the repressive action
will penetrate and the more profound the pathological disturbance" (p.
51).

personality and its latent possibilities—not merely with one half by suppression of the other half. This is just what many patients are doing, for the exclusively rationalistic approach of modern thought leaves man with no alternative.[32] The unconscious is frequently disregarded or ignored.

Neurosis affects the deepest recesses of the human psyche. As a result of the agony produced by the disease, the neurotic may find himself in despair, for he has failed to read the meaning of his existence. He is therefore eager to discover somebody who will reassure him, dispel his misgivings, and help to rebuild a new faith, that is to say, to give meaning, form, and unity to the confusion of his neurotic soul. For this reason, the personality of the doctor, whom the patient trusts, has a curative effect; it is a great healing factor because the shattered existence of the sick demands all the resources of the doctors' capabilities and not personal tricks. If the patient wishes to get unity with himself he has to be united to the doctor first; and if the doctor wants to guide another he must feel with the person's psyche. Only the wounded physician heals; to cure wounds he has to be wounded first. Thus one can easily see what it means to the patient when he can confide his experiences to an understanding doctor. His conscious mind finds in him the moral support he needs, no longer does he stand alone in the battle; he is already united to the doctor. "We have learned to place in the foreground the personality of the doctor himself as a curative or harmful factor; and that what is now demanded is his own transformation—the self-education of the educator. Consequently, everything that occurred in the objective level in the history of our psychology—confession, elucidation, education—passes to the subjective level; in other words, what happened to the patient must now happen to the doctor, so that his personality shall not react unfavorably on the patient."[33]

Therefore therapy makes higher demands on the mental and moral stature of the doctor than a mere application of a

32. *Coll. Works,* X, 286; XVI, 131; VII, 230.

33. *Ibid.,* XVI, 74. Cf. Ibid., XVI, XVI, 88, 132; XVII, 140; XI, 331; X, 159. *Memories, Dreams, Reflections,* pp. 132–133: "Though there is treatment known as 'minor psychotherapy,' in any thoroughgoing analysis the whole personality of both patient and doctor is called into play. There are

routine technique. Naturally a wide knowledge of every aspect of the human psyche is also essential. Science, understanding, and love build up the bridge which leads the sick to a healthy new insight: "Yet seeing the patient grow better as the result of being loved makes it a joy for the therapist to give him his love. It is here that the therapist gets irrefutable evidence of what Christianity has known for ages, namely, that love heals and truth frees.""[34]

And since unity is the goal of therapy the doctor cannot exclude in advance any element of the total pattern of personality. And as every individual is marked by traits of his own, each new therapeutical case should constitute a fresh experience, because the attainment of wholeness assumes in every one traits of irreducible individuality. Hence the fundamental rule for the therapist should be to consider each case as unique and new. He must follow nature as a guide, and what the doctor then does is less a question of treatment than developing the creative possibilities latent in the patient himself. Individual nature rather than art is Jung's first principle of therapy. For example, he tells of the case of an intelligent patient, a woman who looked to him rather a queer customer. The therapy was not hitting the mark, and finally he resolved to speak about it at the next opportunity to his patient, who had not failed to notice this fact. The next night Jung had the following dream: "I was walking along a country road through a valley lit by evening sun. To my right, standing on the steep hill, was a castle, and on the topmost tower, on a kind of balustrade, sat a woman. In order to see her properly I had to bend my head back so far that I got a crick in the neck. Even in my dream I recognized the woman as my patient."[35] From this Jung concluded that if he had to look up so much in the

---

many cases which the doctor cannot cure without committing himself. When important matters are at stake, it makes all the difference whether the doctor sees himself as a part of the drama, or cloaks himself in his authority. In great crises of life, in the supreme moments when to be or not to be is the question, little tricks of suggestion do not help. Then the doctor's whole being is challenged."

34. A.A.A.Terruwe, *op. cit.,* p. 133.
35. *Coll. Works,* VII, 110.

dream, he must obviously have looked down on his patient in reality. From that day on the therapy went ahead beyond all expectation. The compensatory function of individual dreams saved this therapy.

Naturally, the personality of the doctor needs the collaboration and help of the patient who is the one to be cured. Especially for young people Jung accepts Freud's and Adler's therapeutical theories as relatively valid. Psychoanalysis has helped many people and Adler discovered that neurosis is teleologically oriented. In establishing this, Adler has won for himself no small credit. But Freud's and Adler's therapies are insufficient when the therapy demands a positively healthy approach to life, for their exclusive concern with instincts fails to satisfy the deeper spiritual needs of the patient. They do not give enough meaning to life, and it is meaning that liberates. In addition, these theories taken as exclusively approaches to therapy can prevent the understanding, discovery, and exploration of other roads: "An exclusively sexual interpretation of dreams and fantasies is a shocking violation of the patients' psychological material: infantile sexual fantasy is by no means the whole story, since the material also contains creative elements, the purpose of which is to shape a way out of the neurosis. This natural means of escape is now blocked . . . the result is spiritual desolation."[36] This is why it is so important to observe the individual nature of every patient and not to try to steer the therapy within the principles of any "nothing but" theory of neurosis. For example, Morton Prince, in his *Unconscious* tells the case of a phobia—the "bell tower Phobia" —directly connected to guilt as a consequence of a wrong ethical judgment. The patient, a woman, was cured when she was able to resolve her abnormal and irrational guilt. And Morton Prince writes a footnote insisting that sex was not involved in the phobia. At the end of the footnote he says: "This is perhaps made necessary by the violent shaking of the heads of my Freudian friends that I noticed at this point during presentation of this case before the American Psychological Association."[37]

36. *Ibid.*, XVI, 134. Cf. X, 288; XI, 330.
37. Morton Prince, *The Unconscious* (New York, 1921), pp. 392–393.

His Freudian friends did not want to accept guilt as the root underlying the phobia, but sex. The "nothing but" sex's theory of neurosis seems to be a hindrance for the therapy of many neuroses—for all neuroses not caused by abnormal sex.

For many neurotics, life has lost its meaning; this implies that life itself has no meaning. Or it implies, perhaps, that neurosis presupposes a wrong attitude toward life, and the neurosis is warning the ego of its mistaken view. Without neurosis there is no awareness of disease nor possibility of healing. And since the attitude of life depends upon philosophical tenets, therapy requires a reexamination of the basic principles governing human life. To cure a patient it is necessary to touch upon man and life as a whole, including the deepest issues and traditional ideas which influence the psyche. Jung says that nobody can conceive the moral, ethical, philosophical, and religious conflicts that crop up at the problem of neurosis: the facts surpass the imagination.[38] Caruso seems to agree with him when he says: "Just as heresy in religion extends its religious significance to all aspects of life, the 'life heresy' implicit in neurosis is not just an aberration as it were of 'hygiene' but also of ethics and metaphysics."[39] And an aberration of ethics and metaphysics means a mistaken idea of values, a transmutation of the hierarchical subordination of them, thus upsetting the complex unity of man. The lack of meaning of life is often the consequence of the choice of relative values as the ultimate goal of life. Naturally, since relative values cannot replace absolute ones, in the long run the neurotic finds himself frustrated and empty; relative values do not fill the craving of our heart. Accordingly, life loses its meaning. The vital "heresy" has taken its toll. A spiritual philosophy is not a luxury but a necessity if we wish to help permanently a disillusioned personality. The price of unity requires a new system of values. Hence a man's philosophy of life forms the counterpole to the psychologically conditioned psyche, and it ultimately determines the patient's fate. It shapes the spirit of therapy and the doctor must search for the philosophical ideas that best corre-

38. *Coll. Works,* XVI, pp. 76–78.
39. Igor Caruso, *op. cit.,* p. 41.

spond to the patient's emotional states.[40]

And since neurosis presupposes a false suffering, a suffering for a condition that "ought not to be," one of the goals of therapy is to acknowledge the nongenuine suffering of neurosis, the suffering that dissociates and tears man apart, and to try to make the suffering meaningful, a suffering that unites man with his fellow men, with God, and with himself. And though that may seem to cause the individual more suffering, this suffering is genuine and from something real. Genuine suffering is therapeutical and cures; nongenuine suffering does not cure, nor does it produce the desired effect. And since nobody likes to suffer, courage is therefore needed, for "if we want to cure a neurosis you have to risk something. To do something without taking a risk is merely ineffectual, as we know only too well. A surgical operation for cancer is a risk too, and yet it has to be done. For the sake of better understanding I have often been tempted to advise my patients to think of the psyche as a subtle body in which subtle tumors can grow."[41]

Virtues

The neurotic's self-defense mechanism represses the false conscience into the unconscious. Consequently, the patient is not totally aware of the transmutation of the hierarchy of values implicit in many neuroses, nor of the mechanism of projection which burdens others with faults of our own. Therefore humility and self-knowledge are therapeutical prerequisites if the neurotic wishes to clarify and correct a repressed conscience and modify a false ethical attitude. Even in psychoanalytical therapy the resistance that neurotics oppose to the process of analysis can only be overcome with humility and patience. The resolution of the problem of the shadow requires also a similar attitude: "As long as man fails to acknowledge his own immoral and dangerous forces, he will remain on the defensive towards them. But the acknowledgement of the shadow is seldom a

40. *Coll. Works,* XVI, 78–80.
41. *Ibid.,* XI, 341.

smooth and easy process, and it cannot be done at all by merely meditating about responsibility . . . man must experience its progressive discovery and eventual adaptation in his heart, in his flesh and blood."⁴² Therapy requires much more than a mere intellectual confrontation with the shadow, a pure descriptive speculative analysis of its nature; it requires a vital, prudent, and courageous approach to its evils, which, as explained before, requires humility, fortitude, and patience.

When there is resentment (or even worse, hatred) at the root of neurosis, then the tormented soul can only find its cure through forgiving and forgetting; forgiving the enemy often is not enough, it has to be followed by forgetting the offense. Then the dissociated soul, separated from his brothers by hatred, is united to them again by love and comes alive anew from spiritual death; the result of love is healing and union: "Healing," Jung says, "may be called a religious problem. In the sphere of the social or natural relations, the state of suffering may be civil war, and this state is to be cured by the Christian virtue of forgiveness and love of one's enemy. That which we recommend, with the conviction of good Christians, as applicable to external situations, we must also apply inwardly in the treatment of neurosis."⁴³ These words sound similar to those of St. John when he says: "We know that we have passed from death to life, because we love the brethren. He who does not love abides in death. Everyone who hates his brother is a murderer" (1 John 3:13–16). There is no possibility to heal a soul wounded by hatred but by its opposite, by love. Love heals because it unites; hatred sickens because it separates.

Passions

It may occur at times that the source of the rising of the shadow rests on the subordination of the intellect to the powerful emotional passions of man, as a consequence of making pleasure independent to rational judgments and spiritual goals.

42. Igor Caruso, *op. cit.,* p. 120.
43. *Coll. Works,* XI, 341.

Then, as Jung says, a mere suppression of the shadow is as little a remedy as beheading would be for headaches. Passions, emotions, and pleasure are valuable human elements when they operate in the right fashion. For this reason, Aquinas—against Cicero, who calls the passions "diseases of the soul,"—says that passions are not called diseases of the soul save when they are not controlled by reason.[44] Hence, a psychotherapy wishing to give up the making of relative values into an absolute must allow all values to be recognized clearly, and then experience all of them without violence and compulsion in hierarchical subordination to reason. As pointed out before, ignorance of ethical principles and even of the most elemental factors of psychology is at the root of some neuroses: "There is no emotional rapport possible with energy neurotics when it concerns the emotions that have been repressed. Their responses lack the natural feeling tone. If one lets one's feeling go out to them, one is confronted by a wall, impenetrable and unyielding. . . . The energy neurotic is a lonely individual . . . so preoccupied with himself that he is not aware of his loneliness."[45] Their deep ignorance of psychology prompts them to suppress what they need most: their feelings. They are senseless people who wish to live as if they were plants. Healing and integration can be achieved only at the expense of radical change in the psychological viewpoint concerning man.

Finally, since we observe that pride and egoism are the causes of many neuroses, generosity, boundless love, and humility are required to oppose them. For egoism is one of the most tangible evils of the neurotic state: "If I wish to effect a cure of my patients," Jung remarks, "I am forced to acknowledge the deep significance of their egoism."[46] For example, he tells the case of a man about thirty, very clever and highly intellectual, who wrote an accurate psychoanalytic autobiography of his illness and who could not understand why, with his insight, he was not cured: "Please tell me what it is I have overlooked or I am still repressing," he asked. Actually what he had overlooked was to

44. Thomas Aquinas, *Summa Theol.*, I–II, q. 85, a. 3 ad 4; I–II, q. 24, a. 2.
45. A.A.A.Terruwe, *op. cit.*, p. 80.
46. *Coll. Works*, XI, 341.

mention that he was spending the winter in St. Moritz, and the summer at. Nice, at the expense of a woman, a thirty-six-year-old teacher in a council school. "She saved the money by stinting herself, naturally in the hope of a later marriage, which this delightful gentleman was not even remotely contemplating. Don't you think, I asked, that the fact that you are financially supported by this woman might be one of the chief reasons why you are not cured? . . . He was one of many who believe that morals have nothing to do with neurosis and that sinning on purpose is not sinning at all, because it can be intellectualized out of existence." The patient was only a so-called intellectual who believed so much in the power of reason that he even though he could unthink a wrong he had committed. The power of reason, however, cannot violate the feeling values.[47] In other words, we cannot violate without impunity the order of nature; nature reacts, as in Newton's third law, and to every conscious abuse there corresponds an unconscious reaction resulting in neurosis. A "moral" neurosis can be nature's healthy reaction to a false ethics; it warns us of something we are missing or misinterpreting. It is obvious that in this particular case the only possible therapy was a revamping of the patient's ethical viewpoint, followed by a new pattern of behavior more in accord with healthy moral principles.

Religion and Therapy

"Practical experience," Jung says, "shows that many neuroses are caused primarily by the fact that people blind themselves

47. *Ibid.*, XVII, 98–99. From the ethical point of view, a material sin is never advisable. But what about the therapeutical viewpoint? Let us quote the advice of an experienced psychiatrist: "We want to draw the attention that one must not counsel a patient to commit a material sin. This is self-evident from a moral viewpoint, but also, at least according to our therapeutical understanding, from a mental viewpoint. If neurotic patients are advised and prompted to do certain things, their irascible appetite is necessarily brought into action with the result that again they begin to repress, though perhaps in opposite direction from before. The result will then be the reverse: instead of providing relief, the fear, which again has been repressed, becomes worse" (A.A.A. Terruwe, *Psychopathic Personality and Neurosis* [New York, 1958], pp. 159–160 fn.).

to their own religious promptings because of the childish passion for rational enlightment. The religious attitude *per se* . . .
can hardly be overrated."[48] Thus the reason for this contemporary destitution resides in the purely intellectual approach to
man that disregards the needs of the unconscious and makes
man as such into an absolute: "We no longer have any fear of
God and believe that anything is to be judged by human stan-
dards. This 'hybris,' that is, this narrowness of consciousness,
is always the shortest way to an insane asylum. . . . We are still
as possessed by our autonomous psychic contents as if they were
gods. Today they are called phobias, compulsions, and so forth,
or in a word, neurotic symptoms. The gods have become diseases."[49] The source behind the manifestation of these diseases
is subtle and may be hidden even to the therapist, for their
roots rest in a religious connotation of which the patient is
unaware because it is spiritual, difficult to detect, and in many
instances lies in the unconscious. Mircea Eliade expresses this
crucial plight in eloquent words:

> From one point of view it could almost be said that in the
> case of those moderns who proclaim that they are nonreli-
> gious, religion and mythology are "eclipsed" in the darkness
> of their unconscious—which means, too, that in such men
> the possibility of reintegrating a religious vision of life lies at
> a great depth. Or, from the Christian point of view, it could
> also be said that nonreligion is equivalent to a new "fall" of
> man—in other words, that nonreligious man has lost the
> capacity to live religion consciously, and hence to understand
> and assume it; but that, in his deepest being, he still retains
> a memory of it, as, after the first "fall," his ancestors, the
> primordial man, retained intelligence enough to enable him
> to rediscover the traces of God that are visible in the world.
> After the first "fall" the religious sense descended to the level
> of the "divided consciousness"; now, after the second, it has
> fallen even further, into the depths of the unconscious; it
> has been "forgotten."[50]

48. *Coll. Works,* XVI, 46.
49. *Ibid.,* XIII, 37.
50. Mircea Eliade, *The Sacred and the Profane,* p. 213.

In these instances disunity means separation from God, our most important principle; hence, the therapy should revolve around religion. Jung says that of his many hundred of patients, every one of them felt ill because he had lost what the living religions of every age have given to their followers, and none of them was really cured who did not regain his religious outlook.[51] For example, he tells of one treatment he began only after the patient had observed the first series of about three hundred and fifty dreams. Then he got the whole picture of his upsetting illness: "Whenever he tried to be disloyal to his experience or to deny the voice, the neurotic condition instantly came back. He simply could not 'quench the fire' and finally he had to admit the incomprehensibly numinous character of his experience. He had to confess that the unquenchable fire was 'holy.' This was the *sine qua non* of his cure."[52]

Why is religion such an important factor for the therapy of neurosis? Neurosis affects the totality of man, and religion is the strongest and most original of all his spiritual activities; it influences man in the highest degree, even though we may not be conscious of it. Every neurosis is the consequence of suppression, abuse, or distortion of the fundamental values of man which destroy the unity of man. And since the highest dominant role in life corresponds to religion, which unites man to the First source of life and final end of our existence, religion, neurosis, and therapy are necessarily connected and interwoven. Depth psychology has discovered the profound therapeutical implication of some archetypes connected to religion, as Jung has show regarding the archetype of the self, and Caruso regarding the "archetype bringing salvation." This archetype, he says, is the central factor in any psychotherapy, for it makes possible psychotherapy for the neurotic, as well as the analyst; neurosis searches for a redeemer, and depth psychology reveals the archetype of redemption alive within us.[53] Therefore, the emotional disturbances of the patient should activate the corresponding religious and philosophical factors

51. *Coll. Works,* XI, 334.
52. *Ibid.,* XI, 43.
53. Igor Caruso, *op. cit.,* pp. 84, 213, 216; *Coll. Works,* XVI, 121; XI, 172.

in both the therapist and patient. Religions are not enemies of the sick but, on the contrary, they are psychotherapeutic systems in the truest sense of the word, as was explained before. The spiritual bestows fresh vitality to the anemic life of neurotics; faith consoles the believer and unites our intellect to God who is light; hope reassures him and unites the neurotic with the future as possible and attainable; charity fills his heart with new expectations and unites him to God, and through God to all our fellowmen. God is the ultimate source of all unity.

For some, Jung says, Catholicism is the best answer to their needs; for others, the solution lies in Protestantism, Buddhism, or any religious manifestation that fits the concrete psychological spiritual needs. But all religions, not only Christianity—including the primitive, with their magical ritual—are forms of psychotherapy that treat and heal the suffering of the soul, and the suffering of the body caused by the soul. Therapists should search for the religion that corresponds to the patient's emotional states.[54] This is not equivalent to religious relativism, but a simple psychological observation of a psychiatrist accustomed to look at the individual needs of patients—not at the objective evaluation of the different religions as such.

The therapy involving religion is difficult and painful, for deep religious analysis claims the totality of man. Religion, as the most important factor, subordinates all human activity to its service. The lower appetite must be subject to reason, and now reason itself must be subject to God, which usually demands a radical alteration in the pattern of behavior, a radical revision of the human values, and a radical change of the

54. *Coll. Works,* XVI, 80, 16; XI, 347. Every religion presupposes and gives to its followers a certain psychological attitude. For example, Jung says, regarding complexes: "Professor Murray of Harvard University has shown on the basis of extensive statistical material . . . thus confirming my own previously published experiences . . . that the incidence of complexes is, on the average, highest among Jews; second come Protestants; and Catholics third." Jung attributes these statistical observations to the archetypal images of the Pope as the Supreme ruler of Christendom and of the Church which receive the projections. "The Catholic who has been freed from personal ties to his parents returns fairly easy to the mysteries of the Church."

ultimate aims of our existence—from the human to the divine, from immanence to transcendence. This requires an absolute surrender, only possible with the help of grace and the acceptance of suffering. Religious therapy is equivalent to deep spiritual surgery, from which ensues, as its natural consequence, a profound psychological transformation.

The lack of religion is the source of many neuroses, but the conversion does not appear necessarily correct, for the possession of religion is not an infallible guarantee of mental health. There are neuroses caused not by the lack of religion, but by a variety of different agents explained above, like trauma, worries, failures, family difficulties, and so forth, not necessarily related to religion. We observe sincere and devout people who are suffering from scrupulosity, fears, obsessions, compulsions, and many symptomatic manifestations of mild or acute neurosis. How is it then possible to explain these facts? First, on psychological grounds, a religious man before being religious is simply a man, for any specific property presupposes first the existence of the properties that are generic; rationality cannot be given without animality. In like manner a Christian cannot be a Christian unless he is first a man who is, as such, capable of being smitten by the physical and mental diseases afflicting the human condition. Hence some neuroses are caused by factors and circumstances foreign to religion, which in these conditions is powerless to prevent their occurrence, let alone cure them. In this situation disunity does not imply the lack of union of man with God, but merely a dissociation between the different powers of man which tear him apart.

But since grace and nature make up a Christian, who is the unique existent whole, there must always exist a close relationship between grace and nature, religion and man. Therefore it is important to emphasize the following observation. Grace presupposes nature, as faith presupposes an intellect, and other virtues presuppose their corresponding powers. Hence, the healthier the nature, the greater the possibility for holiness and religious development. If in individual cases the parallelism "nature-grace" obviously fails, it fails because pure mental health as such (in the sense the majority takes this concept) is not identical with holiness. A good man is not necessarily a good Christian, and yet it is easier for a gifted nature to become a good Christian and virtuous man than for a crippled nature or dissolute individual. And it is easier for a mentally healthy man to become holy than for a neurotic; the supreme union of man to God is helped by the unity of man in himself: "Anxiety is the soul's greatest enemy, sin excepted," St. Francis of Sales says. "Nothing aggravates evil and hinders good so much as anxiety and worry." And he adds: "The wise man said: 'sadness has killed many, and there is no profit in it' (Eccles. 30:25). . . . Unholy sorrow disturbs the soul, disquiets her, arouses vain fears, overpowers the brain and makes it drowsy, deprives the soul of wisdom, resolution, judgment, and courage, and crushes her strength; in short . . . it deprives the soul of all suppleness, rendering all her faculties of no avail and powerless."[55] And St. Theresa of Avila, doctor in spirituality in the sixteenth century and great connoisseur of the psychology of women, wrote the following warning about neurotic nuns: "And as their illness, not being a fever, forces them neither to keep bed nor to call a physician, the prioress must be their physician, for the disease is more hurtful to perfection than is theirs who, in danger of their life, remain in their beds. The second reason is, that in other illnesses they either recover or die; but it is very rarely that people recover from this or die of it either, but they lose all sense, and that is a death which kills all the others."[56] She advises not to admit nuns subject to neurosis, and to employ them largely in the duties of the house, so that they may have no opportunity of giving way to their imagination, for all the mischief is there.

Therefore, holiness is possible in individuals smitten by psychological weaknesses, as scrupulosity, sadness, fear, and so forth. But as such, these mental diseases are not helpful for holiness, but rather hindrances and even curses, whose disappearance fosters self-confidence and virtue and reassures Christians in their search for God.

55. St. Francis of Sales, *An Introduction to the Devout Life* (New York, 1923), pp. 266–269.
56. St. Teresa of Avila, *The Book of Foundations,* ch. VII, n. 11.

Conclusion

Neurosis is not for the sake of disunity and unhappiness but for the sake of unity and happiness. Thus the ultimate purpose of therapy is unity, a unity that comes with joy and peace, because there is no such thing as a human heart that does not crave for peace. Even when men are plotting to disturb the peace, it is merely to fashion a new peace nearer to the heart's desire. As Augustine says, it is not because they dislike peace as such. It is not that they love peace less, but that they love their kind of peace more.

The peace which the neurotic yearns for is total peace with himself, with his neighbor, with society, with his Maker. Those who are unhappy insofar as they are unhappy are not in peace because they lack unity, the calm of that order which is beyond storm. The total peace which neurotics yearn for is the peace Augustine describes:

> The peace, then, of the body lies in the ordered equilibrium of all its parts; the peace of the irrational soul, in the balanced adjustment of its appetites; the peace of the reasoning soul, in the harmonious correspondence of conduct and conviction; the peace of body and soul taken together, in the well-ordered life and health of the living whole. Peace between a mortal man and his Maker consists in ordered obedience, guided by faith, under God's eternal law; peace between man and man consists in regulated fellowship. The peace of a home lies in the ordered harmony of authority and obedience between the members of a family living together. The peace of the political community is an ordered harmony of authority and obedience between citizens. Peace, in its final sense, is the calm that comes from order. Order is an arrangement of like and unlike things whereby each of them is disposed in its proper place."[57]

The ultimate end of a perfect therapy is perfect peace.

---

57. St. Augustine, *The City of God,* Bk. 19, ch. 13.

VIII

Nietzsche and Jung

If we expect to attain a full understanding of a philosophical system, the chief requirement is an understanding of the ideas and the principles which are its foundation. This is essential but it is not enough. It is also of paramount importance to know the psychology of the thinker, to know the man, and to know his life.

In the case of Nietzsche this is particularly relevant, due to the unusual personality of the German philosopher, the tragedy of his life, and the insanity which befell him at the end of his life. The full explanation of his philosophy and particularly of his last works, which otherwise would be incomplete, requires the investigation of the human elements mentioned above. In this chapter we are trying to analyze some of the landmarks of Nietzsche's thought in connection with depth psychology, his life, and his last disability. We have found in the writing of Jung the main ideas and psychological principles we needed for the understanding of Nietzsche's personality.

If our goal is to understand Nietzsche's psychology and life, we should start by examining his ideas in *The Birth of Tragedy*, the first book he wrote, which contains a psychological study of Greek man with a metaphysico-artistic background.

The problem of suffering, the riddle of suffering, haunted Nietzsche until his death, as it had previously haunted the life of the Greeks. Aware of the terrors and horrors of our contingent existence, Nietzsche searches in the treasures of the Hellenic culture for a possible justification and solution to this bewildering human enigma. How is it possible to overcome the anguish which is congenital to our mortal life? The early Greeks knew and felt vividly the suffering of human existence, and consequently they had a pessimistic outlook on life. "For mortals, not to be born is better than to be born," was their realistic approach to existence, which Nietzsche illustrates by the old Hellenic legend of Silenus: "There is an ancient history that King Midas hunted in the forest a long time for the wise Silenus, the companion of Dionysus, without capturing him. When at last he fell into his hands, the king asked what was best of all and most desirable for man. Fixed and immovable, the demon remained silent; till at last, forced by the king, he broke out with a shrill laughter into these words: 'Oh wretched race of a day, children of chance and misery, why do ye compel me to say to you that it were most expedient for you not to hear? What is best of all is forever beyond your reach: not to be born, not to *be,* to be *nothing.* The second best for you, however, is soon to die."[1]

This was the attitude characteristic of early Greece, but neither Homer nor Nietzsche accept the primitive nihilism of Silenus, for although Homeric man knew the terrors and horrors of existence, in order to live he had to interpose the shining dream birth of the Olympian world between himself and them. Thus the gods, Nietzsche says, justify the life of man in that they themselves live it—the only satisfactory theodicy. Existence under the bright sunshine of gods is regarded as that which is desirable in itself, and the real grief of the Homeric man has reference to parting from it, especially to early parting. "So, it might be said, with a reversion of the Silenian wisdom, that 'to die early is worst of all for them, the second worst is—some day to die at all."[2]

But where does the root of such creation of gods lie? What makes the emergence of the Olympian gods possible? Perhaps there is no better way to introduce us to the solution than Aeschylus' sentence: "Say also this, thou curious stranger: what suffering this people must have undergone, in order to be able to become thus beautiful! But now follow me to the tragic play,

1. Friedrich Nietzsche, *The Birth of Tragedy, The Complete Works of Friedrich Nietzsche* (New York, 1924), p. 34.
2. *Ibid.,* pp. 35–36.

and sacrifice me in the temple of both the deities."[3] Suffering is the primordial root of creation, beauty its form, sacrifice, especially in the Attic tragedy, the outcome. Why? Because art, and not morality is for Nietzsche the properly metaphysical activity of man; the existence of the world is only justified as an aesthetic phenomenon: "The same impulse which calls art into being, as the complement and consummation of existence, seducing to a continuation of life, caused also the Olympian world to arise."[4] To the fearful world of suffering and contingency, of becoming, namely the Dionysian world, is opposed a world of appearance, of illusions and dreams, the Apollonian world, "until at last, by a metaphysical miracle of the Hellenic will, they appear paired with each other."[5]

These two opposite spheres are the expression of two fundamental psychological attitudes and experiences of the Greeks: the Apollonian, which stands for the state of rapt repose in the presence of a visionary world, the world of beautiful appearance designed as a deliverence from becoming; the Dionysian, which stands for strenuous becoming, grown self-conscious in the form of the rampant voluptuousness of the creator who is also conscious of the necessity of destruction. The Apollonian represents the world of dreams, the mastery of everything savage and untamed; while the Dionysian represents the world of frenzy, of highest exaltation, of unmeasured instinct, of identification with nature; it represents horror of annihilation of the Apollonian world; and, again, rapturous delight at its destruction. The Apollonian attitude strives for the eternal happiness of existence, in peaceful terms with himself and all creatures. The Dionysian attitude strives for creation, for the happiness of becoming, of constructing and destroying, a happiness that overcomes the sorrows of existence only in the annihilation of the beautiful world of appearance, in the pessimistic dissipation of illusions.

To these fundamental attitudes correspond two Olympian gods. Apollo is the deity of light, the god of all forming facul-

3. *Ibid.*, p. 187.
4. *Ibid.*, p. 35. Cf. *Ibid.*, p. 183.
5. *Ibid.*, p. 22.

ties, of the inner world of fantasies and dreams in which everything is measured, the glorious divine image of the principle of individuation. Dionysus is the god of drunkenness, of narcotic draught, of song and dance, of pure instinct and music, of primordial unity with nature, the opposite to individuation. He is the god of creation and destruction, of good and evil, of joy and glory, who frees himself from the full anguish of suffering by the redemptive world of appearance, by the Apollonian world of illusion and dream. Hence the Greek man, to the dark realm of suffering and becoming, opposes the serene realm of appearance and dreams which were paired one with the other by art, the true metaphysical activity of man.[6]

The Apollonian art vanquishes the suffering of the individual by the radiant glorification of the eternity of the phenomenon, beauty triumphs over suffering; in Apollo the redemption through appearance is consummated, and he shows us how the world of torment is necessary, that thereby the individual may be impelled to realize the redeeming vision.[7] But again, the Dionysian art makes us understand the joy in the annihilation of the individual, the ceaseless change of phenomena, the eternally creative primordial mother, eternally impelling to existence, self-satisfying eternally with this change of phenomena. Therefore the Dionysian and Apollonian are mutually complementary and dependent on each other. The Apollonian sphere of beauty, the world of appearance, originates as a consequence of the primordial oneness with nature and suffering. But at the same time, the Dionysian depends on the Apollonian, because the essence of the Dionysian lies in the continuous creation and destruction of the sphere of appearance.

Although the union of the opposites is realized through the

6. *Ibid.,* pp. 25–40; p. 10: "Art and not morality is set down as the properly metaphysical activity of man . . . the existence of the world is justified only as an aesthetic phenomenon."
7. *Ibid.,* p. 40; p. 128, pp. 127–128; p. 82: "From the smile of this Dionysus sprang the Olympian gods, from his tears sprang man." P. 130: "That striving of the spirit of music for symbolic and mythical manifestation, which increases from the beginning of lyric poetry to Attic tragedy, breaks off all of a sudden immediately after attaining luxuriant development, and disappears, as it were, from the surface of Hellenic art."

miracle of the aesthetic Hellenic will, Nietzsche ascribes to the Dionysian art of music the dominant role, for "the metaphysical delight in the tragic is a translation of the instinctively unconscious Dionysian wisdom into the language of the scene: the hero, the highest manifestation of the will, is disavowed for our pleasure, because he is only phenomenon, and because the eternal life of the will is not affected by his annihilation. 'We believe in eternal life,' tragedy exclaims; while music is the proximate idea of this life."[8]

Suffering, appearance, beauty, life, death, and the eternal life of the will in the ceaseless change of becoming, are the keys with which Nietzsche understands the features of the Greek man. But the Greeks, Nietzsche says, were not pessimistic, because they got the better of pessimism; they overcame pessimism and redeemed themselves from suffering by means of art, especially music.

In his later works Nietzsche did not essentially change the principles established in the *Birth of Tragedy*. However, he became gradually more and more Dionysian in his approach to life, morality, and aesthetics, developing this daring philosophy to its last consequences. We shall indicate some of the most important principles of these developments.

The Death of God

Nietzsche openly opposes the presence of a living God; God is dead, he says, perhaps because he is too spiritual and ambitious to accept anyone above himself. "If there were Gods," Nietzsche says in *Zarathustra*, "How could I endure it to be no God! Therefore there are no Gods."[9] God is dead, and Nietzsche boasts about his godlessness as if it were a virtue and his greatest wisdom: "Who is ungodlier than I, that I may enjoy his teach-

8. *Ibid.*, pp. 127–128; p. 54: "How does music appear in the mirror of symbolism and conception? It appears as will, taking the word in the Schopenhauerian sense i.e., as the antithesis of the aesthetic, purely contemplative and passive frame of mind."
9. F. Nietzsche, *Thus Spake Zarathustra*, p. 9.

ing?"[10] Perhaps he denies the existence of God to attribute to himself some of the qualities of the Omnipotent, especially the power of creation, which he refuses to yield to God. "Away from God and Gods did this will allure me; what would there be to create if there were—Gods!"[11] Is not Nietzsche, after all, the lyric poet, the man of imagination, the artist who rises effortlessly to the greatest heights, the one who creates the universe and man to the image of his own poetic dreams? "Could ye *create* a God?—Then, I pray you, be silent about all Gods! But ye could well create the superman. . . . Could ye *conceive* a God?—But let this mean Will to Truth unto you, that everything be transformed into the humanly conceivable, the humanly visible, the humanly sensible! Your own discernment shall ye follow out to the end!"[12]

Thus, Nietzsche's philosophy cannot be rooted in what he considers to be pure illusion, namely, God, but rather in the fullness of life, in the desire to live life to its plenitude, and to this goal—"God is our greatest danger," he asserts. But Nietzsche is too positive a thinker to be happy with the pure disappearance of God. The nostalgia of something absolute still rests in the inner recesses of his heart. Hence, to compensate for the demise of gods Neitzsche creates the Superman, the supreme sage, who knows neither God nor devil, the man who masters himself through blind obedience to instincts. *"Dead are all the Gods: now do we desire the Superman to live.*—Let this be our final will at the great noontide!—" And again, "Once did people say God, when they looked out upon distant seas; now, however, have I taught you to say, Superman."[13] Nietzsche rejects the gods, giving birth instead to the Superman.

Recurrence

Man's concept of the absolute cannot be completely uprooted. Men consciously or unconsciously wish to be happy even in this

10. *Ibid.,* pp. 207 and 316.
11. *Ibid,* p. 101.
12. *Ibid.,* p. 99.
13. *Ibid.,* pp. 91 and 98.

life, and to be forever, transcending thus the limitation of our mortal existence. And this is especially true in spiritual men, like Nietzsche. The idea of Eternal Recurrence first came to him in August, 1881. He made a note of the thought on a sheet of paper, with a postscript: "Six thousand feet beyond men and time! That day I happened to be wandering through the woods alongside of the lake Silvaplana. . . . It was then that the thought struck me. Looking back now, I find that exactly two months previous to this inspiration, I had an omen of its coming in the form of a sudden and decisive alteration in my tastes—more particularly in music. It would even be possible to consider all 'Zarathustra' as a musical composition."[14]

Nietzsche harbors in his heart the nostalgia of the absolute, he craves with pain for eternity and utters as though wounded by the desire: "Never yet have I found the woman by whom I should like to have children, unless it be this woman whom I love: for I love thee O Eternity!"[15] And again the poet moans, "O happiness, O pain! Oh break, thou heart! Ye higher men, do learn it, that joys want eternity.—Joys want the eternity of *all* things, they *want deep, profound eternity!*"[16] But how is it possible to attain eternity? Through recurrence, through eternal recurrence, through which "Everything goeth, everything returneth; eternally rolleth the wheel of existence. Everything dieth, everything blossometh forth again; eternally runneth on the year of existence. Everything breaketh, everything is integrated anew; eternally buildeth itself the same house of existence. All things separate, all things again greet one another; eternally true to itself the ring of existence!"[17]

Recurrence is not for everybody; for the miserable, its mere thought is even frightful; recurrence is only for the strong, for those who are able to face life with courage and strength, for those whose life is so valuable that a continually fresh repetition will be a happy thought to them. Recurrence, however,

14. *Ibid.,* pp. xv–xvi.
15. *Ibid.,* p. 280.
16. *Ibid.,* p. 397.
17. *Ibid.,* p. 266.

is not equivalent to the eternity of another life, but of this one, since other lives are pure illusions without existence. "But we do not all want to enter into the kingdom of heaven: we have become men—*so we want the kingdom of earth.*"[18]

Although Nietzsche says in *Zarathustra* and *Ecce Homo* that he was the first to teach the theory of recurrence, that he sought in vain for signs of tragic wisdom even among the great Greeks of philosophy, this is not actually the case. On the contrary, recurrence is well known in Greek mythology, which Nitezsche could hardly have ignored, and is also common all over the world. "The longing for eternity," Eliade says, "is a sort of parallel to the longing for paradise. To the wish to be always and naturally in a sacred place there corresponds the wish to live always in eternity by means of repeating archetypal actions. The repetition of archetypes shows the paradoxical wish to achieve an ideal form in the very framework of human existence."[19] The myth of paradise and recurrence, as all myths, presuppose an attempt to attain reality through the sacred, to which there corresponds a conscious or unconscious yearning for something which transcends our human limitation—for the unknown God.

Furthermore, modern psychiatry has discovered the primary importance of the "paradise archetype" as one of the unconscious and primordial desires of man. Caruso asserts:

> The longing for the state of innocence is at the same time a longing for what has been lost and a desire for what is to come. . . . Longing for the condition of paradise is a longing for the plenitude of being. . . . The total restoration of a condition of perfect pleasure is imaginable only in complete innocence, for guilt entails punishment and loss of pleasure. . . . Neurosis is thus governed by that archetype which links the collective unconscious with the primary state before the original sin; neurosis also attempts to overcome the tragic divorce between good and evil by repressing knowledge. Yet the "paradise archetype" is also a teleological force. We know

18. *Ibid.*, p. 387.
19. Mircea Eliade, *Patterns in Comparative Religion*, p. 408.

that the desire for innocence points not only to repression but also to faith and hope. The aim at innocence may, after all, also imply the assurance that existence will be abolished not by being destroyed, but by redemption of history; and that a redeemer has promised a Kingdom in which no longing, faith or hope shall be needed, but immediate knowledge in love.[20]

So, from the mythical point of view as well as from the psychological, recurrence and eternity call for an absolute being, and for the disappearance of time.

The Will to Power

The eternal recurrence of all things is the highest of all possible formulas to a Yea-saying philosophy. But, what is the significance of a Yea-saying philosophy? The acceptance of life as it is, not the pessimistic attitude of Schopenhauer, of humble resignation to sorrow, but rather a positive attitude towards the totality of life: a pessimism that through bold resolution transforms itself into optimism. "I realized that what my instincts most desired to attain was precisely the reverse of what Schopenhauer's instincts wanted—that is to say, a *justification of life,* even where it was most terrible, most equivocal, and most false: to this end I had the formula '*Dionysian*' in my hand. . . . Schopenhauer did not understand how to deify this will."[21]

Thus Nietzsche teaches us to attain optimism through pessimism, what he calls a tragic pessimism; the tragic man says yes to even the sharpest sufferings, for he is strong, deified enough to do so. Consequently the will to power is the highest affirmation, born of fullness, a yea-saying without reserve to suffering, to guilt, to all that is questionable and even strange in existence itself. To comprehend this, courage and strength are needed, for precisely to the degree in which courage dares to thrust forward one approaches the truth. Hence Nietzsche leads to its

20. Igor Caruso, *Existential Psychology*, pp. 83–84.
21. F. Nietzsche, *The Will to Power*, Vol. II, p. 390.

last consequences the philosophy of Dionysus, which transcending terror and pity realizes the eternal delight of becoming. Nietzsche's initial attitude in *The Birth of Tragedy* has blossomed here into the daring philosophy of the will to power, the philosophy of a tragic poet. And it is tragic because as Nietzsche himself says, the happiness of becoming is possible only in the annihilation of the real, and "with the annihilation of the most beautiful phenomena in the world of appearance, Dionysus' happiness reaches its zenith."[22] It is the will to power which makes life beyond good and evil, death and life, and all the opposites an eternal life. This is especially clear in the text with which he closes his book *The Will to Power*.

> A becoming which knows not satiety, or disgust, or weariness —this, my Dionysian world of eternal self-creation, of eternal self-destruction, this mysterious world of twofold voluptuousness; this, my "Beyond good and evil," without aim, unless there is an aim in the bliss of the circle, without will, unless a ring must by nature keep good will to itself—would you have a name for my world? A *solution* of all your riddles? Do ye also want a light, ye most concealed, strongest and most undaunted men of the blackest mid-night?—*This world is the Will to Power—and nothing else!* And even ye yourselves are this will to power—and nothing besides![23]

If recurrence manifests man's natural longing for eternity, the will to power corresponds to a desperate attempt to make sense out of life, to justify a human condition made up of sufferings, miseries, injustices, frustrations, and pain. To accept life as it is, without—using Nietzsche's own words—the joys of Christian hope, is the achievement of superior men, for pessimism and despair are logical sequels of human existence. Zarathustra teaches his disciples the importance of overcoming these conditions by self-mastery and lofty transcendence of all the opposites: "When ye are exalted above praise and blame, and your will would command all things, as a loving one's will:

22. F. Nietzsche, *The Birth of Tragedy, Introduction,* xxvii–xxviii.
23. F. Nietzsche, *The Will to Power,* Vol. II, p. 432.

there is the origin of your virtue."[24] And it is also the source of happiness, for "Beyond good and evil found we our island and our green meadow—we two alone!"[25] Self-mastery and transcendence are the virtues Zarathustra teaches superior men.

But is this lofty idea attainable? Is he not trying to surpass human capacity? Is it possible to live by sheer effort of the will overcoming thus torments and sufferings? Heroism is not always healthy, for "If heroism becomes chronic," Jung says, "it ends in a cramp, and the cramp leads to catastrophe or neurosis or both. Nietzsche got stuck in a state of high tension . . . for an ecstatic animal is a monstrosity. An animal fulfills the law of his own life, neither more nor less. We can call it obedient and 'good.' But the ecstatic bypasses the law of his own life, and behaves, from the point of view of nature, improperly. This impropriety is the exclusive prerogative of man, whose consciousness and free will can occasionally loose themselves *contra naturam* from their roots in animal nature. It is the indispensible foundation of all culture, but also of all spiritual sickness if exaggerated."[26]

Furthermore, heroism, if unnatural and chronic, may hide on occasions a mechanism of self-defense, a surrogate for a true attitude in regard to life. Then this heroic attitude is but an escape from reality, as happens, for instance, in all heroic neurotic solutions. Perhaps these reasons justify Hannah Arendt's strong criticism of the will to power in *The Human Condition:* "The will to power, as the modern age from Hobbes to Nietzsche understood it in glorification or denunciation, far from being a characteristic of the strong, is, like envy and greed, among the vices of the weak, and possibly even their most dangerous one."[27]

To accept things as they are, is the mark of a realistic and healthy psychology. But to make optimism out of pessimism, bliss out of pain, and eternity out of contingency, comes down to a dream, or at most, to a futile and absurd heroism which

24. F. Nietzsche, *Thus Spake Zarathustra,* p. 87.
25. *Ibid.,* p. 277.
26. *Coll. Works,* VII, 32.
27. Hannah Arendt, *The Human Condition* (New York, 1958), p. 182.

leads necessarily to disintegration. And in the particular case of Nietzsche, this is especially dangerous, because the danger lies hidden in the loftiness and poetic attraction of his extraordinary lyric imagination.

Christianity

Nietzsche did not spare any means to inflict a mortal wound on Christianity. He saw in this religion his first enemy, the antithesis of his philosophical principles and attitude of life. Hence, it is common to find in his writings (especially at the end of his life) a violent attack against Christianity. "Mankind reckons time from the *dies nefastus* when this fatality befell—from the *first* day of Christianity! *Why not rather from its last? From today*—the transvaluation of all values! . . ."[28] This antagonism should surprise no one, because Neitzsche himself suffered in his life a crucifixion of body and soul, and further because Neitzsche's intuitive soul became well aware of the significance of suffering, justification, redemption, salvation, and eternal happiness—all of them crucial both to him and the Christian man. His solution, however, is diametrically opposed to what Christianity proposes. Terrors and sufferings are redeemed by the will to power, not by Christ; beatitude is realized in the Eternal Recurrence, not in heaven; Zarathustra, the magician, replaces Christ; and the "false optimism" of Christian life gives way to the true philosophy of tragic pessimism. This antagonism is dramatic and clear in Nietzsche's own words, especially these, written towards the end of his life:

> Dionysus *versus* "Christ"; here you have the contrast. It is *not* a difference in regard to martyrdom—but the latter has a different meaning. Life itself—Life's eternal fruitfulness and recurrence caused anguish, destruction, and the will to annihilation. In the other case, the suffering of the "Christ as the Innocent One" stands as an objection against Life, it is the formula of Life's condemnation—Readers will guess that

28. F. Nietzsche, *The Antichrist* (New York, 1941), trans., H. L. Mencken, pp. 181–182.

the problem concerns the meaning of suffering; whether a
Christian or a tragic meaning be given to it. In the first case
it is the road to a holy mode of existence; in the second case
existence itself is regarded as sufficiently holy to justify an
enormous amount of suffering. The tragic man says yea even
to the most excruciating suffering; he is sufficiently strong,
rich, and capable of deifying, to be able to do this; the Christian denies even the happy lots on earth; he is weak, poor,
and disinherited enough to suffer from life in any form. God
on the cross is a curse upon Life, a signpost directing people
to deliver themselves from it; Dionysus cut into pieces is a
promise of Life: it will be forever born anew, and rise afresh
from destruction.[29]

But tragic pessimism is powerless to conquer the reality of
death, as explained before; the Eternal Recurrence accounts to
a frustrated nostalgia which tries in vain to overcome the contingency of human existence; and the Superman is simply a
poetic and mythical creation without true reality. "The Christian thought," Eliade says, "tended to transcend, once and for
all, the old themes of eternal repetition, just as it had under-
taken to transcend all the other archaic viewpoints by revealing
the importance of the religious experience of faith and that
of the value of the human personality."[30] Zarathustra is a
dream, the wish fulfillment of Nietzsche. It explains *how* Nietzsche wanted the universe and man to be, not *what* the universe
and man really are.

Psychology

Nobody acquainted with some of Nietzsche's important con-
tributions to philosophy can resist admiring the courage, the
poetic imagination, and the spirit of this outstanding German
thinker. "Whatever his weaknesses," Christopher Dawson says,
"Nietzsche was neither a time-server nor a coward. He at least
stood for the supremacy of spirit, when so many of those

29. F. Nietzsche, *The Will to Power*, Vol. II, p. 421.
30. Mircea Eliade, *Cosmos and History*, p. 137.

whose office it was to defend it had fallen asleep or had gone
over to the enemy. . . . He revolted against the blasphemies of
an age which degraded the personality and denied the power of
the spirit in the name of humanity and liberty."[31]

Nietzsche was a man of superior mind and superior will, a
man of spirit. This was, perhaps, his main danger, and the primary pscyhological factor which explains his philosophy. For
this spirit and the creative poetic imagination of his mind led
him to soar too high, with all the dangers presupposed by this
lofty and heroic altitude. "Do not will anything beyond your
power: there is a bad falseness in those who will beyond their
power. Especially when they will great things!" Zarathustra
advises his disciples. But he forgets the advice himself and the
gnome retorts with the warning: "O Zarathustra, it whispered
scornfully, syllable by syllable, 'thou stone of wisdom! Thou
threwest thyself high, but every thrown stone must fall! O
Zarathustra, thou stone of wisdom, thou sling-stone, thou star-
destroyer! Thyself threwest thou so high,—but every thrown
stone-must fall! Condemned of *thyself,* and to thine own re-
coil!"[32] Identification with heroic heights is death, a deep
plunge into the abyss. This is what Zarathustra teaches his
disciples, but unfortunately forgets himself. Nietzsche, as Zarathustra, tried to will beyond his capacity, risking the stone's
falling upon *himself.*

Nietzsche's dangerous aloofness is also the consequence of a
second false principle, namely, a false idea of instincts, for the
primordial requisite for a healthy man is a healthy psychology
of instincts. "Instinct," Jung says, "is not an isolated thing, nor
can it be isolated in practice. It always brings in its train archetypal contents of a spiritual nature, which are at once its foundation and its limitation. In other words, an instinct is always

---

31. Christopher Dawson, *Christianity and the New Age* (London, 1934), p.
13. Cf. p. 18. "For Nietzsche, who refused to surrender the spiritual element
in the Renaissance tradition, humanism is transcended in an effort to attain
to the superhuman without abandoning the self-assertion and the rebellious
freedom of the individual will—an attempt which inevitably ends in self-
destruction."
32. F. Nietzsche, *Thus Spake Zarathustra,* pp. 188–189, 354–355.

and inevitably coupled with something like a philosophy of life, however archaic, unclear, and hazy this may be. Instinct stimulates thought, and if a man does not think of his own free will, then we get compulsive thinking, for the two poles of the psyche, the physiological and the mental, are indissolubly connected."[33] Archetypes and instincts are interwoven, for the archetypes are the patterns of instinctual behavior. Archetypes, ideas, and instincts have to operate in harmonious correlation if we wish to secure healthy psychology in a man.

The explanation of Nietzsche's final collapse into insanity probably lies in a mistaken philosophy of instincts. He tried to live to its fullness the frenzy characteristic of the Dionysian instinctual state. But he misunderstood the nature of our primordial urges and repressed the content of the collective unconscious by trying to live beyond humanity, which led him to the destruction of his own personality. As Nietzsche himself says, the way of creation entails being burned in our own fire. Nietszche burned himself into ashes in a futile attempt to transcend the instinctual urge, but without getting warmth from the painful sacrifice.

First, he misunderstood the religious instinct of man, as is clearly manifested by his ideas in *The Birth of Tragedy*. For Nietzsche it was the power of the Hellenic art which was able to unite appearance and reality, suffering and joys, illusions and becoming. But neither art nor music is the solution of the Hellenic opposition; the aesthetic ability of the Greek man did not create the Olympian gods. It was rather the congenital religious instinct of man which was the main factor behind the creation of these gods. "The Dionysian satyr-feasts," Jung says, "according to every analogy, were a sort of totem-feast with an identification backward to a mythical ancestor or directly to the totem animal. The cult of Dionysus had . . . in any case exercised a very strong religious influence. . . . Aestheticism is a modern glass, through which the psychological mysteries of Dionysus are seen in the light they were certainly never seen or experienced by the ancients."[34]

33. *Coll. Works*, XVI, 81.
34. *Ibid.*, VI, 176.

Therefore, the aesthetic attitude shields one from being really concerned, from being personally implicated, which would be entailed by a religious understanding of the problem. But as the life of Nietzsche himself has shown, the aesthetic surrogate could not stand the test of time, and Dionysus seems to have taken vengeance upon Nietzsche, for in his later work, *Attempt at Self Criticism,* written in 1886, Nietzsche speaks as the initiated and disciple of his God. "But this was not the Nietzsche who wrote *The Birth of Tragedy;* at that time he was moved aesthetically, while he became Dionysian only at the time of writing Zarathustra, not forgetting that memorable passage with which he concludes his *Attempt at Self Criticism*: 'Lift up your hearts, my brother, high, higher! And neither forget the legs! Lift up also your legs, ye good dancers, and better still: let ye also stand on your heads!'"[35] Thus we are faced with the following paradox: although Nietzsche continually soars higher and higher in a desperate and futile attempt for transcendence, he is, nevertheless, never aiming at the true transcendent God—unless man himself is deified and made absolute. For all its importance the aesthetic instinct can never replace the religious one. In spite of his lofty and heroic exaltation, Nietzsche seems to have repressed his unconscious religious instinct.

Did he repress the archetype of the self? In all his works Jung has emphasized the influence of this archetype upon the conscious life of individuals. And for the Western man, he sees in Christ a symbol of the archetype of the self, a collective figure fulfilling the expectation of the unconscious. Consequent depth psychology has verified experimentally the truth of this important Jungian hypothesis. As Caruso says, neurosis searches for a redeemer, and the "archetype bringing salvation" is the central archetype in all psychotherapy. Therefore, let us ask, what was the extent and the role of the self and Christ in the life of Nietzsche? We are moving in the realm of conjecture, but Nietzsche, like Freud, reveals in his life all the peculiarities of a soul obsessed by Christianity, which suggests the significance of this archetype in Nietzsche's own life. A true atheist ignores

35. *Ibid.,* VI, 177–178.

religion and Christianity, but this is not the case of the German poet. Nietzsche gives the impression that he is fighting desperately against the emergence of the self as Christ. Nietzsche's identification of himself with Christ, as a result of his last insanity, are signs corroborating our assumption. Modern therapy has shown how deep in the inner recesses of our soul lies the need of a redeemer, even in cases of which we are unaware because it rests hidden in the unconscious.

Nietzsche seems also to have repressed those other sources of life that are characteristic of ordinary man. He tried to solve the human problem "by the idea of mastery, through the supreme sage who knows neither God nor devil. With Nietzsche man stands alone, as he himself did, neurotic, financially dependent, godless, and wordless; this is not the ideal for a real man who has a family to support and taxes to pay. . . . Can the neurotic philosopher prove to us that he has no neurosis? He cannot prove it even to himself."[36] Hence, although Nietzsche recommends in theory a blind obedience to instincts, he actually failed to do so in real life, and repressed them. "We must look very critically at the life of one who taught such yea-saying, in order to examine the effects of his teaching in the teacher's own life. When we scrutinize his life we are bound to admit that Nietzsche lived beyond instinct, in the lofty heights of heroic sublimity . . . until the tension shattered his brain. He talked the yea-saying and lived the nay. His loathing for a man, for the human animal that lived by instinct was too great. . . . Hence his life does not convince us of his teaching."[37]

[margin note: Just preach, don't alway follow.]

36. *Ibid.*, VII, 235. *Memories, Dreams, Reflections,* pp. 151–154: "Although I did not properly understand it then, I had observed in Freud the eruption of unconscious religious factors. Evidently he wanted my aid in erecting a barrier against these threatening unconscious contents. . . . Freud shows how the object succumbs to the drive, and Adler how man uses the drive in order to force his will upon the object. Nietzsche, helpless in the hand of his destiny, had to create a 'super-man' for himself. Freud, I conclude, must himself be so profoundly affected by the power of Eros that he actually wished to elevate it into a dogma—*aere perennius*—like a religious numen. It is no secret that 'Zarathustra' is the proclaimer of a Gospel, and here was Freud also trying to outdo the Church and to canonize a theory." 37. *Ibid.*, VII, 30.

Nietzsche wanted to live 6,000 feet beyond praise and blame, good and .evil, and, in consequence, he repressed the basic human instincts, symbolically expressed by this passage of *Zarathustra*: "Meanwhile, however, the higher men had awakened in Zarathustra's cave, and marshalled themselves for a procession to go to meet Zarathustra, and give him their morning greeting; for they had found when they awakened that he no longer tarried with them. When, however, they reached the door of the cave the noise of their steps having preceded them the lion started violently; it turned away at once from Zarathustra and roaring wildly, sprang towards the cave. The higher men, however, when they heard the lion roaring, cried all aloud as with one voice, fled back, and vanished in an instant."[38] The roaring lion of Zarathustra drove back into the cave of the unconscious all the instincts that were clamoring to live, suppressing thus their unconscious regulating influence, and dooming the ego to destruction. No man can live without instincts, and even "the 'higher' man wants to be able to sleep without chloral, to live in Naumburg and Basel despite 'fogs and shadows.' He desires wife and offspring, standing and esteem among the herd, innumerable commonplace realities, and not the least those of the Philistine."[39]

Nietzsche especially repressed the feeling of compassion, which he considers to be the virtue of weak men, not the strong, and which precipitated his final insanity and led him to catastrophe. The psychological cause of his neurosis and final psychosis lies therefore in the repression of the instincts and archetypes of the collective unconscious. Nobody can live without reli-

38. F. Nietzsche, *Thus Spake Zarathustra*, pp. 400–401.
39. *Coll. Works*, VII, 30. Cf. e.c., VIII, 80: "A good example of the suppression of the unconscious regulating influence can be found in Nietzsche's *Zarathustra*. The discovery of the 'higher' man, and also of the 'ugliest' man expresses the regulating influence, for the higher men want to drag Zarathustra down to the collective sphere of average humanity as it always has been, while the ugliest man is actually the personification of the counteraction. But the roaring lion of Zarathustra's moral conviction forces all these influences, above all the feeling of pity, back again into the cave of the unconscious. Thus the regulating influence is suppressed, but not the secret counteraction of the unconscious, which from now on becomes clearly noticeable in Nietzsche's writings."

gion, without society, without friends, without love, without compassion, and without guilt. The final triumph of Zarathustra, his detachment from compassion and from the higher men, represents the downfall of Nietzsche.

> *Fellow-suffering! Fellow-suffering with the higher men!* he cried out, and his countenance changed into brass. Well! That—hath had its time! My suffering and my fellow-suffering —what matter about them! Do I then strive after *happiness?* I strive after my *work!*
>
> Well! the lion hath come, my children are nigh, Zarathustra hath grown ripe, mine hour hath come:—
>
> This is *my* morning, my day beginneth: *arise now, arise, thou great noontide!*
>
> Thus spake Zarathustra and left his cave, glowing and strong, like a morning sun coming out of gloomy mountains.[40]

The archetypes of the collective unconscious were left behind, in the cave of Nietzsche's unconscious, repressed by the roaring of Zarathustra's lion.

Life

This is the end of a great poem, of a dream; namely, Zarathustra. But how different are Nietzsche's own life and the life of Zarathustra, his dream! The life of Nietzsche was a continuous and uninterrupted failure, a life of such total rejection that no lesser man could have possibly endured. He suffered disappointments and loss of friends, loneliness, injustices, many external and internal trials. "His friends," his sister says, "caused him many disappointments, which were the more bitter to him, inasmuch as he regarded friendship as such a sacred institution; and for the first time in his life he realized the whole horror of that loneliness to which, perhaps, all greatness is condemned. But to be forsaken is something very different from deliberately choosing blessed loneliness . . . what he complained of most was his spiritual condition—that indescribable forsakenness—to

---

40. F. Nietzsche, *Thus Spake Zarathustra*, pp. 401–402.

which he gives such heartrending expression in *Zarathustra*."[41]

Not only his sister, but he himself explains the agony of his soul in dramatic words: "I spent a melancholy spring in Rome, where I only just managed to live—and this was not an easy matter." Furthermore, he describes pathetically the sorrow and sadness that were his companions at the time he wrote "The Night-Song," one of the most beautiful passages of *Zarathustra*. "About this time I was obsessed by an unspeakably sad melody, the refrain of which I recognized in the words, 'dead through immortality.'" And he says again: "My 'future' is the darkest thing in the world to me, but as there still remains a great deal for me to do, I suppose I ought rather to think of doing this than of my future, and leave the rest to *thee* and the gods."[42]

The ordinary reader cannot help admiring and pitying the greatness and courage of such a man who, through faithfulness to his principles, suffered martyrdom of soul and body. Both his faithfulness towards a wrong idea of instinct and the continuous blows and disappointments of life explain, at least partially, the gradual development of his last illness which finally developed into a form of incurable insanity.

Nietzsche's Illness

Some critics have condemned the totality of Nietzsche's philosophy as the work of a person who was always insane, but this does not seem to be the case. A. H. Knight says that the failure of *Zarathustra* to arouse interest even among his friends was the cause precipitating his last insanity. What seems more probable, however, is that Nietzsche's personality, by nature prone to mental disorders, gradually weakened, until the illness that was latent openly emerged into consciousness. Whatever the case may be, however, the fact remains that Nietzsche reveals in his symptoms all the characteristic marks of a true identification with the archetypes and the shadow, which was followed by the subsequent unconscious projection of these dis-

41. *Ibid.*, xvii–xxi.
42. *Ibid.*, xix–xxi.

integrated contents. This happens whenever a psychologically crippled personality is prey to abnormal manifestations of archetypes. The pathological element reveals itself by the way the individual reacts to them, and how he interprets them. The characteristic feature of a pathological reaction is, above all, identification with the archetypes. This produces a sort of inflation and possession by the emergent contents, so that they pour out in a torrent which no therapy can stop. And this is what happened to Nietzsche: "The psychology of Nietzsche's Zarathustra," Jung says, "also furnishes a good example. The difference between archetypes and dissociated products of schizophrenia is that the former are entities endowed with personality and charged with meaning, whereas the latter are fragments with vestiges of meaning—in reality, they are products of disintegration. Both, however, possess to a high degree the capacity to influence, control, and even suppress the ego personality, so that a temporary or lasting transformation of personality ensues."[43]

It is an immutable psychic law that when a projection comes to an end, it always returns to its origin. So when somebody hits on the idea that God is dead, or does not exist at all, the psychic God-image which is a dynamic part of our personality finds its way back into the subject and produces a condition of "God-almightiness," that is to say, all those qualities which are peculiar to fools and madmen, and therefore leads to catastrophe.[44] Hence there is a danger, especially in spiritual men, of making the ego the lord of the universe, since the contents that were formerly projected are now bound to appear as personal possessions of the ego. Nietzsche identified himself with God, and this, Jung says, because his God was dead. "The result of this demise was a split in himself, and he felt compelled to call the other self Zarathustra, or, at times, Dionysus. . . . The tragedy of Zarathustra is that, because his God died, Nietzsche himself became a God; and this happened because he was no atheist. He was too positive a nature to tolerate the urban neurosis of atheism. It seems dangerous for such a man

43. *Coll. Works*, VIII, 122.
44. *Ibid.*, X, 214.

to assert that God is dead: he instantly becomes the victim of inflation."[45] And this is what consciously or unconsciously happened to Nietzsche. As he poetically expresses it in *Zarathustra*: "Away with such a God! Better to have no God, better to set up destiny on one's own account, better to be a fool, better to be God oneself!"[46] Upon this idolatric identification, follows the subsequent inflation, the state of wild excitement, the puffed up personality, the ego almightiness: "Now am I light, now do I light, now do I fly; now do I see myself under myself. Now there danceth a God in me."[47] But this is not the end. Upon the identification of the ego with the archetypes follows a second identification, this time with the inferior part of our personality. The psychological observer knows this state as identification with the shadow, a phenomenon that occurs with great regularity at such moments of collision with the unconscious. This is what happened to Nietzsche: "God-almightiness does not make man divine," Jung asserts, "it merely fills him with arrogance and arouses everything evil in him. It produces a diabolic caricature of man, and this inhuman mask is so unendurable, such a torture to wear, that he tortures others. . . . Here we have the picture of the hysterical state of mind, of Nietzsche's 'pale criminal.' . . . That was my other side, my *alter ego,* my all too palpable shadow which can no longer be denied."[48]

Projection is a characteristic mark of the unconscious, because the undifferentiated contents of the collective unconscious are automatically projected upon external objects. This is what occurs with the archetypes and the shadow. The shadow appears in projection, and the projection changes the world

45. *Ibid.,* XI, 85–86. Cf. VII, 70: "Here we see the characteristic effect of the archetype: it seizes hold of the psyche with a primeval force and compels it to transgress the bounds of humanity. . . . This is the reason why men have always needed demons and cannot live without gods, except for a few particularly clever specimens of *Homo occidentalis* who lived yesterday or the day before, supermen whose 'god is dead' because they themselves have become gods—but tin-gods with thick skulls and cold hearts."
46. F. Nietzsche, *Thus Spake Zarathustra,* p. 319.
47. *Ibid.,* p. 45.
48. *Coll. Works,* X, 215; VII, 31–32. For Nietzsche's pale criminal, see *Thus Spake Zarathustra,* VI, "The Pale Criminal," pp. 40–43.

into a replica of one's own unknown face. Accordingly, the judgments we make of the objects and persons upon which we project our feelings are judgments concerning our own unknown unconscious personality. "A whole man knows that his bitterest foe, or indeed a host of enemies, does not equal that one worst adversary, the 'other self' who dwells in his own. Nietzsche had Wagner *in himself,* and that is why he envied his *Parsifal.*"[49] Even Nietzsche himself realizes the truth of this automatic mechanism when he says in *Ecce Homo* that whenever in his early books he spoke of Wagner or Schopenhauer, he meant himself. He was probably sincere, but he was unaware of the extent to which he projected his shadow and undifferentiated archetypes in his bitter criticisms, poisonous diatribes, accusations, and infatuated self-evaluation.

Anthony M. Ludovicy says that in writing *Ecce Homo,* it cannot be doubted the Nietzsche was in a state known in medicine as euphoria, that is to say, that state of highest well-being and capacity which often precedes a complete breakdown. But the contention that the matter, the substance, of his work reveals any sign whatsoever of waning mental health—he adds —is best contradicted by the internal evidence itself.[50] But this is not the contention of a psychiatrist of Jung's stature, who claims the opposite: "Nietzsche's *Zarathustra* is no longer philosophy at all; it is a dramatic process of transformation which has completely swallowed up the intellect. It is no longer concerned with thought, but, in the highest sense, with the thinker of thought—and this on every page of the book."[51] Indeed, God-almightiness, as shown before, clearly manifests itself in *Zarathustra.*

However, it is especially in the *Antichrist* and *Ecce Homo,* both written in Nietzsche's last years, that the projection of his shadow is more evident and clear.

I condemn Christianity: I bring against the Christian Church the most terrible of all the accusations that an

49. *Coll. Works,* VII, 34.
50. Anthony M. Ludovici, in *Ecce Homo,* p. x.
51. *Coll. Works,* XI, 547.

accuser has ever had in his mouth. It is, to me, the greatest
of all imaginable corruptions. . . . The Christian Church has
left nothing untouched by its depravity; it has turned every
value into worthlessness, and every truth into a lie, and every
integrity into baseness of soul. Let any one dare to speak to
me of its "humanitarian" blessings! Its deepest necessities
range it against any effort to abolish distress; it lives by distress; it *creates* distress to make itself immortal. . . . For example, the worm of sin; it was the Church that first enriched
mankind with this misery! The "equality of souls before God"
—this fraud, this pretext for the *rancunes* of all the base-
minded—this explosive concept, ending in revolution, the
modern idea and the notion of overthrowing the whole social
order—this is Christian dynamite. . . . The "humanitarian
blessing of Christianity" forsooth! To breed out of *humanitas*
a self-contradiction, and art of self-pollution, a will to lie at
any price, and aversion and contempt for all good and honest
instincts! All this, to me, is the "humanitarianism" of Christianity—Parasitism is the only practice of the Church. . . .

This eternal accusation against Christianity I shall write
upon all walls, wherever walls are to be found—I have letters
that even the blind will be able to see. . . . I call Christianity
the one great curse, the one great intrinsic depravity, the one
great instinct of revenge, for which no means are venomous
enough, or secret, subterranean and *small* enough—I call it
the one immortal blemish upon the human race. . . .[52]

Was Nietzsche sincere in attacking Christianity in this way?
Did he react against Christianity because he thought he was
defeated? Nietzsche himself, in a chapter of *Zarathustra,* praises
those who destroy out of love and are, therefore, creators, while
he despises others who destroy out of resentment and are, in
consequence, anarchist and fools. "Out of love alone," Zarathustra says, "shall my contempt and my warning bird take
wind; but not out of the swamp!"[53] But against this, A. H.
Knight, following Bertrand, says: "The more I reflect on the
point, the more serious my doubts become. . . . It has been

52. F. Nietzsche, *The Antichrist,* pp. 180–181.
53. F. Nietzsche, *Thus Spake Zarathustra,* p. 216.

remarked that although Nietzsche was often unfair, he was never so unfair as when dealing with Christianity. . . . The tendency to condemn Christianity more and more violently grew upon him steadily through his life. Is it possible that here too Nietzsche was saying that which he did not believe? I think that the almost inexplicable ferocity of the *Antichrist* and *Ecce Homo* . . . is more explicable on this assumption than on any other . . . in which case the madness of his last works was the madness of despair."[54]

This seems likely to be the case. Nietzsche is not judging Christianity, he is rather projecting his hatred and fiery impotency in an attempt to destroy the foundations of the Christian religion. His ferocity may be explained not as a serene and objective philosophical criticism which is foreign to such ferocity, but as a psychological resentment, as a projection of Nietzsche's dark shadow. As Jung explains, the recognition of the shadow is crucial, because our dark side is not harmless; it brings the archaic psyche, the whole world of archetypes into direct contact with the conscious mind, producing neurosis and psychosis. The loathing of Nietzsche for the inferior instincts of man urged him to repress them, thus forcing the latter into revolt. The more the shadow is repressed, the worse; the less conscious it is, the blacker and denser it becomes. The violence of Nietzsche's accusations against Christianity bears the marks characteristic of the shadow.

On the other hand, and as a contrast to this ferocious attack against Christianity, the projection of disintegrated archetypes and inflated ego is patent in Nietzsche's own attempt of self criticism:

> To declare here who and what I am . . . but the disparity which exists between the greatness of my task and the small-ness of my contemporaries . . . *Zarathustra* . . . I gave my fellow-men the greatest gift that has ever been bestowed upon them . . . the loftiest book on earth . . . the deepest

54. A. H. Knight, *Some Aspects of the Life and Works of Nietzsche, and Particularly of His Connection with Greek Literature and Thought* (Cambridge, 1933), pp. 187–188.

book, born in the inmost abundance of truth; an inexhaustible well. . . . I am a master to my backbone. . . . I am myself
with one foot beyond the realm of the living. . . . My humanity is a perpetual process of self mastery. . . . I know more
than other people. . . . I am so clever. . . . I have my readers . . . whithersoever I go every face brightens and softens
at the sight of me. . . . I swoop down from heights into which
no bird has ever soared; I know abysses into which no foot
has slipped. People have told me that it is impossible to lay
down a book of mine . . . that I disturb even their night's
rest. . . . I am capable of many kinds of style . . . in short, the
most multifarious art of style that any man has ever had at
his disposal . . . before me people did not know what could
be done with the German language. . . . With the *Seven
Seals* . . . I soared miles above all that which heretofore has
been called poetry. . . . I cannot doubt but that I should
have to go back thousands of years before I could find another
who could say to me: It is mine also! My destiny ordained
that I should be the first decent human being. . . . I was
the first to discover truth. . . . Mankind can begin to have
fresh hopes, only now that I have lived.[55]

Nietzsche's last accusations against Germany, his motherland,
also bear the mark of frustration. Nobody is a prophet in his
own country and Nietzsche felt bitterly, in his own life, the
bare wisdom of this truth. In the beginning of his life, at the
time he was writing *The Birth of Tragedy,* he had dreamed
of the restoration and rebirth of a new Germany embedded in
the spirit of Wagner's music and Dionysian philosophy. "Let
no one believe that the German spirit has forever lost its
mythical home when it still understands so obviously the voices
of the birds which tell of that home. Some day it will find itself
awake in all the morning freshness of a deep sleep: then it will
slay the dragons, destroy the malignant dwarfs, and waken
Brunnhilde—and Wotan's spear itself will be unable to obstruct
its course. My friends, ye who believe in Dionysian music, ye
know also what tragedy means to us. There we have tragic myth,

55. F. Nietzsche, passages taken from *Ecce Homo.*

born anew from music—and in this latest birth ye can hope for everything and forget what is most afflicting."[56] This was his dream, but subsequent facts did not measure up to his expectations, and Germany was unmoved by his writings and deaf to the voices of its prophet. Nietzsche was embittered by this reproach and accuses his motherland with a violence that is only matched by the one with which he accuses Christianity. "Above all," he says, "I have to direct an attack against the German people, who in matters of spirit, grew everyday more indolent, poor in instincts. I even feel it my duty to tell the Germans, for once in a way all that they have on their conscience. *Every crime against culture for the last four centuries lies on their conscience. . . .* I breathe with difficulty in the neighborhood of this psychological uncleanliness which in every word and expression betrays Germany. The Germans are like women. . . . Have the Germans ever produced even a book that had depth?"[57]

56. F. Nietzsche, *The Birth of Tragedy,* p. 185. Cf. e.c., pp. 150–151. "Out of Dionysian root of the German spirit a power has arisen which has nothing in common with the primitive conditions of Socratic culture, and can neither be regarded by this culture as something terribly inexplicable and overwhelmingly hostile—namely, German music as we have come to understand it, especially in its vast solar orbit from Bach to Beethoven, from Beethoven to Wagner."

57. F. Nietzsche, *Ecce Homo,* pp. 121–130. Cf. e.c., pp. 129–130: "I have considered almost every letter that reached me as a piece of cynicism. I tell every friend to his face that he has never thought it worth his while to *study* any of my writings; from the slightest hints I gather that they do not even know what lies hidden in my books. And with regard even to my Zarathustra, which of my friends would have seen more in it than a piece of unwarrantable, though fortunately harmless arrogance? Ten years have elapsed, and no one has yet felt it a duty to his conscience to defend my name against the absurd silence with which it has been entombed. . . . Admirable; my dear Germans. Allow me to congratulate you." Jung writes about hysteria in the following words: "This spectacle recalls the figure of what Nietzsche so aptly calls the 'pale criminal,' who in reality shows all the signs of hysteria. He simply will not and cannot admit that he is what he is; he cannot endure his own guilt, just as he could not help incurring it. He will stoop to every kind of self-deception if only he can escape the sight of himself. It is true that this happens everywhere but nowhere does it appear to be such a national characteristic as in Germany. I am by no means that first to have been struck by the inferiority feelings of the Germans. . . . This condition

However, for all his accusations and rage, Nietzsche was German to the marrow of his bones, even to the obstructive symbolism of his madness. It was a psychopathic's weakness that prompted him to play the "blond beast" and the "Superman." Furthermore, Nietzsche's personality is close to Wotan, the German god of storm and frenzy, the unleasher of passions, and the lust of battle; the god who is also a magician and artist in illusion. Hence, Jung says, Nietzsche was one of thousands of millions of Germans yet unborn, in whose unconscious the Teutonic wisdom of Dionysus—Wotan—came to birth during the Great War. Zarathustra, too was a soothsayer, a magician, and the storm wind. Thus the God he originally meant was really Wotan, but, being a philologist and living in the seventies and eighties of the nineteenth century, he called him Dionysus, since the two gods have much in common.[58]

As a man of character Nietzsche never compromised with mediocrity, he never gave up his principles to please the crowd. The primacy of the spirit was always his greatest principle. As a poet, as a critic, as a man of imagination Nietzsche is outstanding. But his philosophy is an expression of his neurotic personality and continuous frustrations of his tragic life; a philosophy which does not offer redemption, salvation, or hope.

Nietzsche and Collective Consciousness

The psyche is a reality with which man has to reckon. We believe in physical illnesses because we see scars, wounds, or

---

can easily lead to an hysterical dissociation of the personality, which consists essentially in one hand not knowing what the other is doing, in wanting to jump over one's shadow and looking for everything dark, inferior, and culpable *in others*. Hence the hysteric always complains of being surrounded by people who are incapable of appreciating him and who are activated only by bad motives; by inferior mischief-makers, or crowd of submen who should be exterminated neck and crop so that the Superman can live to his high level of perfection. The very fact that his thinking and feeling proceed along these lines is clear proof of inferiority in action. Therefore all hysterical people are compelled to torment others, because they are unwilling to hurt themselves by admitting their own inferiority" (*Coll. Works*, X, 202–203).

58. *Coll. Works*, X, 212; XI, 28; X, 177–194.

broken bones. But the psyche is invisible and the majority of men, accustomed to rely exclusively on realities perceived by the senses, tend to ignore realities lying beyond the realm of the tangible. When the unconscious is deprived of existence it reacts as the unfailing cause of neurosis, psychosis, inflation, sterility, and sundry other disabilities. But there is something else we did not consider yet; whenever the collective unconscious is repressed, the ego is unable to keep its identity and falls into "conscious collectivism"; the individual man loses his personality to be swallowed by the conscious psyche of the mass. This psychological phenomenon presupposes the disappearance of the individual psyche and the dangerous identification of the subjective consciousness with the collective mass psyche. Therefore, "conscious collectivism" is the social consequence of the denial of the objective psyche.

Man is not merely individual but social, collective. In medieval times this collectivism, Jung says, was represented primarily by the authority of the Church, which is gradually disappearing to be replaced by the collectivism of the State. The Reformation shattered the authority of the Church, and the consequence was an increase in the importance of the individual, which found expression in the modern ideals of humanity, social welfare, democracy, and equality. But following the law of *enantiodromy,* the individualistic trend "is counterbalanced by a compensatory reversion to the collective man, whose authority at present is the sheer weight of the masses. No wonder that nowadays there is a feeling of catastrophe in the air, as though an avalanche had broken loose which nothing can stop. The collective man threatens to stifle the individual man, on whose sense of responsibility everything valuable in mankind ultimately depends. The mass as such is always anonymous and always irresponsible."[59]

Naturally, man needs society not only to survive, but to develop his personality and to attain full individuation. So it is not society as such that Jung blames, but the modern State and the inhuman conditions it imposes. For this reason he

59. *Ibid.,* X, 154.

praises Christianity which in its heydays never subscribed to a belief in the State, but set before man a supramundane goal and gave him an immortal soul. However, if the present State could be personified the result would be an individual similar to a monster, intellectually and ethically below the level of the members composing it, for it represents mass psychology which infallibly swallows up the individual. Anyway, the totalitarian claim is bound to come out somewhere; thus, as the authority of the Church fades away the State becomes the Church. First socialism entered into the Catholic heritage, then Russian communism, quite logically, became the totalitarian Church.[60] And since individuals disregarding archetypes fall victim of the mass psyche, whenever man abandons the psychic equilibrium bestowed on him by institutions of authority, he usually falls victim of some sort of collective mass psyche, as happens, for example, with Christians: "Once Mother Church and her motherly Eros fall into abeyance, the individual is at the mercy of any passing collectivism and the attendant mass psyche. He succumbs to social and national inflation, and the tragedy is that he does so with the same psychic attitude which had once bound him to a church."[61]

The collective emphasis of the contemporary age is a consequence of the conditions in which we live and an accomplished fact that nobody can prevent. As Christopher Dawson put it, the choice that is actually before us is not between an individualistic humanism and some kind of collectivism, but between

60. *Ibid.*, X, 537; XVI, 106; Jung says on authority: "The disintegration and weakening of the salutary institution the Christian Church, goes on at an alarming rate, and the loss of any form of authority is gradually leading to an intellectual, political, and social anarchy which is repugnant to the soul of European man, accustomed as he is to the patriarchal order. . . . If our European social order is not to be shaken to its foundations, authority must be restored at all cost. This is probably one reason for the efforts now being made in Europe to replace the collectivity of the Church by the collectivity of the State" (*Ibid.*, XVI, 103–104). Christopher Dawson shares a similar idea. "The new bureaucratic state, that 'coldest of cold monster,' which exerts a more irresistible and far-reaching control over individual life than was ever possessed by the absolute monarchies of the old regime" (*Op. cit.*, p. 17).
61. *Coll. Works*, VIII, 221.

a collectivism that is purely materialistic and one that is spiritual. It is the lack of spirituality which worries Jung most, for he believes that now the case of Nietzsche is not merely individual and of the historical past, but collective and of the present. Nietzsche is like the exemplar or symbol of the psyche of contemporary humanity, because the unconscious of modern man is endowed with traits similar to the traits of the unconscious of Nietzsche. Hence, "when Nietzsche said 'God is dead,' he uttered a truth which is valid for the greater part of Europe. People were influenced by it not because he said so, but because it stated a widespread psychological fact."[62]

Therefore, it is not primarily his philosophy that bears weight, but the psychological attitude it represents, which is not only that of Nietzsche, but of many individuals whose unconscious is similar to the unconscious of the German philosopher. As a result of the common withdrawal of the projection of the unconscious from God and collective objects, the inflation is now a social phenomenon; and a social phenomenon too, is accordingly the feeling of God-almightiness which follows the inflation. "In recent times this type (Superman) has extended beyond Nietzsche into the field of political psychology, and its incarnation in man has had all the consequences that might have been expected to follow from such misappropriation of power. As human beings do not live in airtight compartments, this infectious inflation has spread everywhere and given rise to an extraordinary uncertainty in morals and philosophy. The medical psychologist is bound to take interest in such matters."[63] Therefore a profound psychological change has

---

62. *Ibid.,* XI, 88. Cf. IX,i, 104; XI, 84: "In our day even the God man seems to have descended from his throne and to be dissolving himself in the common man. That is why his seat is empty. Instead the common man suffers from a 'hybris' of consciousness that borders on the pathological. This psychic condition in the individual corresponds by and large to the hypertrophy and totalitarian pretensions of the idealized State." See also Christopher Dawson, *op. cit.,* p. 100.

63. *Coll. Works,* XI, 315. Cf. XII, 460–461: "Is God dead, because Nietzsche declared that he had not been heard of for a long time? May he not have come back in the guise of a Superman? . . . The fires chilled the air, and the air became the great wind of Zarathustra and caused an inflation of

already taken place and is still going on in the unconscious
of man, the outstanding mark of which is the appropriation
of authority by man himself. Did not Nietzsche announce that
God was dead and that his heir was the Superman? Thus
Nietzsche's Zarathustra brings to light the contents of the collective psyche of our time, and in him the iconoclastic revolt
against the conventional moral atmosphere and the acceptance
of the "ugliest man."[64]

The profound psychological change experienced by humanity is not only a consequence of inflation and iconoclastic
revolt. It is also the result of the rapid development of consciousness through science and technology which left the unconscious behind in a defensive position. The exclusive claims of
consciousness clash with the hidden but real claims of unconsciousness; the result is a man who is torn apart in agony and
who expresses himself in a universal will of destruction, clearly
manifested in art and in the abolition of tradition.

Art, according to Jung, reveals the nature of the unconscious
because art is essentially the unconscious process of symboliza-
tion through the ages. And as a primordial manifestation of the
human spirit and as a genuine creative force of civilization it
anticipates what is to come one or two generations later. Art
reveals a message, and the message that modern art is now revealing is the profound transformation of man's objective psyche.

> This tells us, in plain and universal language, that the pro-
> phetic spirit of art has turned away from the old object-
> relationship towards the—for the time being—dark chaos of
> subjectivism. . . . The development of modern art with its
> seemingly nihilistic trend towards disintegration must be
> understood as a symptom and symbol of a mood of universal

---

consciousness which, it seems, can only be mitigated by the most terrible
catastrophe to civilization, another deluge let loose by the gods upon inhos-
pitable humanity. . . . Nobody realized that European man was possessed
by something that robbed him of all free will. And this state of unconscious
possession will continue undeterred until we Europeans become scared of
our God-almightiness. Such a change can begin only with individuals, for
the masses are blind brutes, as we know to our cost."
64. *Ibid.*, VI, 237; X, 214.

destruction and renewal that has set its mark on our age. This mood makes itself felt everywhere, politically, socially, and philosophically. . . . This peculiarity of our time, which is certainly not of our conscious choosing, is the expression of the unconscious man within us who is changing. Coming generations will have to take account of this momentous transformation if humanity is not to destroy itself through the might of its own technology and science.[65]

For example, the mood of Picasso's painting, his sexuality, his rejection of artistic canons and traditional art, his perennial search for new forms of expression, his always pioneer spirit, love for distortion and ugliness—"the beauty of ugliness," already noted many years ago by Eugenio d'Ors—is analyzed by Jung in these terms: "When I say 'he,' I mean that personality in Picasso which suffers the underworld fate—the man in him who does not turn towards the day world, but is fatefully drawn into the dark; who follows not the accepted ideals of goodness and beauty, but the demoniacal attraction of ugliness and evil. It is these anti-Christian and Luciferian forces that well up in modern man and engender an all-pervading sense of doom, veiling the bright world of day with the mists of Hades, infecting it with deadly decay, and finally, like an earthquake, dissolving it into fragments, fractures, discarded remnants, debris, shreds, and disorganized units. Picasso and his exhibition are a sign of the times."[66] Modern art is perhaps the best manifestation of the profound metamorphosis of our unconscious.

The second symptomatic manifestation of destructive tendencies of our unconscious is revealed by the systematic abolition of tradition, which Jung considers a tragedy: "Naturally the present tendency to destroy tradition or render it unconscious could interrupt the present tendency of development for several hundred years and substitute an interlude of barbarism. . . . Loss of roots and lack of tradition neuroticize the masses and prepare them for collective hysteria. Collective hysteria calls

65. *Ibid.*, X, 303–304.
66. *Ibid.*, XV, 138. Naturally, this is only an analysis of Picasso's psyche, not of his work of art. Personally I believe that Picasso is the greatest artist of the twentieth century.

for collective therapy, which consists in abolition of liberty and terrorization. Where rationalistic materialism holds sway, states tend to develop less into prisons than into lunatic asylums."[67] Therefore, secularization, desacralization, escape from the mythical, industralization, and the overgrowing power of the State are robbing man from history, from tradition, from God, and from the elements of unconscious. The result is an individual who is unstable, insecure, and suggestible.[68]

Hence Jung draws a picture of modern man whose characteristic mark is that of crisis and renewal, of deep transformation—the outcome of which no one is capable to foresee. Every crisis and every profound metamorphosis contains new possibilities as well as dangers; dangers because every new human experience presupposes the hazards and uncertainties of the unknown; new territories are always uncharted and hazardous. But on the other hand new discoveries have never been achieved

67. *Ibid.*, IX,ii, 181. Cf. XVI, 103–104; XI, 342: "Consider for a moment what it means to grant the right of existence to what is unreasonable, senseless and evil! Yet it is just this that the modern man insists upon. He wants to live with every side of himself . . . to know what he is. That is why he casts history aside. He wants to break with tradition so that he can experiment with his life and determine what value and meaning things have in themselves, apart from traditional presuppositions. Modern youth gives us astonishing examples of this attitude. To show how far this tendency may go, I will instance a question addressed to me by a German society. I was asked if incest is to be reprobated, and what facts can be adduced against it!" *Memories, Dreams, Reflections,* p. 236: "The less we understand of what our fathers and forefathers sought, the less we understand ourselves, and thus we help with all our might to rob the individual of his roots and his guiding instincts, so that he becomes a particle in the mass, ruled only by what Nietzsche called the spirit of gravity." Victor Frankl, *op. cit.,* p. 168: "The traditions that had buttressed his behavior are now rapidly diminishing. No instinct tells him what he ought to do; soon he will not know what he wants to do. More and more he will be governed by what others want him to do, thus increasingly falling prey to conformism."
68. *Ibid.*, X, 222, 254. Alex Carrel, in his well-known best seller, *Man the Unknown* (New York, 1961), pp. 23–25, holds similar views to Jung's. He writes: "Besides, they are haunted by the fear of losing their employment, their means of subsistence, their savings, their fortune. They are unable to satisfy the need for security that exists in the depth of each of us. In spite of social insurances, they feel uneasy about their future. Those who are capable of thinking become discontented. . . ."

without a certain spirit of adventure and without the feeling that although unknown, the adventure will provide a better solution than the one abandoned, no matter how much the cost in hardship and sufferings. Granted the plausibility that "the symbolism that depth psychology decipher are for the most part made up of scattered fragments and of the manifestation of a psyche in crisis, if not in a state of pathological regression,"[69] then, the spiritual factors of man ought to lead him towards the discovery of his true self that cannot be a totality without spiritual factors and God. The outcome of the modern psychological plight will depend in the last analysis on the kind of philosophy we choose, whether materialistic or spirtualistic.

69. Mircea Eliade, *Images and Symbols,* p. 37.

IX

Summary

It is far from easy to synthesize in a few pages the contents of Jung's writings. The complexity of the elements making up his ideas is so great, and his work, as a pioneer one, is so new that many years shall be required to know the exact implication of his voluminous writings. But insofar as religion goes, the importance of his work rest precisely in his initial viewpoint, different from the initial viewpoint of theology. The theologian's initial viewpoint is rooted in faith, and his principles are the articles of faith known to us by God's revelation. Jung's initial point of view is man, and his method is empirical. He delves into the deep layers of our unconscious in order to explain man's personality and the patterns of man's behavior. And in this unconscious he finds factors of primordial significance for understanding these patterns, and for the development of human personality to its fullness. These elements, called archetypes, reveal in us the existence of collective factors shaping our behavior in ways similar to previous generations and to other races, even in ways similar to primitive man.

What is the relation of archetypes and the patterns of religious manifestations known to us through history? Mircea Eliade is cautious, and rightly points out the difference of archetypes as factors of the unconscious, and archetypes in the way he uses them, namely, as paradigms shaping the history of religion. But although their meaning differs, this does not imply that they are unrelated. In fact, it is possible to believe that the paradigms discovered in religion may have their foundation and ultimate explanation in the archetypes of the unconscious discovered by Jung. Thus the confrontation of depth

251

psychology and the patterns in comparative religion is a fascinating problem in which much remains to be investigated.

But regardless of whether this correspondence is a fact or
not, Jung's discoveries in psychology are of great implication
in theology. Why? Because these discoveries, which the theologian is ready to welcome, prove that religion is man's most
important instinct and, furthermore, they prove that the symbols, dogmas, and images of Christianity are archetypal and—
save the exception of the quaternity—in perfect agreement with
the needs of our unconscious. There lies Jung's greatest contribution to theology. Christianity fits perfectly the psychological
needs of man, even the needs unknown to us because they are
unconscious. The archetypes of the collective unconscious find
the objects upon which they can project their contents on the
dogmas proposed by Christianity. The importance of this conclusion rests not only in its objective truth, but also in the fact
that it has been discovered beginning with man and after many
years of painstaking empirical observation.

In the sphere of neurosis and therapy Jung's contribution is
also a major one, for although the psyche and God are invisible, the psyche and religion exist. Accordingly Jung ascribes to
the lack of religion a major influence causing neuroses, and he
also stresses the great significance of religion as a therapeutical
factor which psychiatrists have to reckon with. To ignore the
importance of religion can only be done to the damage of the
patient's mental health and even to the damage of society,
because when religion is repressed the energy corresponding to
it is freed and reappears in ways not always easily controlled
by the ego, not by the civil authority.

Jung has also observed in his experience with his patients
the connection between morality and mental health, the importance of pride, the danger of God-almightiness, the need of self-
examination, the necessity of recognizing the shadow, and the
importance of evil. Naturally evil cannot be a "positive" factor
for individuation, as Jung believes to be the case; but evil is
a factor with which we have to deal in life and in society, just
as we have to reckon with guilt, punishment, healing, struggle,
disappointments, and the sheer facts of life. Life is sometimes

even brutal, and Jung does not promise happiness and redemption to those who have not the courage to face it and suffer. A soft approach to life, a dreamlike life, will please the majority who sooner or later will find themselves victim of their wrong outlook.

Jung has also revealed the primary importance of paradigms, of archetypes, as against the motley variety of the contingency of daily experience. There exist natural tendencies in man to escape from the particular and contingent in order to attain the universal, the permanent, the absolute. Even the intuitive experience of the primitive concerning myth, although existential and spontaneous, is chiefly paradigmatical and exemplar. In this sense Jung is not an existential philosopher; for him, the essence is more important than the concrete existence, and the general patterns bear more weight in life than the concrete situation in which they appear.

In a time of artistical and liturgical renewal, the importance of symbols and images can hardly be overestimated. Eliade asserts that the symbol is the point of departure for the spiritual renewal of modern man in total agreement with Jung. Jung unceasingly stresses the psychological richness of the symbols and images appearing in Christianity, because they are in perfect correspondence with the needs of the collective unconscious of man. A better psychological understanding of the elements of the Christian liturgy can enhance the deeper understanding of the Christian religion as such, for all religions reveal themselves spontaneously in symbols and images. And as Austin Ferrer says, Christianity meant not an abandonment, but a transformation of primordial images. Hence the study of the symbols irrelevant to race and age that have appeared continuously over the centuries can help the understanding of the full significance of them when they appear in the sacraments, in the Christian ritual, and other manifestations of Christian life. The determination of the exact meaning of these symbols is the exclusive work of Christian theology; but the better we understand the psychological implications of Christian symbolism the better we can appreciate the deep religious meaning of the elements composing the Christian symbolism.

Jung's empirical method is not exempt from dangers, because the insufficiency of the experimental approach and the difficulties entailed in understanding nature lures the scientist in general, and the psychologist in particular, to speculate far beyond the narrow realm of observed data. When scientists do not find in nature the explanation of facts, they themselves provide the tentative hypotheses that nature is reluctant to yield. And as scientists get older, they usually fall into the tendency of becoming less empirical and more speculative and philosophical in their approach to nature. This is not necessarily a wrong attitude, but simply risky, especially for those scientists not sufficiently trained in theoretical thinking. Albert Einstein was blamed by Max Born and other colleagues for abandoning in his later years what they believe to be the experimental method in physics. Perhaps Jung is not an exception to this common attitude, and some of his speculations (for example, on flying saucers, on synchronicity, on alchemy, and on astrology) leave the majority of his readers cool, if not disappointed, and prevent a better appreciation of the rest of his work.

Jung, always modest but sincere, asks for a hearing on the ground of his unique experience, when he says the following in *Civilization in Transition*: "I hope, therefore, that a psychiatrist, who in the course of a long life has devoted himself to the causes and consequences of psychic disorders, may be permitted to express his opinion, in all modesty enjoined upon him as an individual, about the questions raised by the world situation today. I am neither spurred on by excessive optimism nor in love with high ideals, but I am merely concerned with the fate of the individual human being—that infinitesimal unit on whom a world depends. . . ." Jung certainly deserves that hearing.

Appendix
Dreams and Christian Life

In a book recently published in America, *Dreams The Dark Speech of the Spirit,* Morton T. Kelsey tries to prove the great significance of dreams for the full understanding of the Christian message. Religious men, he says, from Solomon to St. Augustine, all believed that dreams and visions were vital mediums through which God revealed Himself to man and in which man found a spiritual communication with his Creator.

Then in the Middle Ages this attitude completely changed. St. Thomas Aquinas closed almost every entrance to revelation of unconscious spiritual realities. This negative attitude regarding the importance of dreams has lasted up to the present, hampering the full understanding of religion; for dreams do play a significant role in the life of man and allow him to communicate with God: "Dreams are so important to mental health that simply being deprived of them may lead to mental breakdown and even psychosis. These findings, particularly those of Jung, certainly suggest that the dream—which has been valued and interpreted by all religious groups, Christianity included—is worthy of serious consideration and may be one very important access to knowledge."[1] "The Christian clergy, the theologians are still silent," Dr. Kelsey remarks, "and this is surprising when we realize how much there is about dreams in the Christian tradition from the Old Testament on. . . . Once the dream is taken seriously, as something given, with religious significance, then it is inevitable that there is some direct and natural contact with reality other than material or rational. Dreams

1. Morton T. Kelsey, *Dreams The Dark Speech of the Spirit* (New York, 1968), p. 6.

may well be a doorway to religious significance and a new theology, as well as to the unconscious."[2]

Morton Kelsey primarily blames St. Thomas Aquinas for this state of affairs, for he created a theology based upon only half of the Christian story. "Because of his philosophical background," he says, "it was impossible for Aquinas to believe that the human psyche could communicate directly with any reality that was not physical, not just angelic or demonic abstraction, a 'thinking thought'. . . . Aquinas then concluded that dreams were really not significant or sure, because he believed that we have no direct, immediate contact with spiritual reality. A rather important conclusion, with all sorts of implications for modern theology."[3]

What is to be said about this imputation? We do not intend to explain here Aquinas' theory of knowledge and the way he explains how we attain a certain knowledge of God and spiritual substances through analogy. We merely wish to explain a few ideas about dreams, inasmuch as they are connected with the Christian religion and the Christian revelation.

All psychologists, beginning with Freud and Jung, agree on the great importance of the analysis of dreams in order to explore the unconscious. Dreams are indeed crucial factors with which we must deal if we wish to discover the psychological damage implied by the repression of religious elements, as well as the religious needs of both sick and healthy individuals. The cause of neurosis, psychosis, or emptiness may perhaps be the repression of religious factors which we are reluctant to admit, let alone assimilate, impeding thus their integration into our conscious personality. For this reason it is of primary significance to take into account our dreams and to analyze them. Dreams are "goal" oriented, and they warn our conscious self of something which is hidden, repressed, or simply ignored. Aquinas, convinced of the intimate union between soul and body, indicates the importance of dreams for the knowledge of our inner self: "Sometimes the inward cause of dreams involves

2. *Ibid.*, pp. 10–12.
3. *Ibid.*, pp. 175–176.

the body because the inward disposition of the body leads to
the formation of a movement in the imagination consistent
with that disposition. . . . And for this reason physicians say
that we should take note of dreams in order to discover internal
dispositions."[4]

Furthermore, Aquinas, following Aristotle, explains the
unique significance of dreams in apprehending the hidden realities of our psyche, realities difficult to reach when we are awake
or engrossed in external things: "When the soul is withdrawn
from corporeal things, it is more susceptible to the subtle
motions which take place in the human imagination through
the impression of natural causes, whereas it is hindered from
receiving them while occupied with sensible things."[5] This is
also extended to the knowledge of future events which are
sometimes better known in dreams.[6]

In conclusion, dreams are important elements upon which we
must rely to know ourselves, especially the needs of our unconscious, needs that are often of a religious kind. Therefore
Aquinas would have agreed heartily with Jung, who says: "Practical experience shows that many neuroses are caused primarily
by the fact that people blind themselves to their own religious
promptings because of the childish passion for religious enlightenment."[7] When the gods have become diseases, when the root of
disease rests on some religious factor of which the enlightened
individual himself is unaware because it is spiritual and in the
unconscious, then dreams are of great help because they warn
individuals of the spiritual elements missing in the conscious
personality. For example, Jung tells of one patient he began to
treat only after he had observed the first series of about three
hundred and fifty dreams. "Whenever he tried to be disloyal to
his experience or to deny the voice, the neurotic condition
instantly came back. He simply could not 'quench the fire,' and
finally he had to admit the incomprehensible numinous character of his experience. He had to confess that the unquench-

4. Thomas Aquinas, *Summa Theol.*, II–II, q. 95, a. 6.
5. *Ibid.*, II–II, q. 172, a. 1 ad 1. Cf. *De Ver.*, q. 12, a. 3 ad 1.
6. *Ibid.*, q. 172, a. 1 ad 2.
7. C. G. Jung, *Coll. Works*, XVI, p. 46.

able fire was 'holy.' This was the *sine qua non* of his cure."[8]
Therefore dreams are of crucial significance in discovering the
religious need of individuals, especially when the religious elements are hidden in the unconscious and are, nevertheless, the
principle factors causing neurosis and emptiness.

On the other hand, as long as the normal development of
Christian life goes on, dreams can never be essential factors
which we have to trust if we wish to grow in holiness. The first
reason is because dreams, visions, miracles, gifts of tongues,
prophecies, and the rest of the extraordinary graces which are
sometimes bestowed on souls, are not essential for the normal
development of Christian life. The essential element is sanctifying grace, of which St. Thomas declares that "the good of
grace in one is greater than the good of nature of the whole
universe."[9] Grace is really a participation in the divine nature
precisely insofar as it is divine: "Human souls and angels are
by nature made to the image of God and resemble Him by
analogy insofar as he is intelligent; but no creatable nature can
resemble Him as He is God. Grace alone can make us participate really and formally in the Deity, in the intimate life of
Him whose children we are by grace."[10]

Hence the slightest degree of sanctifying grace is infinitely
superior to the extraordinary graces, charisms, or graces freely
bestowed, enumerated by St. Paul, and which are so dear to
certain Christians: "Now there are diversity of graces but the
same Spirit. . . . To one through the Spirit is given the utterance
of wisdom; and to another the utterance of knowledge according to the same Spirit; to another faith, in the same Spirit; to
another gift of healing, in the one Spirit; to another the working of miracles; to another prophecy; to another interpretation of tongues. But all these things are the work of one and
the same Spirit, who allots to everyone according as He will"
(1 Cor. 12:4–11; Cf. Rom. 12:6).

These graces are ordained primarily to the benefit of the

8. *Ibid.,* XI, p. 43.
9. Thomas Aquinas, *Summa Theol.,* I–II, q. 113, a. 9 ad 2.
10. Garrigou Lagrange, *Christian Perfection and Contemplation* (St. Louis,
1937), p. 56.

neighbor, and although sometimes they are granted for the benefit of the recipient, they are not essential elements for Christian life. The normal development of Christian life depends upon the sacraments, the life of prayer, especially contemplation, and the exercise of the Christian virtues, chiefly faith, hope, and charity. For this reason, not only Aquinas as a theologian, but many saints who were themselves endowed with these charisms always emphasized the superiority of faith, and the dangers entailed on visions, miracles, prophecies and other charisms for the soul striving for perfection. St. Teresa of Avila and St. John of the Cross, both doctors and mystics and who had personal experience of them, advise the faithful to detach themselves from charisms to follow the road of pure faith: "I do not deny that the memory of spiritual visions may raise the soul to some love of God and contemplation," John of the Cross says, "but pure faith and detachment in darkness from all this stimulus raises the soul much more thereto, without the soul's knowing how and whence it comes . . . whence it follows that the more eager the soul is for obscurity . . . the more increases in faith, and also hope and charity, inasmuch as the three theological virtues form a unity."[11]

The second reason dreams cannot be essential factors in our growth in holiness concerns revelation. Divine revelations are supernatural manifestations of a hidden truth by means of a vision, a word, or a prophetic instinct. Revelation therefore consists in knowledge, because prophets know things that are hidden from man's knowledge;[12] and since this kind of knowledge surpasses natural reason, it follows that prophecy requires an intellectual light surpassing the light of natural reason. This prophetic light is in the prophet's soul by way of a passion or transitory impression[13] and is chiefly about future events.[14]

The only official revealed doctrine the Church admits is contained in the Bible and is proposed to the faithful by her

---

11. John of the Cross, *Ascent to Mount Carmel,* II, ch. 24. Cf. Teresa of Avila, *Interior Castle,* 6. ch. 9.
12. Thomas Aquinas, *Summa Theol.,* II–II, q. 171, a. 1.
13. *Ibid.,* a. 2.
14. *Ibid.,* a. 4.

teaching authority. With the death of the last Apostle the official revelation was closed, although the development of Catholic dogma was not. Hence, in the same way that the only essential element which makes us Christians is sanctifying grace, the only essential revelation needed is contained in the Bible and it is interpreted officially by the Church.

But what about private revelations, especially revelations received by means of dreams? God reveals Himself continuously in many ways to countless numbers of individuals to whom He grants the gift of hidden knowledge. Revelations presuppose the gift of prophecy and they are called private when they are ordained for the particular benefit of those who are favored with them, at least sometimes. Private revelations, no matter what their importance, do not belong to the deposit of Catholic faith.

The cause of divine prophecy is supernatural: the Holy Spirit; thus prophecy is a gift of the Holy Spirit. God manifests this gift according to His will in diverse manners; and man too, as a living instrument in God's hand, can receive this knowledge in a variety of ways, for everything which is received is received after the manner of the recipient. Hence since we have three kinds of knowledge, the revelation may be received in three different cognitive ways: one by the eyes of the body, another by the soul's imagination, a third by the eyes of the mind. And the prophet may be awake, asleep, or in ecstasy; occasionally, in fact, a sensible, outward sign appears to the eyes or an exterior voice is heard.[15]

The most important revelation is intellectual revelation, for the intellect is the most perfect power of man. Besides, the devil cannot interfere in exercise of the activity of the intellect, for spiritual substances do not directly penetrate the mind; it is beyond angelic or demonic power to form ideas in our mind. "The demons reveal what they know to men, not by enlightening the intellect, but by imaginary vision, or even by audible speech."[16]

For this reason it is difficult to be deceived by intellectual reve-

15. *Ibid.,* q. 174, a. 1 ad 3.
16. *Ibid.,* q. 172, a. 5 ad 2. Cf. *Ibid.,* I, q. 111, a. 3; *De Ver.,* q. 12, a. 10.

lation. But intellectual revelation is unusual. The imagination is par excellence the vehicle of revelation, and Aquinas says that prophecy requires goodness of imagination and abstraction from the senses, "lest the things thus seen by images in the imagination be taken for objects of external sensation. . . ."[17] Revelation produced in our imagination by God or by the angels are granted when a person is either awake or asleep. St. Joseph was on several occasions supernaturally instructed in a dream, and the lives of the saints contain similar instances.

Since the withdrawal from corporeal things enhances the activity of the imagination, dreams play an important part in this kind of revelation. "Knowledge of the future by means of dreams," Aquinas says, "comes either from the revelation of spiritual substances, or from corporeal causes. . . . Now both these causes are more applicable to a person while asleep than while awake, because while awake, the soul is occupied with external objects, so that it is less receptive of the subtle impressions either of spiritual substances, or even natural causes."[18]

But in order to clarify the significance of dreams in regard to revelation Aquinas points out an important distinction: "There are two things to be considered in knowledge: reception and judgment about that which is received. Accordingly, in the matter of judgment the cognition of one who is awake is preferable to that of one who is asleep, for the judgment of one who is asleep is preferable for reception, because internal impressions from external movements can be received better when the senses are at rest. This is so whether they come from the separated substances or from heavenly bodies. Thus we can understand in this sense that which is said of Balaam in Numbers (24:16): 'Who falling,' that is sleeping, 'hath his eyes opened.' "[19]

This is so, because when the exterior senses are bound in sleep, the interior powers are, as it were, free from the bustle of the external senses and can better perceive the internal impressions made on the understanding or the imagination by a divine or angelic light, or by anything else. But since the

17. *Ibid.*, q. 173, a. 3.
18. *Ibid.*, q. 172, a. 1 ad 2.
19. *Ibid. De Ver.*, q. 12, a. 3 ad 1.

senses are the first source of knowledge, we must in some way reduce to sense everything that we judge. Since then the senses are fettered in sleep, there cannot be perfect judgment, so that a man is deceived in some respect, viewing the likeness of things as though they were the things themselves.[20]

Consequently, it is the judgment which is essential in revelation. "One is not called a prophet if this knowledge is supernatural only in reception, just as Pharaoh who supernaturally received a sign of abundance and famine under the figure of oxen and ears of corn was not called a prophet. But if someone has supernatural judgment, or reception and judgment together, he is called a prophet."[21] This idea is crucial, for the bare reception of images in dreams is not sufficient for prophetic revelation. There is always, however, infused prophetic light for the judgment, and indeed it alone suffices, as in the case of Joseph when he interpreted the dreams of Pharaoh.

The revelation through dreams seems to be a valid prophetic revelation when the dreams are coming from God. "And God indeed," Aquinas says, "reveals certain things to men in their dreams by the ministry of the angels, according to Numbers (12:6): 'If there be among you a prophet of the Lord, I will appear to him in a vision, or I will speak to him in a dream.' . . . Accordingly, we must say that there is no unlawful divination in making use of dreams for the foreknowledge of the future, so long as these dreams are due to divine revelation. . . . But it will be an unlawful and superstitious divination if it be caused by revelation of the demons. . . ."[22] That a dream may be supernatural, it should not be explicable exclusively by the laws of memory and imagination. To be divine, it should not contain anything contrary to revealed doctrine or to good morals.

These two considerations, namely, reception and judgment on one hand and the source of revelation on the other, are the necessary factors that should be considered in evaluating the significance of revelation by means of dreams. Consequently, it is easy to see that the difficulties of interpretation of divine

20. *Ibid.,* ad 2.
21. *Ibid.,* a. 7.
22. *Summa Theol.,* II–II, q. 95, a. 6.

revelation by means of dreams are numerous. First, because even in revelation coming from God it is far from easy to distinguish what is coming from Him and what is proper to the prophet. The saints themselves attribute to the Spirit of God what sometimes proceeds from the depths of their own souls, or may falsely interpret the meaning of the truly divine revelation: "Though sayings and revelations may be of God," John of the Cross says, "we cannot always have confidence in them, for we can very easily be greatly deceived by them because of our manner of understanding them."[23] The saint illustrates how this happens with examples taken from the Bible itself.

Second, because imaginary revelations and visions are subject to the illusions of the devil. "It is to these senses of imagination and fancy that the devil habitually betakes himself with his wiles—now natural, now supernatural; for they are the door and entrance to the soul. . . . And for this reason it is hither that both God and the devil always come with their gems of supernatural forms and images, to offer them to the understanding."[24]

Third, because the imagination itself is difficult to control: "As not only three or four, but a large number of people have spoken to me on the subject [revelations and visions]," Teresa of Avila says, "I know by experience that there are souls which, either because they possess vivid imaginations or active minds, are so absorbed in their ideas as to feel certain they see whatever their fancy imagines. . . . They themselves fabricate, piece by piece, what they fancy they see. . . ."[25]

Therefore for all these reasons John of the Cross reproves the desire for revelations, in complete accord with St. Vincent Ferrer and the majority of the saints: "The soul imagines that something great has taken place, that God Himself has spoken, when in reality there is very little, or nothing, or less than nothing. . . . This is why I affirm that these illusions offer a great obstacle to divine union, for if the soul makes much of them, this fact alone drives it very far from the abyss of faith. . . . The most perfect recollection is that which takes place in

23. John of the Cross, *op. cit.,* II, ch. 18.
24. *Ibid.,* ch. 16.
25. Teresa of Avila, *op. cit.,* 6, ch. 9.

faith. . . . Charity is infused in the proportion to the purity of the soul in a perfect faith: the more intense such charity is the more the Holy Ghost enlightens the soul and communicates His gifts to it."[26]

Augustine, who was interested in prophetic dreams, is fully aware, however, of the dangers of visions and dreams: ". . . since the examples of such visions (of men misguided by delusions) closely resembling the visions of pious and holy men are so numerous, that if I wished to quote them, time, rather than abundance of examples, would fail me."[27]

Let us say in conclusion that although revelations by dreams come sometimes from God and are helpful, it is better not to desire them, and to follow instead the way of pure faith.

"The philosopher won and the Bible lost," Kelsey says referring to Aquinas. "He created a theology based upon half of the Christian story. He simply ignored not only the dreams, but the experiences of the angels and demons, the healing, tongues speaking, and miracles in general in most of the New Testament, particularly the Book of the Acts."[28] These words indicate ignorance of the work of Aquinas, and a false interpretation of his theological principles. In the *Summa* alone, Aquinas wrote three hundred pages on angels and demons, and many more about the very things Kelsey imputes him to have ignored.

The philosopher did not win; it was indeed the theologian and common sense that won. The Bible did not lose, but perhaps the losers were all those who would like to base Christianity on the extraordinary or accidental. We thus return again to sanctifying grace, the teaching of the Church, the theological virtues, and the eminence of charity. There is no way to go astray holding fast to these principles, all of them rooted in the Bible.

26. John of the Cross, *op. cit.,* II, ch. 29.
27. St. Augustine, quoted by N. Kelsey, *op. cit.,* p. 265.
28. N. Kelsey, *op. cit.,* p. 174.

Bibliography

ADLER, A. *The Practice and Theory of Individual Psychology* (London, 1955).

ADLER, G. "The Psychological Approach to Religion," *Studies in Analytical Psychology* (1948).

ARENDT, H. *The Human Condition* (New York, 1958).

ARINTERO, J. *The Mystical Evolution* (Saint Louis, 1950).

ARISTOTLE. *The Works of Aristotle,* ed. W. D. Ross (Oxford, 1928).
    I. *Logic.*
    II. *Philosophy of Nature.*
    III. *The Soul.*
    VIII. *Metaphysics.*
    IX. *Ethics.*

ARTOLA, J. M. *Creación y Participación* (Madrid, 1963).

AUGUSTINE, SAINT. *Writings of Saint Augustine* (New York, 1953). *Patrologiae Migne,* Vols. XXXII–XLVII.

AYLWARD, J. "Archetypes and Natural Law," *Proc. 2nd Int. Congress Analytic Psychology* (Zurich, 1962).

CARREL, A. *Man the Unknown* (New York, 1961).

CARUSO, I. *Existential Psychology* (New York, 1961).

CASSIRER, E. *An Essay on Man* (New Haven, 1944).

_____. *Language and Myth,* trans. Susanne K. Langer (New York, 1946).

COX, H. *The Secular City* (New York, 1966).

DALBIEZ, R. *Psychoanalytical Method and the Doctrine of Freud,* transl. T. F. Lindsay (London, 1948).

DAWSON, C. *Christianity and the New Age* (London, 1934).

DUHEM, P. *The Aim and Structure of Physical Theory* (Princeton, 1954).

ELIADE, M. *Cosmos and History* (New York, 1959).

_____. *Images and Symbols* (New York, 1961).

————. *Myth, Dreams, and Mysteries* (New York, 1960).

————. *Myth and Reality* (New York, 1963).

————. *Patterns in Comparative Religion* (New York, 1958).

————. *The Sacred and the Profane* (New York, 1961).

————. *The Two and the One* (London, 1965).

FORDHAM, F. *An Introduction to Jung's Psychology* (Baltimore, 1956).

FORDHAM, M. *Contact with Jung,* ed. Michael Fordham (London, 1963).

FRANCIS DE SALES, SAINT. *An Introduction to the Devout Life* (New York, 1923).

FRANKL, V. *Man's Search for Meaning,* trans. Ilse Lasch (New York, 1968).

FRAZER, J. G. *The Golden Bough* (London, 1907).

FREUD, S. *A General Introduction to Psychoanalysis* (New York, 1957).

————. *Moses and Monotheism* (New York, 1959).

————. *The Future of an Illusion* (London, 1928).

————. *Totem and Taboo* (New York, 1956).

FROMM, E. *Psychoanalysis and Religion* (London, 1951).

————. *The Forgotten Language* (New York, 1951).

GARRIGOU LAGRANGE, R. *Christian Perfection and Contemplation,* transl. Sister M. Timothea Doyle, O.P., (Saint Louis, 1937).

GLOVER, E. *Freud or Jung?* (New York, 1957).

GOLDBRUNNER, J. *Individuation* (London, 1955).

HILLMAN, J. *Insearch: Psychology and Religion* (New York, 1967).

HOSTIE, R. *Religion and the Psychology of Jung,* trans. G. R. Lamb (New York, 1957).

JACOBI, J. *The Psychology of C. G. Jung,* trans. K. W. Bash (New Haven, 1954).

————. *Complex, Archetype, Symbol in the Psychology of C. G. Jung,* trans. Ralph Manheim, (New York, 1959).

JAMES, W. *The Varieties of Religious Experience* (London, 1962).

JOHN OF THE CROSS, SAINT. *The Complete Works of Saint John of the Cross,* ed. Allison Peers (Westminster, 1949).

JUNG, C. G. *The Collected Works of C. G. Jung,* Pantheon Books (New York).

    I. *Psychiatric Studies.*

    II. *Experimental Researches.*

    III. *Psychogenesis in Mental Disease.*

IV. *Freud and Psychoanalysis.*
V. *Symbols of Transformation.*
VI. *Psychological Types.*
VII. *Two Essays on Analytical Psychology.*
IX,i. *Archetypes and the Collective Unconscious.*
IX,ii. *Aion: An Historical Inquiry into the Symbolism of the Self.*
X. *Civilization in Transition.*
XI. *Psychology and Religion.*
XII. *Psychology and Alchemy.*
XIII. *Alchemical Studies.*
XIV. *Mysterium Coniunctionis.*
XV. *The Spirit in Man, Art, and Literature.*
XVI. *The Practice of Psychotherapy.*
XVII. *The Development of Personality.*
XVIII. *Miscellany.*
XIX. *Bibliography and Index.*

————. *Memories, Dreams, Reflections,* trans. Richard and Clara Winston (New York, 1963).

————. *Modern Man in Search of a Soul* (New York, 1933).

————. *Spirit and Nature,* ed. J. Campbell (London, 1955).

————. *The Secret of the Golden Flower* (London, 1965).

————. *The Interpretation of Nature and the Psyche* (with W. Pauli), (London, 1955).

————. *Essays on a Science of Mythology* (with C. Kerenyi), (New York, 1949).

KELSEY, M. *Dreams, the Dark Speech of the Spirit* (New York, 1968).

KERENYI, C. *Essays on a Science of Mythology* (with C. G. Jung), (New York, 1949).

————. *The Gods of the Greeks* (London, 1951).

KNIGHT, A. H. *Some Aspects of the Life and Works of Nietzsche and Particularly of His Connection with Greek Literature and Thought* (Cambridge, 1933).

LEO XIII. *The Holy Spirit.*

LEONARD, A. "La psychologie religieuse de Jung," *Supplement de la Vie Spirituelle* (1951).

MALINOWSKI, B. *Magic, Science, and Religion* (New York, 1955).

————. *Sex and Repression in Savage Society* (New York, 1959).

MARITAIN, J. "Freudianism and Psychoanalysis—A Thomist View,"

Freud and the Twentieth Century, ed. Benjamin Nelson (New York, 1957).

MEIER, C. A. *Antike Inkubation und Moderne Psychotherapie* (Zurich, 1949).

NEUMANN, E. *Amor and Psyche* (Princeton, 1962).

―――. *The Great Mother,* trans. Ralph Manheim (New York, 1955).

―――. *The Origins and History of Consciousness* (London, 1954).

NIETZSCHE, F. *The Complete Works of Friedrich Nietzsche,* ed. Oscar Levy (New York, 1924).

―――. *The Antichrist,* trans. H. L. Mencken (New York, 1941).

OTTO, R. *The Idea of the Holy,* trans. John W. Harvey (Oxford, 1943).

―――. *Mystique d'Orient et Mystique d'Occident* (Paris, 1951).

PHILIPON, M. M. *The Spiritual Doctrine of Sister Elizabeth of the Trinity* (Westminster, 1947).

PHILP, H. L. *Jung and the Problem of Evil* (New York, 1959).

―――. *Freud and Religious Belief* (London, 1956).

PIUS XII. *The Mystical Body of Christ.*

PROGOFF, I. *Jung's Psychology and Its Social Meaning* (New York, 1953).

RAMIREZ, S. *De Hominis Beatitudine* (Madrid, 1947).

RHINE, J. B. *Extra-sensory Perception* (Boston, 1934).

―――. *The Reach of the Mind* (New York, 1947).

RUMKE, H. C. *The Psychology of Unbelief* (1952).

RUSSELL, B. *Introduction to Mathematical Philosophy* (London, 1960).

SANFORD, J. *Dreams, God's Forgotten Language* (Philadelphia, 1968).

SCHAER, H. *Religion and the Cure of Souls in Jung's Psychology,* trans. R. F. C. Hull (London, 1951).

SNOECK, A. *Escrúpulo, Pecado, Confesión,* trans. C. Ruiz Garrido (Madrid, 1960).

STERN, K. *The Flight from Woman* (New York, 1967).

―――. *The Third Revolution. A Study in Psychiatry and Religion* (New York, 1955).

STRAUSS, R. "A Personal Recollection," *Contact with Jung.*

TERESA OF AVILA, SAINT. *The Interior Castle,* trans. Benedictines of Stambrook (New York, 1921).

―――. *Life* (New York, 1921).

―――. *The Book of Foundations* (New York, 1921).

TERRUWE, A. A. A. *The Neurosis in the Light of Rational Psychology* (New York, 1960).

————. *Psychopathic Personality and Neurosis* (New York, 1958).

THERESE OF LISIEUX, SAINT. *Autobiography,* trans. Ronald Knox (New York, 1958).

THOMAS AQUINAS, SAINT. *Summa Theol.,* trans. Fathers of the English Dominican Province (New York, 1947).

————. *Summa Contra Gentiles,* trans. Charles J. O'Neill (New York, 1957).

————. *De Veritate,* ed. Marietti (Roma, 1951).

————. *In Post. Analit.,* (Roma, 1955).

————. *In Ethic.,* (Roma, 1964).

————. *De Potentia* (Roma, 1953).

————. *Scriptum Super Sent.,* ed. Lethielleux (Paris, 1929).

TONQUEDEC, J. *Les maladies nerveuses ou mentales et les manifestations diaboliques* (Paris, 1938).

VAN DER HOOP, J. H. *Character and the Unconscious,* trans. Elisabeth Trevelyan (London, 1950).

WHEELWRIGHT, J. "A Personal Experience" *Contact with Jung.*

WHITE, V. *God and the Unconscious* (Cleveland, 1965).

————. *Soul and Psyche* (London, 1960).

————. "Answer to Job," *Blackfriars* (1955).

WICKES, F. G. *The Inner World of Childhood* (New York, 1966).

ZIMMER, H. *Myths and Symbols in Indian Art and Civilization* (New York, 1946).

Index

Abnormality: a continuum, 200

Active imagination: as proof of archetypes, 6

Agony: of Nietzsche's soul, 235

Alchemy: importance of, 36; and mysticism, 82

Anima: feminine archetype in man, 47; as the archetype of life, 49; role of anima in marriages, 49–50; symbols of, 49–50; power of, 51; projection of, 51; the anima compensates the persona, 53; assimilation of, 53; and Eros, 54; and religion, 56

Animus, 50

Antichrist, 94

Anxiety: greatest enemy of soul, 214

Archaic man: importance of, 9–10; prelogical state of primitives, 15; and myth, 18

Archetypes: term borrowed from St. Augustine, 3; definition, 3–4; proof of existence, 4–6; importance, 7; produce primitive images, 7; and reduced intensity of consciousness, 8; are not peculiar symptoms of psychotic states, 8–9; interwoven with conscious material, 9, 21; and myth, 18; origin of, 18–20; properties of, 20 ff.; and scientific ideas, 22; and dreams and fantasies, 23; as principles of religion and political life, 25; and instincts, 26; and individuation, 34; and power of, 34; the shadow, 39; the anima, 47; the "wise old man," 57; and religion, 74; identification with archetypes in Nietzsche, 235

Arendt, H., 226

Aristotle, 1, 13, 195

Art: importance in Nietzsche's philosophy, 217; anticipates what is to come, 247; and disintegration, 247; reveals the unconscious, 247; and Picasso, 248

Augustine, St., 3, 35, 41, 44, 56, 57, 116, 117, 125, 127, 135, 145, 147, 150, 152, 153, 155, 157, 160, 179, 192, 215

Authority, 244

Baptism: and rebirth, 59, 122; benefits of, 65

Baynes, H. G., 108

Benoit, P., 48

Bohme, J., 144

Born, M.. 254

Caruso, I., 7, 120, 128, 131, 132, 137, 187, 194, 197, 205, 211, 223

Cassirer, E., 34

Christ: as the living myth of our culture, 76, 91, 174; expresses the needs of the archetypes of the unconscious, 91, 119; Jung's ideas on, 91; as an embodiment of the self, 92; and individuation, 93; critique of Jung's ideas on, 119; and needs of depth psychology, 120; and incarnation, 121; Dionysus versus Christ, 227–228

Christianity: and myth, 173–175; and Nietzsche, 227, 238

Church: and sin, 41; and dogmas, 77–78

Cicero, T., 208

Coincidence of opposites, 132–134

Collective consciousness: definition, 244

Collective unconscious: nature, 2; thinks in terms of millennia, 24; reveals itself in form of symbols, 35; and religion, 73

Collectivism: two kinds of, 245–246

Compassion: considered by Nietzsche the virtue of the weak, 233

Confession, 43–44

Connelly, C., 70n

The United States Occupation of Haiti, 1915-1934